BROTHERS IN ARMS

BROTHERS IN ARMS

The Epic Story of
the 761st Tank Battalion,
WWII's Forgotten Heroes

Kareem Abdul-Jabbar
and Anthony Walton

BROADWAY BOOKS | NEW YORK

PRINTED IN THE UNITED STATES OF AMERICA

BROADWAY BOOKS and its logo, a letter B bisected on the diagonal, are trademarks of Random House, Inc.

Visit our website at www.broadwaybooks.com

First edition published 2004.

Book design by Richard Oriolo

Cataloging-in-Publication Data is on file with the Library of Congress under the control number 2004-045063.

ISBN 0-385-50338-5
10 9 8 7 6 5 4 3 2

To Colonel Paul Levern Bates

and the men

of the 761st Tank Battalion

Men, you are the first Negro tankers to ever fight in the American Army.
I would never have asked for you if you weren't good. I have nothing but
the best in my Army. I don't care what color you are, so long as
you go up there and kill those Kraut sonsabitches. Everyone
has their eyes on you and is expecting great things from you.
Most of all, your race is looking forward to your success. Don't
let them down, and, damn you, don't let me down!

—GEORGE S. PATTON, NOVEMBER 2, 1944
NEAR NANCY, FRANCE

Contents

PREFACE   xi

JANUARY 9   1

1.   Volunteers   5
2.   Soldiers   35
3.   ETO   63
4.   Blood Brothers   79
5.   Field of Fire   113
6.   The Saar   137
7.   The Bloody Forest   163
8.   Tillet   187
9.   Task Force Rhine   205
10.   The River   227
11.   Home   249

ENDNOTES   273

SELECT BIBLIOGRAPHY   283

ACKNOWLEDGMENTS   289

INDEX   291

Preface

Leonard "Smitty" Smith was a Transit Police officer with my father, F. L. "Al" Alcindor, for more than two decades, beginning in the mid-1950s. They were good friends, and would often hang out together after they had finished their shifts. Sharing an enthusiasm for the Big Band sounds of their youth, they most enjoyed going to the jazz clubs together to hear Lionel Hampton, Count Basie, Benny Carter, Maynard Ferguson, and the Thad Jones–Mel Lewis Big Band.

Smitty was like a surrogate uncle to me. He is one of those people who has an intense opinion on just about any subject and he is never reluctant to share his views. The district office for the New York City Transit Authority Police in upper Manhattan was located at the 145th Street subway station, and I would often have to change trains there to get to whatever game I was playing in the Bronx. My Dad had asked Smitty and other fellow officers to keep an eye out for me, to make sure that I didn't get into any of those minor schoolboy hassles that occasionally turn ugly. Many a time Smitty would suddenly materialize at my side as I waited on the platform. His first words to me were always "Hey, young man." We would chat while I waited for my train. He would ask about my grades or how my Mom was doing, or wisecrack about how badly the Knicks were playing.

On one occasion, some of my friends were riding with me to check out that evening's game. Smitty gave them the once-over and told my friend Little Bob that should any trouble start, he wouldn't hesitate to shoot whoever was involved. Little Bob, not knowing Smitty's playful nature, took him seriously. He told Smitty that shooting a kid would get him fired from the police force. Smitty replied that Little Bob would be dead and so wouldn't get any satisfaction from that fact. It was a couple of days before I could convince Little Bob that Smitty had been pulling his leg.

Black men on the New York City police force were unusual in the 1950s. My Dad, Smitty, and the few other blacks in the Transit Police were pioneers. They had to endure the critical eyes of the public, the hostility of some of the white cops, and occasionally the resentment of black people who felt that they were sellouts. The fact that they were eventually able to earn the respect of both the police hierarchy and the black community says a lot about their achievement. My Dad went on to become a sergeant, and later a lieutenant, advancing through the ranks: Smitty was always supportive; he was proud to see a black cop take up the challenge and succeed.

Smitty's personal story never surfaced while he and my Dad were on the force together. Although he was a friendly face and welcome presence, I saw him as a grown-up; it never occurred to me that he even had a story. I never thought to ask about his life. I had no idea that Smitty, years before, had been a pioneer in an even more significant context.

WHEN I MOVED OUT TO California to attend UCLA and later to play for the Lakers, I didn't see Smitty for many years. All that changed one night in 1992 at Lincoln Center. The lights had just been dimmed, and I was rushing to find my seat in the concert hall. The featured event was a documentary film about a black tank unit that had fought in WWII. I had been enlisted to assist in a number of public-speaking appearances in which members of the unit would describe their combat experiences. I'd been interested for some time in the struggle of black veterans to gain the recognition they deserved, in part because of my father's experience in the Army.

Dad was trained in artillery at Fort Bragg—specializing in the 155mm howitzer—and was qualified and eager for an opportunity to fight the Germans. But like many African Americans in what was still a segregated Army, he never got that chance. Most blacks were allowed only to train; it was hoped that this limited gesture would be enough to ensure the black community's support for the war effort. Accepting the inevitable, my Dad chose to serve in a band unit and never left the States for the duration of his tour of duty. His experience in the Army had another, unexpected benefit, however, because it was during his military service that he met my Mom. He always said it was the high point of his time in uniform.

African Americans in support roles performed important tasks from the outset of the war, including loading convoy ships, carrying out mess duties, driving supply trucks and ambulances through combat zones, and constructing military highways. Later, as Allied casualties mounted and replacements became an issue, some African American units were finally given the chance to fight. The 761st—the heroic tank battalion chronicled in the documentary film I was about to watch—was one of these units.

One special aspect of the 761st's role in the war concerned their involvement in the liberation of some of the Nazi concentration camps. That night at Lincoln Center, Harlem Democrats Percy Sutton and Charles Rangel, who both served with the Tuskegee Airmen, were in attendance, as were such notables as Lena Horne, Roy Haynes, Sidney Lumet, Dr. Ruth Westheimer, and other highly regarded members of New York's black and Jewish communities. As I hurried to my seat, I heard an oddly familiar voice call out, "Hey, young man." Something about that voice transported me back in time, to my teenage years. I turned, and there was Leonard Smith.

"What are you doing here?" I asked him in surprise. Smitty replied that he had been a member of the 761st. With the lights flickering on and off, signaling the imminent start of the film, we had to get to our separate seats. Running into Smitty after all those years was a pleasant shock. But what I saw in the film left me speechless. Smitty had been involved as a tank gunner in some of the most intense fighting of World War II. He had fought in five countries and had been awarded a Bronze Star for valor.

When I found Smitty after the screening, I was unable to adequately express how deeply I'd been affected by what I had just seen. Being exposed to a side of a person you've known that has been hidden or ignored for so long can be very disorienting. Smitty had never mentioned his war record, even to my Dad. In the years since I learned of his service, I've come to find out that many soldiers, both black and white, who returned from the war never mentioned the ordeals they faced in combat. They all seemed to feel that they were just doing their jobs and deserved no special acknowledgment for performing their duty.

Unfortunately, some of the events referred to in the documentary I saw that night, *Liberators: Fighting on Two Fronts in World War II*, had not been adequately researched. The film was produced with the best of intentions, but crucial facts were incorrect or transposed. The resulting controversy tarnished the record of one of the most highly decorated and courageous combat units in the war, and made me aware of the need to tell the 761st's story in a way that would attempt, insofar as possible after almost sixty years, to set the record straight.

THAT EVENING IN 1992 SENT me off on a twelve-year journey to find out more about the battalion, and the more I learned, the more I wanted to know. I began to collect memorabilia, which included articles and the first book written about the 761st, *Come Out Fighting*, by war correspondent Trezzvant Anderson, as well as photographs of battalion members and of the unit in action. A later book, *The 761st*

"Black Panther" Tank Battalion in World War II, written by Joe W. Wilson Jr., the son of a unit member, became an illuminating and invaluable resource. I continued to research the 761st's combat record; the records of the infantry divisions they fought beside; the history of African Americans in the United States military; and the history of the Second World War in general, so that what the men witnessed and achieved could be seen and appreciated in the largest possible context. I began to arrange and conduct a series of audio and video interviews with several of the battalion's surviving members. Beginning in 2002, I worked along with Anthony Walton to arrive at a way of telling this story that would reflect the courage, honor, and integrity of these men.

In telling the story of the 761st Tank Battalion, we have chosen to focus on three members of the 761st in particular. In so doing, we in no way mean to diminish the bravery and contributions of the other soldiers in the unit. Rather, these three men serve as guides into and through the experiences of a distinguished group of American citizens and soldiers during one of the most difficult periods of our nation's history.

I believe theirs is a story that should be known.

Kareem Abdul-Jabbar
Los Angeles
January 1, 2004

BROTHERS IN ARMS

January 9

The German Mark IV Panzer tanks, concealed by dense pine woods, waited until the Sherman was halfway across the snow-covered field, fully exposed. They opened fire with a barrage of machine guns and artillery. The stillness of the morning was shattered by the explosion of shells and whistling bullets.

On the ragged, disorganized battlefield, the American tank and its supporting infantry had somehow found themselves behind enemy lines. Several infantrymen fell at the opening onslaught; the rest fled in disarray. The Sherman tank's commander, Teddy Windsor, yelled for the gunner, William McBurney, to return fire with armor-piercing and high-explosive shells, while frantically directing his driver to turn. Leonard Smith, the loader, rammed one shell after another into the breech as the Sherman fired back into the trees. Suddenly, the tank was rocked by an explosion as it struck a German land mine. It shuddered to a stop.

A rain of high-velocity 75- and 88-millimeter artillery began falling all around it. Smith, McBurney, and Windsor fled the paralyzed vehicle, diving out the turret hatch. Their driver, however, hesitated. He stood up in his seat but didn't move. The others called his name, begging him to jump. A moment later, he was virtually decapitated by a direct artillery hit; the explosion also ignited the ammunition stowed on board. Smith wept openly as he watched flames lift from the turret. His friend McBurney grabbed him and pulled him back.

"I don't belong here," twenty-year-old Leonard Smith thought to himself. He was supposed to be back in bivouac, repairing "Cool Stud," the tank in which he had landed on the debris-strewn aftermath of Omaha Beach two months earlier and driven across France. But after sixty straight days on the front lines, "Cool Stud," like more than half the tanks of Charlie Company, one of the five companies of the 761st Tank Battalion of George Patton's Third U.S. Army, had broken down.

The unit itself had been dangerously thinned during Patton's fall Saar Campaign, with casualties approaching 40 percent. Patton's attack had been halted by a surprise German counteroffensive, the Battle of the Bulge. On Christmas Day, the 761st had rushed north across the icy roads to Belgium to help stop the Germans.

They had been fighting for over a week in the Ardennes Forest during the coldest winter in Europe in thirty-five years, a cold beyond imagining. They had no winter gear, garbed in regular combat fatigues and boots without lining. After another brutally cold night, the crew of "Cool Stud" had been more than happy for a short break from the action, huddled around the fires the GIs made from twigs, boards, fences, anything that would burn. Smith, who in the folly of youth had continued to view the war as an extended game of Cowboys and Indians, had eagerly volunteered that morning to round out the depleted crew of his friend's tank.

SMITH, MCBURNEY, AND WINDSOR crawled slowly across the open field, past the bodies of infantrymen fallen moments before, as well as bodies frozen solid in grotesque poses from the previous day's fighting. The bitter cold had turned the skin of the dead the purplish red color of wine. Smith found himself face-to-face with a dead German soldier whose eyes were a vivid clear blue. Windsor and McBurney, dragging their .45-caliber submachine guns with them, returned fire at intervals on the German tanks and white-clad infantry as they struggled to make their way. Mortar fire burst behind and in front of them. Machine guns spat at their feet. In their green regulation uniforms, they were easy targets against the freshly fallen snow.

Windsor led, followed by McBurney, with Smith at the rear. They had gone about three hundred yards when McBurney stopped. It was so cold it hurt to breathe. His fingers were now too numb to pull the trigger of his submachine gun. The edge of the woods they were painfully making their way toward was still a mile away—impossibly far. Smith came up beside him. "Come on, man, come on—think about the Savoy. We got to get back there and do some more dancing." The Savoy was a legendary ballroom in Harlem, known for its Big Band roster and polished oak floors.

"You go on," McBurney told him.

Smith persisted. "We got to get the hell out of here so we can get back and party."

McBurney wasn't thinking about the Savoy; he certainly wasn't thinking about dancing; he was thinking they were going to die here, in this hell on earth, thousands of miles from home. He was thinking Smith must be out of his mind. But Smith refused to leave him. Exhausted past the point of caring, McBurney simply wanted to lie there, close his eyes, and go to sleep. But at Smith's insistence, he started moving again.

Three green targets in the open white field, three miles from any aid or shelter, the bullets continued falling all around them, sending up mists and vapors in the waist-deep snow.

1

VOLUNTEERS

The atmosphere of the whole country was

to get in the service and help.

I wanted to do my part.

—William McBurney

When seventeen-year-old Leonard Smith stepped off the United States Army troop train in Rapides Parish, Louisiana, in the fall of 1942, it was the first time he had been outside of New York State. For the last three days, he had been traveling with fourteen other recruits, headed to Camp Claiborne, seventeen miles southwest of Alexandria. There, they were to join a recently established armored unit. To Smith's surprise, the train stopped in an open field. The sergeants on the train threw the young soldiers' bags out and told them to get off. Smith and his companions, in full dress uniform and carrying their regulation duffel bags, waited for four hours in the empty field on the outskirts of the Kisatchie National Forest, watching the sun move across the sky. Finally, two of them set off on foot to find help.

Leonard Smith was one of the more than six hundred men who would come together at Camp Claiborne during the Second World War to form the 761st Tank Battalion. They would hail from over thirty states, from small towns and cities scattered throughout the country, from places as varied as Los Angeles, California, and Holtulka, Oklahoma; Springfield, Illinois, and Picayune, Mississippi; Billings, Montana, and Baltimore, Maryland. Most had volunteered. Some were the middle-class sons of doctors, undertakers, school-teachers, and career military men; among the officers were a Yale student and a football star from UCLA who would later make his mark in American sports and American history. Many more were the sons of janitors, domestics, factory workers, and sharecroppers.

Their combat record in Europe during the war was noteworthy. They were to earn a Presidential Unit Citation for distinguished service, more than 250 Purple Hearts, 70 Bronze Stars, 11 Silver Stars, and a Congressional Medal of Honor in 183 straight days on the front lines of France, Germany, Belgium, Luxembourg, Holland, and Austria. These accomplishments carried a significance, however, beyond the battlefield. The unit's official designation was "The 761st Tank Battalion (Colored)." As they waited in that hot Louisiana field, Leonard Smith and his fellow recruits were on their way to becoming part of the first African American unit in the history of the United States Army to fight in tanks.

IN THE FALL OF 1942, the battlefields of Europe and the Pacific seemed far from the backwater post of Camp Claiborne, Louisiana. They were as far from Leonard Smith's experience as Camp Claiborne had been before he boarded the train in New York City. Smith was born in Harlem Hospital on November 2, 1924; he was a sickly child at birth, weighing less than five pounds, with both colic and a heart murmur. His mother abandoned him shortly after he was born. Lulu Hasbruck, who worked for New York City taking in children with medical complications, cared for Smith during those early, precarious years. Other foster children regularly moved in and out of Hasbruck's home, but Smith and two girls, Thelma and Flora, remained. Smith would come to regard Lulu as his mother, though she never formally adopted him.

Despite his short, skinny frame and the heart murmur that kept him from playing school sports, Smith became an active, adventuresome child, regularly challenging other kids in his Brooklyn, and later Queens, neighborhood to footraces around the block. The neighborhood kids didn't seem to mind losing to him. There was something about him that adults and classmates immediately responded to, a combination of good-naturedness, irrepressibility, and naïveté that made him impossible to dislike.

He loved singing, and was good enough even at age eight to solo with the senior choir at local churches. But his obsession was airplanes. A favorite teacher rewarded students for exceptional performance by buying them a toy of their choice from the neighborhood five-and-dime. Smith hated arithmetic, but he worked hard to get high marks so that she would have to buy him a toy. He invariably picked out model planes, pictures of planes, and books about planes. Though he had never seen an airplane up close, there was something about the idea of planes and flying, the freedom of movement flying symbolized, that endlessly fired his high-spirited imagination.

Money was scarce. Clothes for foster children were provided by the city, a source of some discomfort for the children: People knew they were "home" children, wards of the city, because of the way they dressed. But the only thing Smith really missed was not having a father. When other kids in the neighborhood would talk about things they'd done with their fathers, he would make up stories about fishing trips and family outings. When asked why his father wasn't around, he would tell his friends his father was traveling on business. He made an imaginary father out of Mrs. Hasbruck's deceased husband, George, collecting countless details about him: Mrs. Hasbruck told him that George had smoked a pipe with Prince Albert tobacco, and Smith vowed that when he grew up he'd do the same. Mrs. Hasbruck's two brothers gave Smith spending money from time to time, but they rarely provided him with fatherly guidance. He had to learn everything for himself, and he often made mistakes.

One such mistake contributed to his decision to enlist in the Army. As a teenager, he had enrolled at Chelsea Vocational High School to study aviation mechanics. There he fell in with a group of older boys, budding delinquents who played hooky every Friday, shoplifting tools from local stores. It was typical of the guileless Smith that he continued going to class long after the boys he hung out with had stopped. It was also typical that while Smith's adventuresomeness led him to skirt the edges of disaster, his good-naturedness and good luck just as often kept him out. A neighborhood cop who knew and liked Smith pulled him aside, telling him that the boys he was running around with were going to wind up in prison one way or another. "Have you ever considered joining the Army?" he asked.

Smith had considered it—it was May 1942, and the United States had been at war for six months—but at seventeen, he had thought he was too young to enlist. American troops were already engaging in bloody combat in the Pacific, surrendering after a hopelessly one-sided struggle in the Philippines on May 6, but stalling the advance of the Japanese two days later in the Battle of the Coral Sea. Like millions of families across the country, the Hasbrucks listened to the radio every night for war updates. When he went to the local cinema, Smith avidly watched the early newsreels of combat. He knew exactly what he wanted to enlist as: a fighter pilot. He imagined himself streaking through the skies, on the lookout for Japanese Zeros, engaging in dogfights, dropping bombs on enemy aircraft carriers. In Smith's young mind, war was a kind of game. He had no concept of war's brutality, and he was eager to join the fight. At the policeman's suggestion, he went to the induction office on Whitehall Street in lower Manhattan carrying a permission form signed by his foster mother.

The doctor administering the Army physical failed to notice his slight heart murmur, and passed him. Smith told the recruiter who processed his application that he wanted to be a pilot. The sergeant told him that was not possible—the Army Air Corps did not accept blacks. Smith barely managed to swallow his disappointment. Citing his training in high school, he then said he wanted to be an aviation mechanic. Again, he was told that was not possible. The Army's rigid color line took Smith by surprise. Growing up in the New York City of the 1920s and '30s, he had encountered his share of discrimination: There were certain neighborhood pools where he was not permitted to go swimming, and certain stores where the entrance of anybody black was announced by ringing bells to rouse white clerks to extra vigilance. But despite such small daily indignities, it had somehow never occurred to him that the color of his skin would impact his future, his lifelong dream of working with planes.

He had scored high marks on the Army's IQ screening test. "Infantry you definitely don't want," the sergeant advised him. The next-best thing to the air force was armored, the sergeant said. "Armored?" Smith asked. The sergeant replied, "Tanks. They're starting a couple of colored tank battalions. How would you like that?" Smith had never seen a tank—in fact, he had no idea what a tank was. But he was game for anything. The sergeant told him that as a volunteer, "if that's what you want, that's where you're going to go."

WILLIAM MCBURNEY WAS AS RESERVED and cautious as Leonard Smith was naive and adventuresome. Although the two men didn't know each other, McBurney took the subway to the induction office just days after Smith. His motives in doing so were mixed. Like Smith, he had watched the news updates of the war: A wave of patriotism had swept the country in the wake of the bombing of Pearl Harbor, and thousands of young men across the country enlisted every day. McBurney was eager to do his part for the war effort. But he also saw the Army as an escape.

McBurney was born in Harlem on May 21, 1924. His parents divorced when he was very young; his mother moved away to Florida, and he saw her only rarely after that. He was raised by his father and stepmother. When he was twelve years old, his younger brother died of scarlet fever. Though devastated by the loss, McBurney did what he had watched his father do all his life: bury the pain deep inside, and keep moving.

William had always been in awe of his father. A smart, determined, and ambitious man, his father had been born dirt poor around the turn of the century in Titusville, Florida. Seeing no prospects for advancement there, he had worked his way north to New York City as a railroad porter. At the outbreak of World War I, he had volunteered for the Army, serving in a quartermaster unit in Europe. When he returned to New York, still searching for a means of steady employment and advancement, he had worked his way through school to become a dental technician. But in the 1920s it was very difficult for blacks to find work in professional jobs. With a young wife and a growing family to support, he had no choice but to turn to manual labor, working on the docks and, later, with the advent of the Great Depression, for the Civilian Conservation Corps, one of the massive public works programs started by the federal government.

William McBurney was an intelligent, active boy. Despite his large size, he was not coordinated or good at sports: His one physical gift was a powerful right hook. Though he never went out of his way to seek out a fight, neither did he ever turn away from one. He got into the usual number of scrapes for a kid in Harlem in the 1930s—often chasing or being chased by Italian kids from adjacent neighbor-hoods—but he was also always at one remove from whatever he was doing, thinking several steps ahead. He had already noticed the kinds of trouble young black men often got into, especially with the police, and he intended to avoid it. With his air of watchfulness, his quiet, steady intelligence, and his physical courage, he stood out in his group of friends as the one you wanted watching your back.

Like Smith and countless other African Americans at that time, McBurney was tracked early in his school career toward shop class, regardless of his intelligence or academic success. Given the options available to him at New York Vocational High School, like Leonard Smith he chose to study aviation mechanics. A female cousin was tak-ing flying lessons at Floyd Bennet Field, and watching that plane take off and sail away made McBurney dream of becoming a pilot. But as time went on, it was a dream he seemed to have less and less hope of attaining. After school and on Saturdays he worked at a paintbrush factory for twenty-five cents an hour, helping his family to weather the Depression. Many of his friends had taken similar menial jobs. As high school graduation approached, many more of his friends, with no real opportunities for advancement, were falling into gambling and petty theft. McBurney saw himself and his friends moving steadily toward dead-end lives.

Like many young men, he had romanticized his father's service in World War I—the more so because his taciturn father never talked about it. He saw the Army as a way of creating a new life for himself, and of realizing his secret dream of flying. When he told his father he wanted to join the Army Air Corps, he was surprised to find his father immediately dismissive. He didn't believe the Air Corps would accept an African American. This only made McBurney more determined. Three days after his eighteenth birthday, he took the train to the recruitment center on Whitehall Street.

His father's warning about the Air Corps turned out to be all too true—as Leonard Smith had already discovered, no blacks were allowed to join. To McBurney, it was a slap in the face. Nonetheless, he decided to enlist. Like Smith, he had scored high marks on the Army's intelligence test. Though he also had no idea what a tank was, he found himself, like Smith, steered by the recruiter into armored.

AFTER PASSING HIS PHYSICAL AND being given his shots, McBurney was sent by train with several other fresh recruits to Camp Upton, a processing center surrounded by open potato fields in Suffolk County, Long Island. Thousands of Army recruits would move through the sprawling complex between 1941 and 1945. The recruits spent two weeks living in tents, where they were given close haircuts, uniforms, and basic gear; then they were moved into barracks. They performed a series of marching and close-order drills each day, learning the basics of military procedure and decorum, as well as carrying out KP duty and cleaning the grounds of the camp. Finding themselves with a great deal of free time on their hands, they held a series of boxing and softball tournaments as they waited endlessly, it seemed to McBurney, for their orders to come. During orientation, they had seen motivational documentaries chronicling the reasons the country was at war, highlighting the battles that had been fought to date, and firing them up against Germany and Japan. All were eager to get overseas and get started. They wanted in on the action.

The close friendships that would characterize the men in combat were already beginning to form. William McBurney first met Leonard Smith at Camp Upton. Despite, or perhaps because of, their vast temperamental differences—Smith was the sort who leapt before looking, while McBurney was the one who held back; Smith's humor tended toward open-hearted playfulness, McBurney's toward irony and observation—the two became fast friends. Soon they became close to another recruit as well, soft-spoken Preston McNeil.

At nineteen, McNeil was a year or two older than the other new recruits. Something about his patience and gentle, reflective manner made him seem older still. His gaze was direct but kind; deeply empathetic, he was always willing to give others the benefit of the doubt, taking care to make sure that no one in the group felt left out. Though McNeil had joined the Army in New York, he had been born and raised in Raleigh, North Carolina, a segregated southern city. His mother worked as a live-in maid, and McNeil grew up in his grandmother's house. He never knew his father.

His grandmother was a staunch Baptist, a "Holy Roller" who made certain that McNeil went to church every Sunday. The generosity that came to be characteristic of McNeil was more than a religious conviction, however: In the Depression-era South, he daily witnessed people like his grandmother sharing what little she had with neighbors who had less. Much of McNeil's early life was spent taking care of others, performing whatever odd jobs he could to earn money for his family. At the age of thirteen, he left home to join the Civilian Conservation Corps. There he earned a dollar a day, thirty dollars a month. Twenty-five of that was sent home to his grandmother. He stayed at the CCC camp in North Carolina for three years before moving north to New York City to live with his aunt and cousins.

Segregation had been such a permanent fact of McNeil's early life that he'd never thought much about it, and he was stunned by the relative freedom of New York. He could sit on the bus beside a white person; if he was first on line at the grocery store, he could pay for his goods and leave—he didn't have to keep moving back for whites. He could sit at a lunch counter and be served. To him, it was heaven. He briefly attended New York Vocational High School, but had to leave after a few months because of the pressing need to send money back to his family. He got a job at a CCC camp in upstate New York, where he worked for another three years before joining the Army in the spring of 1942.

EACH DAY AT CAMP UPTON, the men gathered excitedly before the tin-roofed PX to learn who had been given orders to be shipped out. Leonard Smith received his orders to Camp Claiborne relatively quickly. He reluctantly bid good-bye to his newfound friends, thinking he would never see them again, and headed with fourteen other recruits for that hot Louisiana field, beginning his basic training at Claiborne shortly thereafter.

McBurney and McNeil remained stationed at Camp Upton for so long that they stopped paying attention to the daily roll call. In time, their excitement turned to apathy. The war would surely be over, they began to think, before they shipped out. Then came the day that would alter their lives forever: McNeil heard the first name called on the day's list—Thomas Brisbane, whom he knew to be a member of his group of recruits. The men were shipping out to Kentucky to begin specialized training.

The Armored Force Replacement Training Center at Fort Knox was located in the rolling countryside approximately thirty-five miles south of Louisville. It was there that McNeil and McBurney would see a tank for the first time. However, they had several weeks of trial and tribulation to suffer first. Any impression they may have formed during their long sojourn at Camp Upton that the military would be easy was dispelled the moment they set foot on the grounds at Fort Knox: Drill sergeants screamed at the new recruits. The men were drilled anew in formations. The smallest infractions in dress code or bearing were punished not with lighthearted assignments to KP, as at Upton, but with shouted insults, push-ups, and more push-ups. They went on forced daily marches in rain or sun, heat or cold; they took apart and reassembled guns blindfolded, navigated obstacle courses, crawled under barrages of live machine-gun fire. Upon returning from this daily torment, they would troop back to their quarters up "Misery Hill," a mile-long incline, in full gear.

Preston McNeil survived by repeating to himself and laughing at the irony of something the Army recruiter had told him months before—the sole reason he had allowed the sergeant to sign him up for armored as opposed to a quartermaster or infantry unit: "You won't have to do any walking." This phrase became his mantra as he walked, ran, crawled, vomited, sweated, and willed his way through basic training.

Leonard Smith, on the other hand, six hundred miles away at Camp Claiborne, had with characteristic ingenuity and good fortune found a way out of the more grueling aspects of training. He volunteered for the battalion's military band. He had no experience on any instrument, but, relying on his childhood talent as a singer, he figured he could fake his way through on drums. He played for the other soldiers as they headed out on long forced marches, then joked around with the rest of the band in the PX until they were called on to play the exhausted, sweaty, mud-soaked troops back in.

Finally, after several weeks of training, the men at Camp Claiborne and Fort Knox were marched to their respective motor pools. Most of them—like Smith, William McBurney, and the vast majority of Americans in the Depression years—had grown up in varying degrees of poverty and had never driven a car before. They had to be trained from scratch in the basic maintenance of motor vehicles, lectured repeatedly on the function and significance of everything from headlights and motor oil to fan belts and spark plugs. They were taught how to drive motorcycles, followed by jeeps and trucks, with a sergeant watching over their every move, riding beside or pacing behind them. Finally, they were brought before a tank.

The men of the 761st initially trained on a model known as the M-5 Stuart Light Tank. This was a smaller, less powerful vehicle than the M-4 Medium Tank they would drive to battle across Europe; but to Leonard Smith, seeing a tank for the first time, the M-5 was something to marvel at. Powered by twin 220-horsepower Cadillac V-8 engines, weighing approximately 12 tons, the M-5 was armed with a 37mm cannon and three .30-caliber machine guns.

The men were given time on the tank range to get used to their new equipment, driving for three or four days with an instructor beside them and then a day or two alone. The only breaks in this hands-on training were to receive instruction in the basics of map reading, compass reading, and battle strategy. In the day room, they'd discuss problems in tank placement and command. Officers would present the men with various hypothetical battlefield situations, such as "What would you do if you were a tank commander and you were out to recapture a town overlooked by an enemy-controlled ridge?" A sand bin contained miniature tanks with which the trainees would demonstrate their plans of attack; the officers would then talk them through what they could have done differently, how another maneuver might have been more effective.

As they became more familiar with their equipment, the men began to learn how to work together as a crew. The crew of the M-5 Stuart consisted of a tank commander, driver, gunner, and replacement gunner. Each man learned to master all four positions. Quarters were close: In early models without radios, the tank commander, positioned above and just behind the driver, communicated with him by tapping his foot on the driver's left shoulder to turn left, on his right shoulder to turn right, and by giving him a firm kick in the center of his back to make him stop suddenly. The men learned how to zero in on both static and moving targets, "bracketing" to find the correct range. The tank commander spotted targets through the telescopic sight and gave orders to the gunner beside him—left, right, steady on—and then he'd estimate the range to the target, say, 110 yards. If the round was short, the commander would tell the gunner to go up fifty yards. If it was long, he'd tell him to come down fifty.

Though they learned the rudiments of operating and firing a tank cannon, the African Americans did not shoot live ammunition; they were told they were going through "dry runs." In their final week of training, they were permitted to fire a single round of ammunition.

That was all. White recruits at Fort Knox, by contrast, fired live rounds throughout the majority of their training period. At Knox, as at Upton, the men had grudgingly accepted their segregated quarters, but this particular disparity in training was hard to take. Officers assigned to train African American recruits often expressed concern for the well-being of their men: How were the soldiers supposed to learn the intricacies of bracketing targets—firing a first shot long, a second shot short, then calibrating and adjusting to hit the target—if they could fire only once? If, in actual combat, they missed and didn't know how to correct, they were dead.

THOUGH THEY WERE UNAWARE OF the historical implications of their activities, Leonard Smith, William McBurney, and Preston McNeil were in the vanguard of a change with ramifications that would bear enormous consequences for the American armed forces. The 761st Tank Battalion, created by the War Department on April 1, 1942, would not only become the first African American armored unit in the nation's history to land on foreign soil; it would also become one of the first black combat units in the modern Army to fight side by side with white troops. The unit's actions, and those of their fellow black soldiers, would ultimately lead, in 1948, to the desegregation of the American military.

African American soldiers had served with the highest distinction in nearly every major conflict since the Revolutionary War. But by the outbreak of World War II, this storied legacy had been all but forgotten by military commanders. There were black casualties at the Boston Massacre of 1770, and several black soldiers received special commendation for extraordinary heroism in the Battle of Bunker Hill. Five thousand slaves and freemen served beside white troops in George Washington's Continental Army, in battles from Lexington and Concord to Yorktown. In the War of 1812, black seamen made up at least a tenth of all naval crews on the Upper Lakes; blacks in the Army fought both scattered among white troops and in separate all-black units, including two black battalions that executed counterattacks critical to Andrew Jackson's victory at the Battle of New Orleans. Slaveholders, however, had always bitterly protested the arming of black troops, and following the American victory in 1814, the enlistment of African Americans was discouraged in every branch of the service except the Navy.

This was the status quo until the Civil War. Abraham Lincoln resisted the use of black troops until manpower requirements and the persuasion of Frederick Douglass led him to authorize the creation of black regiments. Black Union soldiers would see combat in almost every southern state, with more than 38,000 losing their lives by war's end; Major General Q. A. Gilmore and six other major generals would testify to the bravery of African American soldiers under their command. After the war, four all-black units were set up permanently, two infantry and two cavalry. The cavalry regiments, the Ninth and the Tenth, became the famed "Buffalo Soldiers" who took on the Apaches and the Cheyenne in the American Southwest, fighting with such notable skill that the commander of the Army, William Tecumseh Sherman, argued before Congress—unsuccessfully, as it turned out—for the full integration of the armed forces. Elements of the Ninth and Tenth Cavalries later served with Teddy Roosevelt at San Juan Hill, and with General John "Black Jack" Pershing in the expedition against Pancho Villa in Mexico.

But as Southern whites regained political power in the early 1900s, asserting Jim Crow stereotypes and legislation, this history was virtually erased. African Americans in both the Army and the previously integrated Navy found themselves increasingly relegated to inferior quarters and to menial service and support roles. Two separate race riots involving black soldiers in training—one at Brownsville, Texas, in 1906 and one at Houston, Texas, in 1917—were used by

Southerners to justify this policy, though both incidents had been sparked by the brutality of local white police toward uniformed blacks. Of the 380,000 African Americans who served in World War I, all but 42,000 were assigned to support roles.

General Pershing—the same general who had been well-served by the Buffalo Soldiers—sent the all-black 92nd and 93rd Infantry Divisions to France with insufficient equipment, after what was at best a rudimentary course of training. The 92nd, operating largely under the command of white Southerners who were openly contemptuous of its men, received an unjust yet enduring reputation for cowardice—though the secretary of war himself later disputed these claims, and though twenty-one of its soldiers earned the Distinguished Service Cross, more than were awarded to the soldiers of comparable all-white divisions fighting nearby. The combat record of the 93rd Infantry Division, the "Men of Bronze," was extraordinary. Turned over early in 1918 to the command of the French, the men of the 93rd served in the trenches for six straight months, not yielding a single foot of territory, earning 550 medals from the French and the Americans, including 180 Croix de Guerre. Seven hundred and fifty African American soldiers were killed in World War I, and more than 5,000 were wounded.

In the 1920s and '30s, the number of blacks in the military diminished greatly as vacancies in black units, due to budget-cutting decisions, were left unfilled and as innovations in warfighting strategy resulted in newly created whites-only branches, such as the Army Air Corps. But the attack on Pearl Harbor on December 7, 1941, altered the course of American history. In the subsequent flood of volunteers, one out of seven were African American, a much greater ratio than the ratio of blacks in the general population. Among them were the 761st Tank Battalion's Leonard Smith, William McBurney, and Preston McNeil.

The 761st, along with black units such as the 758th and 784th

Tank Battalions and the 99th Fighter Pursuit Squadron (also known as the Tuskegee Airmen), had been created not to fight but rather to placate black voters and the Negro press. The belief held by most Army officers and War Department officials at the outset of World War II was that African Americans lacked the intelligence and physical skills necessary to perform specialized combat operations. President Franklin Delano Roosevelt, War Secretary Henry Stimson, and other national leaders saw the mobilization of these showcase units primarily as a way of solidifying Democratic Party gains in the black community.

While FDR's motives were political, those of Eleanor Roosevelt and Harry Truman (at the time a senator and working behind the scenes) were more altruistic and forward thinking. Mrs. Roosevelt publicly agitated for the full and equal utilization of African American manpower, and she used her bully pulpit with her husband to advocate as well. Her sentiments mirrored those of African American leaders, who resented the restriction of blacks in the military to noncombat roles. For generations, African Americans had argued that black soldiers be given the right to shoulder their portion of the burden in order to gain full purchase as citizens. As Frederick Douglass had stated during the Civil War, "The colored man only waits for honorable admission into the service of the country.—They know that who would be free, themselves must strike the blow."

AS THEY SWEATED THROUGH BASIC TRAINING, Leonard Smith, William McBurney, and Preston McNeil did not yet know, or even suspect, that the Army never intended that they go overseas or see combat. In the heat of the autumn in the South, amid intense physical hardship as they climbed up Misery Hill to their quarters carrying full packs day after day, McBurney and McNeil formed close ties. The fellow New Yorkers shared a special bond, if one formed in mutual adversity:

Some of the Southern sergeants at Fort Knox seemed to have it in for them. They would make the New Yorkers stand apart from the others, snickering, "You New Yorkers think you're smart, but we got something for y'all." They'd make them do extra drills, extra push-ups, and march extra distance. Smith encountered the same reaction from sergeants at Camp Claiborne.

But it was not just the New Yorkers who began to band together into a cohesive fighting unit. All of the men were developing a tight camaraderie. As they moved through basic training, African American recruits from New York, Chicago, South Carolina, Oklahoma, and virtually every other corner of the country were starting to think of themselves as a single unit. Warren Crecy of Corpus Christi, Texas, and northerner Horatio Scott of Lynn, Massachusetts, for example, became the closest of friends.

Warren Crecy's serious manner and striking good looks tended to make him stand out in any group. Crecy was a study in contrasts: A former high school football star known for his gutsy willingness to throw his 150-pound frame in harm's way, he was nonetheless introspective, at times almost painfully shy. Though ferociously competitive and determined to be the best at whatever task he applied himself to, Crecy was universally considered the nicest man in the battalion. He was rarely heard to use a word stronger than "damn." Horatio Scott mirrored Warren Crecy in his seriousness, his quiet intelligence, and deep-seated kindness, if not his ferocity and force of will. The two became as close as brothers, taking a solemn oath that they would refuse promotions in rank until the other man had made the same rank.

AFTER THEIR THIRTEEN WEEKS OF training at Fort Knox, the men of the 761st boarded a troop train for the six-hundred-mile journey through the winding hills of Kentucky, Tennessee, and Mississippi to rejoin Leonard Smith and the others already at Camp Claiborne. Louisiana was an alien land to most of these young men. For William McBurney and Preston McNeil, seeing their old buddy Leonard Smith was the only pleasant aspect of the relocation.

What struck them most, as they marched from the train to their new quarters, was the smell. The segregated black quarters were located near the camp's sewage-treatment plant. When the wind came from the right direction, the smell could be overpowering; on the best of days it was foul, assailing the men anew each time they came back to their quarters from the range. Second only to the smell in its sheer physical unpleasantness was the mud. The camp itself was situated in a swampy area, and their quarters—a scattering of field tents and ramshackle wooden structures—were located on the low grounds. They lived in a sea of mud. They hadn't realized mud could be so various, changing day by day to cover the entire range of textures from soupy to thick and claylike. The ever-present substance made walking difficult, found its way over the tops of their boots, and soaked their clothes when passing motor vehicles spun their wheels.

The rough physical conditions were not the only thing they had to adjust to. They also had to adjust to life in the South. Preston McNeil, who had spent his childhood in North Carolina, was anxious for the others. He tried repeatedly to warn his comrades from the north about Jim Crow, explaining the unwritten codes dictating who they could and could not interact with, where they could and could not go. Some of his friends listened and some of them—including Leonard Smith—had to learn the hard way.

On the base, the battalion's training in the M-5 Stuart tanks intensified. Almost daily, the men were timed in mounting and dismounting the tanks. Each had to be able to get in and out of position by a certain time. They were told repeatedly by screaming sergeants that in combat situations their quickness in dismounting could mean life or death. They grew to hate this exercise—jumping in and out of the tanks so often in the oppressive heat that they started slipping on their own pooled sweat—but they did get faster. They also continued their instruction in vehicle maintenance. They were taught to take apart and reassemble the 37mm cannon and .30-caliber machine guns. They learned the importance of oiling the bogie wheels—the wheels that turn the undercarriage—which otherwise could freeze and disable the tank. In field exercises, they learned how the vehicle responded to various types of terrain. Surrounded on all sides by swampland, the terrain type they came to master above all others was mud. The trick, they discovered, was to keep moving; it was usually only when you stopped or slowed that you got stuck.

Men who had learned all four positions in the tank in basic training were now assigned to one role, based on character evaluations made by their sergeants and lieutenants. William McBurney, ever reserved, composed, and steady under pressure, was assigned to the position of gunner, operating the 37mm cannon and coaxial .30-caliber gun. Preston McNeil and Warren Crecy were both chosen as tank commanders—McNeil because of his steadfast concern for others and the loyalty he earned in return, Crecy because of his steely determination, his thoughtfulness, and his consistently excellent marks throughout training.

Leonard Smith had also received high marks on most of the physical and technical challenges of training—but found himself assigned to the junior position of assistant gunner. He was regarded by his superiors as something of a rebel. Nobody in the battalion spent more time at punitive KP duty than did Smith, whose naïveté and high-spiritedness often bordered on seeming insouciance. He regularly forgot to salute officers, greeting them instead with a nod, a smile, and a "Hey, how you doing?" He frequently reported late for duty. The officers and sergeants nonetheless found it impossible not to like him, believing he had the potential to become an accomplished soldier if he could just learn to settle down.

The men were given not only tank position but also company assignments. The 761st Tank Battalion at the time consisted of five companies: Headquarters, Service, and the letter companies—Able, Baker, and Charlie—as well as a medical detachment. The letter companies contained three platoons, each platoon made up of five tanks. Leonard Smith and William McBurney were sent to Headquarters Company. Headquarters consisted of three tanks, a mortar platoon, and an assault gun platoon, and included the battalion's commanders and support staff. Preston McNeil and Warren Crecy were sent to Service Company, containing an assortment of tanks, half-tracks, and jeeps responsible for resupplying the men.

Whatever their company assignment, the young soldiers identified themselves first and foremost as part of the battalion. An all-black engineer battalion was quartered nearby, and the men set up wrestling events and other minor competitions to see who had the best unit. They were proud of the armored patch displayed on their shoulders— a triangle in three colors, yellow, blue, and red, containing the picture of a cannon with a jagged red lightning bolt drawn across it, and at the top their battalion number, 761.

Within the battalion there continued to develop smaller, close-knit groups of friends. Leonard Smith remained tight with William McBurney and Preston McNeil. But Smith's best friend became a young man whom he first met at Claiborne, the driver of McBurney's tank, Willie Devore. There was an instant affinity between Devore and Smith. Devore, from Greenwood, South Carolina, was gregarious, charming, and intensely loyal to his friends. Quick on his feet, he was able to find humor in any situation. Handsome, with a rakish confidence, he had several different girlfriends writing him from home. Smith, who by that time had barely kissed a girl, was greatly impressed. Devore hooked Smith up with a girlfriend, a young woman from Greenwood who wrote him letters throughout the war. Devore was like a big brother to him, and the two looked out for each other.

THE NEARBY CITY OF ALEXANDRIA, like the entire South at the time, was strictly segregated. William McBurney thought that Preston McNeil was exaggerating when he described the danger. Ever watchful by nature, however, he took his friend's advice and made his first trip to town as part of a large group. He looked in amazement at the signs marking "White" and "Colored" drinking fountains, and noted the naked hostility with which white civilians glared at the uniformed members of his group and treated them in stores. He didn't go into Alexandria much after that, figuring the hell with it, choosing instead to read a book and stay on base.

On his first trip to Alexandria, Leonard Smith became involved in an incident that almost ended his military career. Like McBurney, he had been warned to take a black Southerner with him so he wouldn't get into trouble. With his inveterate tendency to leap before looking, he had blithely disregarded the advice. A white bus driver took offense at Smith's open, friendly greeting on boarding the bus—Smith apparently wasn't deferential enough to suit him—and deliberately let him off on the wrong side of town. It was a potentially deadly act. Smith walked into the nearest store and picked out a few small gifts, including a pillow embroidered with the word "Mom," to send home to his foster mother and sisters. Two white MPs entered the store and told him he wasn't supposed to be there. Smith told them this was where the bus driver let him off. The MPs drove Smith to the black side of town, where they handed him over to five black MPs.

Common practice in the military at the time was to leave problems of discipline with black soldiers to black MPs—more specifically, to certain black MPs who were selected because of their low IQs and propensity to violence. This allowed white officers to keep what they considered to be "order," while protecting themselves from direct charges of racism. A white captain of the 761st who was openly contemptuous of the men voiced this policy to a newly arrived fellow officer by saying "You got to have a mean coon . . . to keep these boys in line."

The two white MPs who handed Leonard Smith over to the black MPs explained to them that Smith hadn't done anything wrong, that he'd just gotten let off in the wrong place. After the whites left, one of the black MPs pushed Smith up against the wall, saying, "You're one of them New York wise boys." When Smith shoved back, the rest of the black MPs jumped on him, beating him badly before locking him in the stockade. Nursing his wounds in a solitary cell wasn't exactly what Smith had bargained for when he'd volunteered. The MPs reported that he had been drunk and disorderly. He came very close to being court-martialed. But his boundless luck came through in the end: The two white MPs were located to testify on his behalf, explaining that Smith couldn't have been drunk, as he had been in town for less than five minutes.

VIOLENT ENCOUNTERS BETWEEN UNIFORMED BLACK servicemen and MPs, local citizens, and police were legion throughout the South, and could turn deadly. At Fort Benning, Georgia, in April 1941, the body of Private Felix Hall was discovered hanging from a tree just outside the base. Investigators ruled the death a probable suicide, though the dead soldier's hands had been tied together behind his back. In Tampa, Florida, in July 1941, an argument between white MPs and black soldiers escalated to blows; a white city policeman, learning of the fracas, shot one of the black soldiers while he was lying on the ground. Near Fort Bragg, North Carolina, in August 1941, a dispute over seating on a bus led to a gun battle in which one black soldier and one white MP were killed. Also that month, near Gurdon, Arkansas, dozens of members of the 94th Engineer Battalion were attacked by a mob of white civilians and state troopers.

Other racial disturbances occurred at or near Fort Jackson, South Carolina; Camp Davis, North Carolina; Camp Stewart, Georgia; Fort Bliss, Camp Wallace, and Clark Field, Texas; Camp Shelby,

Mississippi; and Camp Breckenridge, Kentucky. Outside of Camp Van Dorn, Mississippi, on May 30, 1943, an unarmed black private arguing with a white MP was shot to death by a local white sheriff; rumors of mass violence by white soldiers and civilians against black soldiers at Camp Van Dorn in the following months have never fully been disproved.

The violence of such assaults—and the suspicion that many more went unreported—led African American federal judge William Hastie to undertake a fact-finding mission throughout the South on behalf of the Justice Department. His report to Secretary of War Stimson on September 22, 1941, stated that "bullying, abuse and physical violence on the part of white Military Policemen are a continuing source of complaints. . . . In the Army the Negro is taught to be a man, a fighting man; in brief a soldier. It is impossible to create a dual personality which will be on the one hand a fighting man toward a foreign enemy, and on the other, a craven who will accept treatment as less than a man at home."

In January 1942, several months prior to the creation of the 761st, a violent race riot occurred in Alexandria, Louisiana. After witnessing the brutal arrest of an African American soldier by white MPs, members of three black units stationed nearby decided to fight back, throwing rocks and bottles in the town center. Local police organized to repulse the black troops, and a large number of white townspeople joined in on what became a melee. The black soldiers were beaten, tear-gassed, and fired on by shotguns and pistols. In the aftermath, the president of the New Orleans Press Club reported to the executive secretary of the NAACP that as many as ten black soldiers may have been killed in what became known as the Lee Street Riot.

The Army refused to investigate the incident, and would not allow soldiers who were involved to participate in interviews with the press. Later that same year in Alexandria, an African American soldier was murdered by a Louisiana state policeman. Louisiana law-enforcement officials ignored the incident and did not discipline the officer involved. The Army also failed to call for an investigation, though the slain soldier, Raymond Carr, was a military policeman in good standing and did not have a weapon.

The soldiers of the 761st came to understand the kinds of things that could happen in Alexandria. Many, like William McBurney, chose to stay on the base. The others generally kept to themselves on the black side of town.

BUT THE PROBLEMS THEY ENCOUNTERED in Alexandria were far from the defining element of their experience at Claiborne. The men of the 761st were fast on their way to becoming soldiers. The training was rigorous. Their instruction in tank warfare intensified. While ammunition was kept strictly under lock and key, the men were allowed to fire live rounds, correcting for some of the limitations of their initial training at Fort Knox. They learned to refine their skills, to fire and maneuver the tanks under pressure.

There were the usual tensions between officers and enlisted men, as well as tensions related to issues of race. When the 761st Tank Battalion was activated, few black officers had been trained in armored warfare. The unit began under the command of white officers who came primarily from the Deep South. These officers were gradually replaced, according to the initial design for the unit, as black officers received the requisite armored training at Fort Knox.

Many of the original white officers resented their assignment to the 761st. They considered the post a purgatory, biding their time until they received promotions to other units. "White Christmas" was leading the pop charts in 1942 and '43, and these officers frequently sang "I'm dreaming of a white battalion" to the melody of "White Christmas" in the presence of the black enlisted men who worked in the Officers' Club.

There were two notable exceptions. David J. Williams came to the battalion as a young lieutenant just out of Yale. Williams was the son of a prominent Pittsburgh industrialist. Other white officers told him his father must have used his political influence to situate him with the 761st so that he wouldn't have to go overseas to combat, and Williams resented the assignment, as he was gung ho and eager to join the fight. Williams had been raised with an ethic of racial tolerance, but he had little experience interacting directly with blacks. He was nervous and unsure. Wanting to appear confident and in control, at times he could be standoffish, overly strict. The men regarded him warily and were not quite sure what to make of him. Despite his strictness, however, they believed him to be fair.

The officer who came to be most beloved of and respected by the battalion also happened to be white. Lt. Col. Paul L. Bates started as the 761st's executive officer and later became its commander. A former All-American football star from Western Maryland College, Bates had worked for ten years as a high school teacher and coach before joining the service. He was fundamentally decent, honest, modest, and compassionate. He saw and treated the men of the battalion with a simple, direct humanity, and they responded in kind. Unlike other commanders of the battalion, Bates lived on the post with the soldiers. He went with them on marches and runs, listening to their comments and complaints. There was nothing he could do to alter the underlying attitudes of other white officers, but he did forbid any direct mistreatment of his soldiers, and he insisted they be given nothing but the highest caliber of armored training. He believed in them.

The men could never find enough words of praise to describe Paul Bates. He would have said he was just doing his job. When Bates's eighteen months of duty as executive officer and commander with the 761st were up, he asked to remain with the unit, refusing a promotion in rank from lieutenant colonel to full colonel to do so.

The first three African American officers of the 761st joined the battalion on July 16, 1942. Ivan H. Harrison of Detroit, Michigan, was assigned to Leonard Smith and William McBurney's Headquarters Company, eventually becoming company commander. Harrison was a strict disciplinarian, nicknamed "Court-Martial Slim" because of his insistence that things be done the right way, by the book, each and every time. Harrison was at first suspected of being anti-black, although over time the men softened their harsh judgments of him as they realized that what lay behind his seeming rigidity was in fact a deep concern for their safety and well-being.

More African American second lieutenants joined the battalion in the following months, among them Charles A. Gates of Kansas City, Missouri. Gates was put in charge of the assault gun platoon of Headquarters Company. A graduate of Virginia's Hampton Institute, Gates had joined the service in April 1941 and trained with the Buffalo Soldiers at Fort Riley, Kansas. He was tough, principled, resolute: When told by white MPs in Alexandria that black officers were not permitted to carry side arms off the base, Gates quoted from the rule books he had memorized in detail, which made no such distinctions of race. Threatened with court-martial, he nonetheless maintained his position and ultimately won the right to carry his gun.

Thirty-one when he joined the 761st, Gates was given the affectionate nickname of "Pop." The nickname said more about the extreme youth of his men than about Gates's age. Gates took a particular liking to the spirited, headstrong Leonard Smith, and became determined to make a soldier out of him.

When Gates learned that Smith did not know how to swim, he immediately moved to rectify the situation. He took Smith along with some of the other men to a nearby pond. The water was deep. Gates held Smith over the side of the rowboat, and somebody yelled out, "Water moccasin!" (Water moccasins were a common threat in the Kisatchie Forest.) Smith jerked away, and Gates lost his hold. Gates was about to dive in after Smith when he looked up and saw him, dripping wet, sitting on the rocks by the shore beside the others. "How the hell did you get up there?" he asked. Smith told him, "I fell straight down to the bottom and ran. I didn't come all the way from New York City just to get killed by a snake."

Pop Gates laughed and said, "Can't you do anything right?"

AS THE MEN CONTINUED TO master their equipment and to mold their identity as a fighting unit in the early months of 1943, tensions rose between members of the battalion and the MPs, as well as between the battalion and white citizens of Alexandria. The men began to avoid traveling into Alexandria on weekend leave, going in on Mondays if they had to go at all. A rumor floated around the battalion— impossible to verify, as the Army refused to investigate such incidents—that a black soldier from one of the units at nearby Camp Polk and Camp Livingston was killed every weekend.

In March 1943, several weeks before the first anniversary of the 761st's activation, these tensions came to a head. A few members of the battalion had recently been severely beaten in Alexandria. Word went through the unit that another black soldier had been killed. His body had been discovered cut in half on the railroad tracks in Alexandria. The investigators claimed that he was intoxicated and stumbled onto the tracks himself. But men who knew him insisted he was a strict Baptist and a complete teetotaler.

When they learned of the killing, Leonard Smith, William McBurney, Preston McNeil, and several others went down to the motor pool, commandeered six tanks and a half-track, and started down the road toward Alexandria. They didn't care what happened to them; they were determined to roll to town as a show of strength, to demonstrate to local citizens that if they wanted they could blow the entire city off the map. If the Army wasn't going to do anything for them, they would look out for their own.

Lieutenant Colonel Bates stopped them at the gate leading out of the camp. He told them, "Let me go to town and see if I can straighten this out. If anything like this ever happens again, I swear I'll lead you into town myself." Bates was as good as his word: In their remaining three months at Camp Claiborne, Louisiana, the men of the 761st were never again harassed by the MPs or by the citizens of Alexandria.

ON APRIL 8, 1943, the 761st Tank Battalion joined the 85th Infantry Division, the 93rd Infantry Division, and the 100th Infantry Battalion of the 442nd Regimental Combat Team (consisting of "Nisei" Japanese American troops) for Third Army maneuvers in the Kisatchie National Forest. The maneuvers were designed by the Army to give its constituent units direct experience of the varying types of conditions and situations they would encounter in real combat.

The armored field operation in the swampy, densely vegetated terrain continued for almost two months. The men conducted combat simulations, working for the first time with infantrymen to take assigned objectives, learning to communicate with them via radio and hand signals. They rolled down narrow roads at night without the use of their headlights to prepare for surprise attacks. They further mastered the art of extricating tanks from stubborn mud holes. They learned how to bivouac in hostile territory, positioning the tanks in a circle around the battalion's headquarters and service elements, with the vehicles approximately twenty-five yards apart and facing outward from the center. They experienced countless details of life in battle: digging latrines, surviving on C rations, keeping the tanks functioning smoothly in the face of adverse weather conditions, scouting locations for camp beyond the range of enemy mortar and artillery fire.

Both Lt. Gen. Ben Lear, the commanding general of the Army Ground Force Reinforcement System of the European Theater of

Operations, and Lt. Gen. Leslie McNair, the chief of the Army Ground Forces, observed the 761st on several occasions. By every account, the battalion conducted itself well.

The 761st returned to Camp Claiborne with a road march of eighty-three miles. Two months later, on September 14, the battalion was moved to Camp Hood, Texas, for its final months of training. On October 29, 1943, by order of the War Department, a key piece of equipment of the 761st Tank Battalion was changed: The battalion was upgraded from the M-5 light tank to the M-4 medium, or Sherman, tank.

2

SOLDIERS

Wars may be fought with weapons,

but they are won by men.

—GENERAL GEORGE S. PATTON

The M-4 Sherman tank—named after Civil War general William Tecumseh Sherman—was the mainstay and chief hope of the United States Army ground forces on the eve of the Allied invasion of Europe. At thirty-two tons, more than twice the weight of the M-5 Stuart, the Sherman was armed with a 75mm cannon, a .50-caliber machine gun, two .30-caliber machine guns, and a two-inch smoke mortar. The turret at its thickest point boasted 3.94 inches of armor; the V-8 500-horsepower engine powered the massive vehicle at speeds of up to forty-five miles per hour; the eighteen-inch-wide treads provided high maneuverability over difficult terrain. The first Sherman to roll off the assembly line at the Chrysler Arsenal in Detroit in February of 1942 was hailed as a masterpiece of engineering, a definitive match against the German Panzer.

Looking at his new tank in the motor pool at Camp Hood, Leonard Smith couldn't help but feel like a kid on Christmas morning. The battalion had seen training films of Sherman tanks rolling straight through walls, knocking down trees, annihilating armored targets from distances of five hundred yards and more. This was *power*, on a level that compared—for both Smith and William McBurney—with their unfulfilled dreams of piloting fighter planes. They spent several days on the dusty driving range just getting used to the new equipment. They felt unwieldy at first in the strange machines that handled like large farm tractors—but then, as they mastered the ins and outs of the controls, invincible. Like other young American tankers in training at the time, they had no way of knowing that the Sherman's reputation was a lie. The M-4 General Sherman tank would prove to be one of the deadliest military design failures in history.

Armored vehicles, in the form of plated horse-drawn chariots, had been a highly effective force in combat from the time of the ancient Greeks; the first mechanically powered armored vehicle was designed in 1482 by Leonardo da Vinci, who developed a sketch of a crank-operated covered chariot. But mechanized, armored track–laying vehicles were not introduced to combat until 1916, by the British in World War I. The name "tanks" comes from the crates in which these top-secret weapons were shipped to the front in France, labeled as "water tanks." The first tanks were not much more than mobile steel-encased boxes equipped with machine guns and a cannon. They showed promise, however, as a means of breaking the bloody stalemates of trench warfare. Tanks could roll straight across the trenches to penetrate deep behind enemy lines—though early models were severely hampered by the thinness of their armor, by the short range of their weapons, and by the lack of any means of communicating with the outside world, which all too often left them cut off from infantry and artillery support in hostile territory.

After the war, an isolationist United States Congress voted to abolish the Army's nascent Tank Corps. It was deemed a waste of money. Two young captains—George Patton and Dwight Eisenhower—were virtually alone in recognizing the advent of mechanized warfare. In a 1920 *Cavalry Journal* article, Patton wrote, "The tank is a special, technical and vastly powerful weapon . . . give it half a chance, over suitable terrain and on proper missions and it will mean the difference between defeat and victory." This perception was, as historian Stephen Ambrose wrote, "exactly right," but unfortunately "decades ahead of most military theorists."

The Army did continue, albeit by fits and starts, to probe the new technology. But it was hamstrung by its limited vision for the use of tanks, seeing their primary role as providing reconnaissance and support for traditional cavalry and infantry tactics. In 1931, Army engineers chose—with what would prove to be tragic ramifications—not to adopt the new ideas proposed by eccentric inventor Walter Christy, which included a revolutionary suspension system that would have allowed for wider tracks, thicker armor, and far greater maneuverability. Christy subsequently took his designs to Europe, where they became a cornerstone of the German armored force. The American cavalry, with its emphasis on scouting and pursuit, developed a series of quick, lightly armored vehicles armed with 37mm cannons, precursors of the M-5 Stuart light tank. The infantry, with its focus on supporting riflemen in assaults against defensive positions, developed the heavier (though still relatively light) twenty-ton M-2 medium tank, armed with a hodgepodge of .30-caliber machine guns and a 37mm cannon. Compared with the emergent German fleet, both tanks were children's toys.

In postwar Germany, the development of armored technology had become the first priority of the state. By the late 1930s, Germany had secretly amassed an arsenal of medium Panzer (or Panther) tanks, equipped with high-velocity 75mm cannons, as well as an impressive air force, and was far along in the development of the fifty-five-ton 88mm Tiger tank. Of equal importance was Germany's development of radio technology allowing for close communication among the different elements of the military—tanks, aircraft, motorized infantry, artillery, combat engineers, and headquarters. This technology fueled the previously unimaginable mobility and highly coordinated assault of the blitzkrieg across Europe in 1939. In a panicked response, on June 10, 1940, the United States Congress authorized the creation of an Armored Force, and Army ordnance engineers began a desperate game of catch-up.

Hope for stopping the advance of the German fleet came to rest on the rapid modification of the infantry's existing M-2 medium tanks. The cavalry's light tanks were too thinly armored to withstand the German tank guns (though they proved useful in reconnaissance, and were deployed to great effect against Japanese infantry in the Pacific). The M-2 medium's 37mm cannon would clearly be no match against the 3.5-inch German armor. A 75mm cannon already in the Detroit Chrysler arsenal was mounted on the body of the M-2. With further modifications, including thicker armor and a turret that could rotate on a 360-degree axis, this became the M-4 Sherman. The first Shermans were deployed in combat by the British in North Africa in September 1942, and by the Americans in Tunisia in December; pitted against the Panzers, they achieved at best only bloody stalemates. Allied tankers shared stories of watching in horror as their 75mm shells bounced harmlessly off the sides of German tanks. Members of the U.S. Armored Force argued for replacing the Sherman with the prototype M-26 Pershing, a forty-two-ton tank with an improved suspension system that carried thicker armor and a 90mm cannon.

A command decision was made, by Lt. Gen. Leslie McNair among others, to continue with the Sherman. Army doctrine held that head-to-head combat against Panzers would be the function of tank destroyers, not of tanks. While tank destroyers (lightly armored vehicles with high-range, high-velocity guns) held off the German tanks, the Shermans—in theory—would spread out to make sudden, surprise spearheads across enemy infantry lines, and in its intended role the Sherman was believed to hold the advantage over the prototype M-26 because of its greater mobility. The Sherman's relative lightness also made it easier to manufacture and ship overseas in bulk. The prototype M-26 was shelved. By the summer of 1942, more than 2,000 Sherman tanks were being produced in Detroit each month.

HEADING BACK TO THE MOTOR POOL from the tank range at Camp Hood, William McBurney constantly pestered Willie Devore to let him take the driver's seat. There were "governors" inside the Sherman's engine to limit training speeds to a maximum of twenty-five miles per hour, but it had taken the men only a day or two to figure out how to disable them. Without governors, the 32-ton vehicles could fly. It was an incredibly powerful feeling. Battalion tanks would race each other back to the motor pool doing forty to fifty miles an hour.

The young soldiers found themselves spending most of their time at Camp Hood inside their new tanks in the scorching Texas heat. On its arrival at Hood in the fall of 1943, the 761st was designated the "enemy" in maneuvers. It performed the crucial function of "school troops"—in essence, playing the Germans—for the tank destroyer units that rotated through the camp in the final weeks before those units were shipped overseas and into combat. As a result, the men were on near-constant maneuvers both on the base and throughout the surrounding Texas countryside, learning to master their M-4 Shermans under simulated battle conditions.

The Sherman tank was operated by a five-man crew: a tank commander, gunner, bow gunner, driver, and loader (in the light tank, the commander doubled as loader). The men kept positions comparable to those they'd held in the M-5 Stuarts: William McBurney was a gunner. Leonard Smith, with his continued knack for staying in trouble with officers and sergeants, found himself situated in the most thankless position of a tank crew, that of loader. Standing in the left rear of the turret, the loader followed the gunner or tank commander's orders as to which type of ammunition to pull off storage on the floors and walls and load into the cannon. He also had to eject the spent shell casings out of a small side hatch. Typically, the loader worked like hell in battle; as fast as he could load the shells and duck away from the cannon's recoil, the gunner would fire and demand another.

The tank commander sat or stood in the right rear of the turret. He wore radio headphones through which he remained in constant contact with platoon and company commanders. He communicated with his own crew via a handheld microphone, as the Sherman's engine made so much noise that even yelling at the top of his lungs he might not have been heard. He could fire the .50-caliber machine gun attached to the turret roof, turning it upward if necessary for antiaircraft use. The tank commander had the best periscope, with the widest field of vision. Except during heavy combat when the tank was "buttoned up"—the turret hatch closed, to guard against artillery bursts and mortar fire—he rode with his head and shoulders sticking out the top of the turret for an even better field of view. On maneuvers in the Texas heat, though ordered to button up for combat simulations, tank commanders usually left the hatches open. The inside of the tank could get as hot as an oven.

The gunner sat just in front of the tank commander. His vision was limited to the window of a periscope and a small telescopic sight on the turret. He couldn't see much of anything, and he depended on the eyes of the tank commander, who'd tell him to rotate the turret, say, thirty degrees right or sixty degrees left, and then order, "Hit that half-track over there," or "Get that sniper in the tower." After firing, the tank commander would tell him if the round fell short or long so he could raise or lower his aim to correct. The gunner could fire either the 75mm cannon or the coaxial .30-caliber machine gun. To preserve his 75mm shells, the gunner would often use the machine gun as a tracer, judging by where those bullets struck whether or not he had his target locked.

The bow gunner rode in the right front hull of the tank and controlled a .30-caliber machine gun. The driver was positioned in the left front hull of the tank. The bow gunner and driver entered and exited through their own hatches; when the tank was buttoned up, each had the use of a periscope. Like the tank commander, when the Sherman was not in combat the two would frequently stand with their heads and shoulders protruding from the hatches for better vision.

The task of driving could be physically exhausting. The Sherman didn't have a steering wheel but rather two levers, right and left, which, when pushed or pulled, would stop the movement of their respective tracks on the undercarriage. To turn right, the driver would pull the right lever, stopping the right tracks while the left continued to rotate. To turn left, he did the opposite. To shift gears to increase or decrease the vehicle's speed, the driver had to double-clutch, pushing down with his full weight on two pedals. At just 135 pounds, Leonard Smith had trouble managing it. But like William McBurney, he constantly pestered the driver of his tank, Hollis Clark, for the chance to race the Sherman back from the range. The thrill was worth the effort.

The shift in the 761st's principal equipment from light to M-4 medium tanks was accompanied by a battalion reorganization. The 761st still contained Headquarters Company, Service Company, and Able, Baker, and Charlie Companies; but an additional letter company was added, consisting of fifteen of the old light tanks. Dog Company would be used primarily for reconnaissance missions. The Sherman tankers, proud of their new equipment, couldn't help but tease Dog Company's members a bit—calling the light tanks the "mosquito fleet" because of their small size, and referring to the 37mm guns as "pea shooters" next to the 75mm cannons. On maneuvers, however, they learned the critical role light tanks could play in a mission's success or failure. Battalion officers, fully aware of this, transferred two of the battalion's most responsible members, Warren Crecy and soft-spoken Preston McNeil, into Dog Company to serve as tank commanders and platoon leaders.

WHEN THE MEN RECEIVED PASSES to travel off base, they tended to avoid the nearby town of Killeen. After a few times, even the adventuresome Leonard Smith refused to take his chances there. Local whites wouldn't just glare at the men, as in Alexandria; they'd shout epithets out the windows of their cars. There was no black side of town: African Americans had been openly discouraged from living in Killeen since its founding in the late 1800s (the town would have no black residents until after 1950). Instead, during their travels off base, members of the 761st went to the towns of Lampasas, Belton, and Temple, or traveled the eighty miles to Austin, where there was a USO for African American soldiers. Black soldiers didn't have any trouble in Austin as long as they kept to their side of the city.

Travel, however, could prove troublesome. Preston McNeil had grown up in the segregated South: Knowing the injustice of its various laws and codes, he nonetheless accepted them as a part of life. But the constant mistreatment he received from white bus drivers at Camp Hood infuriated even him. The back seats of the buses, where black soldiers were forced to ride, held six to eight people. Civilian bus drivers insisted there be six black soldiers present at the base bus stop before they'd let any blacks on. Even a group of five soldiers would be told they had to wait. McNeil, wearing the uniform of his country, had no choice but to stand and wait while busloads of white soldiers and white civilian employees came and went.

Trying to make it back to the base could be even worse. The last bus back at night was always full of soldiers. Several bus drivers made a regular practice of stopping the bus when they were still two or three miles from the post, suddenly announcing that the vehicle was overloaded and ordering the black soldiers off. Leonard Smith found the walk back far from pleasant. Watching the taillights of the bus recede, he knew there was nothing he could do about it. Even with a group of friends around him, he didn't feel quite safe. There weren't any streetlights to speak of. On the rare occasions when car headlights approached, he felt a quick tightening of his stomach. He refused to hide or crouch out of sight—but he was well aware that in this part of the country anything could happen to him. After a hard day of maneuvers, heading toward the start of another such day, it could feel like a very long walk home.

THE YOUNG TANKERS DEVELOPED a fierce sense of proprietorship toward their vehicles, akin to a teenager's outsized feeling of ownership toward his first car. Most of the 761st's members were, in fact, still teenagers. But the Sherman tank—at twenty feet by nine feet by eleven feet—was cooler by far than any car any of them would ever own. Leonard Smith loved to stand in front of his Sherman, looking up at its turret, thinking, "This is *mine.*" Smith had never before gone out of his way to seek extra duty, but he chose to stay late in the motor pool, cleaning the tank, checking its tracks, making sure that all its component parts were well-oiled. The men hadn't given names to the M-5 Stuarts in which they'd trained, but they named their Shermans. In Headquarters Company, William McBurney's tank was the tank Lt. Col. Paul Bates would command on the battlefield. Bates named the vehicle after his girlfriend, "Taffy." McBurney might have preferred something with a bit more of an edge: Other tanks carried monikers like "Thunderbolt," "Hurricane," and "Widow Maker." The irrepressible Leonard Smith's tank was christened "Cool Stud."

When they were first assigned the Shermans at Camp Hood, the men were told that these were the vehicles they'd drive if the battalion went to combat. But as the months passed, the prospect that the battalion would experience real combat seemed increasingly remote. While the white tank destroyer units against which they were pitted rotated regularly through Camp Hood to be shipped overseas, the 761st received no such orders. In Texas, as in Louisiana, they couldn't help but overhear the derisive term by which many whites, including some of their own officers, referred to them—"Mrs. Roosevelt's Niggers," a designation referring to the First Lady's continued insistence in the press that blacks be given the opportunity to fight on equal footing. The phrase implied that the 761st was a mascot existing only for show, that they weren't going anywhere.

Training periods for armored units varied greatly in duration, depending on the date of their creation and the theater of operations for which they were intended. Tank units that were authorized, like the 761st, after America's official entrance into the war rarely trained in the States for more than a year. Some were shipped overseas to North Africa and the Mediterranean, some to the Pacific, some to England to train in preparation for the invasion of Europe. By the winter of 1943, the 761st Tank Battalion had been in existence for twenty months, and no arrangements were being made on any level of command for its deployment. The men continued to listen to what war updates they could (information was restricted for units in training), but they had less and less of a sense that they themselves would become directly involved. For Leonard Smith, William McBurney, and Preston McNeil, who had volunteered with such high hopes, the feeling that the battalion would not get the chance to fight was deeply disappointing.

AMERICA'S OVERARCHING BATTLE PLANS for the remainder of the war had been firmly established at a conference in Teheran, Iran, in the four days from November 28 to December 1, 1943, the first official meeting of Allied leaders Winston Churchill, Franklin Roosevelt, and Joseph Stalin. By this time, after a series of bitter desert battles in 1942 and early 1943—including El Alamein, Kasserine Pass, Tunis, and Bizerta—American and British forces had succeeded in pushing the Germans out of North Africa and Tunisia. They continued to wage a costly campaign against German forces in Italy, launching numerous unsuccessful assaults against a defensive perimeter known as the "Winter Line" near Cassino and Anzio. In 1942, Russia had come close to losing Moscow to the invading Germans but had succeeded in turning the tide after brutal fighting at Stalingrad and Kursk, and was making plans for its own large-scale offensive. In the Pacific theater of operations, American and Japanese forces were at a stalemate, though America seemed finally to be gaining momentum after tough naval and infantry battles from Guadalcanal to the Solomon Islands and New Guinea.

The three heads of state meeting in Teheran had varied, at times conflicting, strategic interests: Stalin wanted supplies from America and Britain to fill his vastly depleted arsenals, and he pushed for a second front in Europe to relieve pressure from the Soviets; the British, depending for many of their supplies on colonies accessed through the Suez Canal, wanted to maintain a heavy presence in the Mediterranean; the Americans wanted to contain and roll back the Japanese presence in the Pacific, and also pushed for a cross-Channel invasion of Europe to be launched at the earliest possible date, believing that such an assault would bring the war against Germany to the quickest end. At the conclusion of the Teheran Conference, the Allies agreed that the Americans and British would together carry out a massive invasion across the English Channel in the spring of 1944; in exchange for continued British and American support, Stalin would commit the Soviet Union to fight against Japan when the war in Europe was over; and the Americans would continue fighting in Italy, though limiting the scale of these operations in favor of the European invasion.

ALTHOUGH THEY HAD COME TO BELIEVE that it was unlikely they would see combat, the men of the 761st were determined to train hard—to prove that they *could* fight. In their ongoing, at times seemingly endless, maneuvers at Camp Hood through the winter and early spring of 1944, they were becoming a crack outfit. The crews of the M-4 Shermans became expert at judging terrain and spotting threats peculiar to tanks: ground that could be heavily mined—a tactic at which the Germans were particularly adept—and "tank traps," trenches dug in the ground and covered with branches and dirt that the heavy tanks would sink into and be unable to maneuver out of. Such traps were almost always watched by hidden tank destroyers, gun emplacements, or concealed infantry holding bazookas.

Each of the battalion's companies had its outstanding performers. In Dog Company, the platoon commanded by the tough, determined Warren Crecy executed scouting and screening maneuvers with particular distinction. In Headquarters Company, the assault gun platoon—a platoon consisting of five 105mm howitzers mounted on M-4 Sherman chassis—commanded by Leonard Smith's mentor, Charles "Pop" Gates, destroyed its assigned targets with such pinpoint accuracy that a visiting white colonel who had fought extensively in North Africa chose to stay with the unit for several weeks, working with them on a hillside in the dry Texas heat. He arranged for Pop Gates's crews to get extra ammunition so that they could further perfect the art of shooting indirect fire, a technique using mathematical calculations and forward spotters to hit targets the gunners could not see.

As "school troops," the Sherman crews of the 761st had been instructed not to hold any punches, to perform to the best of their ability in order to provide the tank destroyers with the highest possible level of combat training. They took this instruction quite literally, regularly outmaneuvering the tank destroyer teams. Lt. Col. Paul Bates, who had continued his practice of living on the post and spending time with the soldiers, greatly admired and took pride in the accomplishments of his men. When Bates was walking through the motor pool one afternoon, he overheard a group around one of the tanks laughing loudly. He asked the soldiers what they were laughing about. The Tank Destroyer motto at the time was "Seek, Strike and Destroy." One of the men told him, "You know what those tank destroyers call themselves? . . . When we appear it is 'Sneak, Peek and Retreat'!"

The commander of Headquarters Company, Capt. Ivan Harrison, worked together with battalion members to come up with an official insignia and motto for the 761st. The insignia of the tank destroyer force at the time was a black panther crushing a tank in its jaws. The men drew from this, choosing for their own insignia a snarling black panther. German tanks were known as "Panzers" or "Panthers," and (with typical GI swagger) the battalion's M-4 Sherman tankers considered themselves more than a match for the enemy, hence the name "black panthers."

For their unit motto, they decided on "Come Out Fighting." It was taken from a quote by boxer Joe Louis, who had been foremost among the heroes of many of the men when they were growing up, and it conveyed their sense of themselves as scrappy, underestimated underdogs. In his second match against German Max Schmeling in 1938—a match widely touted by the press as a test of democracy against fascism—Joe Louis had destroyed his opponent, knocking him out in the first round. No one had thought beforehand that he had a chance of winning. Asked just prior to the match by reporters how he was going to fight Schmeling, Louis said, "I'm going to come out fighting!"

Entering into this tightly bonded group, fresh recruits could feel like the awkward new kid on the first day of school. The battalion received a number of recruits just out of the Armored Force Replacement Training Center in January 1944, bringing the unit's total number up to 713 enlisted men. Floyd Dade, an eighteen-year-old from Texarkana, Arkansas, who'd been drafted out of high school, was assigned to act as loader in an Able Company tank. Dade listened to the company's longtime members tell jokes and stories about their previous training in Louisiana and at Camp Hood, shyly asking them to explain references and terms he didn't understand. Dade worked extraordinarily hard to catch up; he was diligent to a fault, always seeking out extra tasks to perform in training, but he escaped the resentment of his peers for this dutiful trait because he had an excellent sense of humor.

Close friendships continued to develop throughout the battalion. Warren Crecy's wife, Margaret, lived not far from the base, and on weekend passes Crecy would invite his best friend, the quiet, reflective Horatio Scott, to spend time with them in Temple. Leonard Smith's buddy, charismatic Willie Devore, received letters from various girlfriends almost every day and read choice excerpts aloud to Smith. Smith continued his correspondence with the young woman Devore had hooked him up with from Greenwood—though he started to think she was eccentric if not downright crazy, as she never wrote to him on regular paper but rather on assorted scraps and pieces of tissue paper, which spilled out of the envelopes when Smith tore them open.

Despite Pop Gates's continued efforts to shape him into a soldier, Smith was constantly skirting the rules. The others in his tight group of friends—including McNeil, McBurney, and Devore—made the rank of technician or sergeant while at Camp Hood; Smith was promoted and then demoted. Gates thought that he might teach Smith responsibility by recommending him to act as Captain Harrison's jeep driver. It was a very short stint. One day, driving fast, Captain Harrison suddenly said, "Turn here." Smith turned—and the captain went flying out of the jeep. Smith backed up, and Harrison said, "What is wrong with you?" Smith replied, "You gave me an order. I obeyed it." Harrison said, "You're trying to get out of this Army, aren't you?" Smith protested, telling the captain honestly that he loved the Army. Harrison asked, "You do?" Smith nodded vigorously. And Harrison said, "You're not crazy, Smith, you're just plain simple!"

OFFICERS CONTINUED TO ROTATE through the battalion. Many of the original white officers who weren't pleased to have been attached to an African American unit were awarded transfers out—though Charles Wingo, who viewed the men with contempt, had remained and been promoted to the rank of executive officer. David Williams, the young lieutenant from Yale who had longed to leave the unit because he wanted the chance to fight, was granted his request for a transfer out to train with a paratrooper outfit—but several months later was disappointed to receive orders to transfer back in, and found himself put in charge of Able Company.

Another white officer, Russell C. Geist, from Germantown, Pennsylvania, had first been transferred to the unit at Camp Claiborne. Geist had immediately requested a transfer out. When group photographs were taken, Geist opted not to participate because he did not want to be pictured with the men. He gradually came to know the men, however—largely through his love of radios and the inner workings of military equipment. The Army had a new device known as a gyrostabilizer, designed to keep the 75mm cannon locked on target even when the Sherman was crossing rough terrain. Only a small number of soldiers with top-secret clearances were supposed to have the level of technical expertise to repair it. But one of the men in Headquarters Company, Thomas Ashly, would break the seal on the equipment whenever something went wrong and fix it. Geist was amazed that a black man could do that; it contradicted everything he'd been taught to believe growing up. Over time he fell in love with his men and did a complete about-face.

The unit was joined by several black officers while at Camp Hood, officers switched over to the unit from the newly formed 784th Tank Battalion. As per the Army's original plan, the battalion now contained more black officers than white, with three of its five companies—Charlie, Dog, and Headquarters—headed by African Americans. Among the new black officers was Capt. Garland "Doc" Adamson, who was put in charge of the medical detachment. Doc Adamson, by far the unit's oldest member at the age of fifty, had been an instructor in obstetrics and gynecology at Meharry Medical School in Tennessee before joining the Army.

Leonard Smith's first meeting with Adamson could have been disastrous. Hood, like all other Army bases at the time, was segregated even in its entertainment facilities. African American soldiers were strictly forbidden from entering the white movie theater on base. But members of the 761st would sometimes sneak undetected into the balcony to see the movies not shown in their theater. One evening, William McBurney, Preston McNeil, Leonard Smith, and others were in the balcony when Smith slipped and fell. He was lucky: He might have been killed, but instead he escaped without serious injury. He was lucky, too, in that whereas he could have been court-martialed for breaking the rules, when he went to see Doc Adamson to treat his rather extensive bruises, the kindly doctor turned a blind eye and did not file a report.

IN APRIL 1944, THE 761ST was joined by several more black officers, among them 2nd Lt. John Roosevelt Robinson, better known in the pantheon of American history as "Jackie." Robinson, who was born in 1919 in Cairo, Georgia, had been a standout football player and track star at Pasadena and UCLA before being forced to leave school to help support his family during the Depression. On April 3, 1942, he answered his induction notice and was sent to Fort Riley, Kansas, for basic training. Robinson was an intense, sober, and quiet young man who had been known since his youth as an intelligent loner who was deeply loyal to his loved ones and the causes he believed in. He was ready to join the fight for the service of his country, but he was leery of the poor treatment blacks received in the American military.

On joining the 761st, Lieutenant Robinson was immediately assigned to lead a tank platoon, although he had received no instruction in armored warfare at Fort Riley. As the unit was on near-constant maneuvers, there was little room for error. Robinson decided the only way to avoid disaster was simply to tell the men the truth, that he had never been inside a tank before and knew absolutely nothing about how a tank battalion operated. He knew enough from his training at Riley to attach himself to an experienced sergeant and to follow his lead. During maneuvers, Robinson spoke constantly with the sergeant via the two-way radio in his tank. The sergeant did a tremendous job of explaining things to him, and Robinson learned as he went along. The men had been impressed from the outset by Robinson's willingness to be honest with them, to admit what he didn't know and learn from them. They threw themselves into their work. After training with his platoon for several weeks, Robinson received an order to visit Lieutenant Colonel Bates at Headquarters. He still felt he knew nothing about armored warfare, and he was expecting to receive a reprimand. "Robinson," Bates told him, "I want to commend you and your outfit on your work down here. You have the best record of all the outfits at the camp, and I am singling you out for special mention."

Robinson was too stunned to answer right away. He decided, though, to tell Bates the truth—that the platoon's success had nothing to do with him but was instead due entirely to the efforts of the men. Bates considered his confession for a moment before saying, "Robinson, I don't care how you accomplished what you did, but the fact of the matter is that you still have the best outfit of all down here. That's all that counts."

Impressed with the rapport that Lt. Jackie Robinson had established with the men, Bates appointed him the unit's morale officer. Robinson organized pickup softball games with both the officers and the enlisted men on the base. When Robinson himself was at bat, the entire infield moved back about fifty feet.

BUS TRAVEL CONTINUED TO BE a problem for members of the 761st. At Camp Hood and throughout the South, clashes occurred repeatedly between black soldiers and white civilian bus drivers. Civilian Aide to the Secretary of War Truman K. Gibson called the bus situation in 1943 "one of the most serious problems facing the Army," reporting that for black soldiers "[i]ntercity travel is a source of constant peril or uncertainty."

William McBurney responded, as at Claiborne, by choosing to remain on the base in his free time. There was enough injustice on the post itself to make him angry. Camp Hood served at the time as a detainment center for German prisoners of war (holding as many as 4,000 by 1945), many of them part of Field Marshal Rommel's Afrika Korps. The German POWs had light work detail, and most were allowed to roam through the camp unguarded. They were permitted to walk in and out of the PX and special services clubs from which McBurney himself was barred. German prisoners were given more freedom than were the black American soldiers.

THE HIGH MARKS THE 761ST earned in training and on maneuvers at Camp Hood did not escape the notice of the Army's higher echelons. Brig. Gen. Ernest A. Dawley, the commanding general of the Tank Destroyer Center, had reported to Washington on the unit's training and had addressed the men on several occasions. Lt. Gen. Benjamin Lear had also observed the battalion repeatedly. During a mass post formation—in which all units present at Camp Hood were lined up in strict formation for inspection—Lear paid the battalion a signal honor. He called the officers and first sergeants of the 761st to step forward, saying, "All the reports coming up to Washington about you have been of a superior nature, and we are expecting great things of your battalion in combat."

It is unlikely that even at this late stage of the war the 761st was actually intended to see combat. The Allies were slowly gaining ground on the Italian peninsula, having staged a series of landings

SOLDIERS

behind the impenetrable "Winter Line" defenses south of Rome; on May 18, 1944, Cassino fell, to be followed by Anzio on May 23. The Russians were defeating the Germans in battle after battle on the eastern front, reclaiming Kiev, Leningrad, and the Crimea, and by the summer of 1944 were poised to force the Germans back across Poland into Germany. In the Pacific in the winter and spring of 1944, the Allies fought island by island closer to Japan itself, facing ever-more-resolute, then desperate, Japanese soldiers, determined to defend the home islands to the death. In the Marshall Islands, Saipan, and Guam, the Japanese lost tens of thousands of men. The Japanese fared no better at naval warfare, suffering heavy losses of men, aircraft carriers, and battleships in the Battle of the Philippine Sea.

On June 4, the Americans captured Rome, though the fighting in Italy was far from over. Then, on June 6, the Allies implemented Operation Overlord, the D-Day invasion of Europe. After the largely horrific landings at Gold, Juno, Sword, Utah, and Omaha Beaches, the Allies commenced what they believed would be a tough but inexorable march to Berlin. Coming across Normandy, however, American forces experienced unexpected difficulties and devastating casualties—particularly among the M-4 Sherman tanks and their crews, which were being lost by the hundreds. The 761st was the best-trained and most able-bodied armored unit remaining in the United States.

On June 9, 1944—three days after the Allied landings in Normandy—the 761st Tank Battalion was put on full alert for movement overseas. All communications from the men were now strictly monitored and censored; the activities of the unit from this point forward were considered top secret.

AMONG THE OFFICERS AND enlisted men in combat in World War II, a wound that was serious enough to warrant evacuation back to the

States, but not serious enough to cause permanent harm, was termed a "million-dollar wound." Second Lt. Jackie Robinson had suffered his million-dollar wound before he entered the Army: His right ankle had been wrenched during a football scrimmage at Pasadena Junior College in 1937, leading to a condition diagnosed as "arthritis, chronic, nonsuppurative, moderately severe." In January 1944, the Disposition Board of Brooke General Hospital at Fort Sam Houston in San Antonio, Texas, stipulated that Robinson be "physically disqualified for general military service, but qualified for limited service."

This meant Robinson did not have to fight if he did not so choose. When the battalion was put on alert, Lieutenant Colonel Bates, who had been so impressed with Robinson's rapport with the men, asked that he consider going overseas as a morale officer. Robinson agreed. He took the first steps toward obtaining the Army's consent, signing waivers relieving the Army of any responsibility in the event of further injury. On June 21, as part of this process, Robinson reported for examination at McCloskey General Hospital in Temple. X rays showed that his condition had not changed. Nonetheless, on June 26 the hospital's board cleared Robinson to travel overseas. He was required to remain at McCloskey General Hospital for further treatment. Several days later, on July 6, he was granted a night's leave. That evening he left the hospital for Camp Hood. What happened next would alter the course of Jackie Robinson's life and, as it turned out, the course of sports and American history.

Robinson boarded the bus back to the post, eventually heading to the Negro Officers' Club. The battalion had been sent out on maneuvers, and he found the club almost empty. A later blood test would show that he consumed no alcohol. At 11 P.M., he boarded a bus from outside the club to make the trip back to the hospital. He joined the wife of a fellow lieutenant with the 761st, Virginia Jones, who was heading back to her home in Belton, halfway between the base and the hospital. Jones had made what was to prove a fateful decision on where to sit. She got on and sat down in the fourth row from the rear. Lieutenant Robinson got on next and sat beside her.

The bus traveled two more stops on the base before filling with civilian workers leaving Camp Hood. Someone pointed out to the driver that a black officer was not sitting at the back of the bus; he was sitting in the middle of the bus, apparently beside a white woman (Jones was extremely light-skinned). The bus driver looked back at them and asked Lieutenant Robinson to move. Robinson told the bus driver, according to Mrs. Jones's testimony, to "go on and drive the bus." The driver demanded that Robinson move, and Robinson refused. The driver stopped the bus, walked down the aisle with his fist balled, and said, "Will you move to the back?"

In the weeks prior to this, the War Department had been forced to acknowledge the potential explosiveness of the bus situation for black soldiers stationed in the South. Joe Louis and Sugar Ray Robinson, both soldiers assigned to Camp Siebert in Alabama, had recently been harassed and threatened by white MPs while waiting outside a bus depot. The incident was widely publicized. In June, in Durham, North Carolina, a black soldier had been shot and killed by a white bus driver when he refused to move to the back of a bus; the driver was subsequently acquitted by an all-white civilian jury. The Army responded to public pressure by issuing an order— without fanfare, in order to avoid a firestorm in the South—barring segregation on any vehicle operating on an Army post. Aware of these regulations, Robinson would not be intimidated. But while Robinson knew of the order, the bus driver apparently did not—or chose not to honor it.

According to Robinson, the driver told him that if he didn't go to the back of the bus there would be trouble. Robinson replied coolly that he knew his rights. At the last stop on the post—the central terminal, where Jones and Robinson were intending to transfer to the city bus that would take them on to Belton and Temple—the driver jumped off the bus and quickly returned with the dispatcher and several drivers. "There's the nigger that's been causing me trouble," he shouted. Robinson pointed his finger at the driver and said, "Quit fucking with me."

The MPs were called to the bus station by the dispatcher, at the driver's request. The white MPs treated Robinson with proper courtesy: "They were enlisted men," Robinson would later say, "and they called me 'sir' and seemed only interested in doing their duty under the circumstances." They asked Robinson to accompany them to the military police guard room. There, Robinson encountered a sergeant and a private, Ben Mucklerath, who asked one of the MPs if he had that "nigger lieutenant" with him. Robinson took exception to Mucklerath's language. The MPs summoned the duty officer, Captain Wigginton, to the station; Wigginton proceeded to ignore Robinson and to question Mucklerath, who knew nothing but what he had heard secondhand about the bus incident. Both men referred to Robinson as a "nigger." When Robinson protested, Captain Wigginton ordered him outside.

Finally, Capt. Gerald M. Bear, the head of the base's military MPs, arrived. Robinson followed Captain Bear into the guard room to give his account of the incident, but Bear ordered him out. Robinson, who could see both Mucklerath and Wigginton inside, objected to being excluded from a process that could have serious implications for his future. Robinson would testify that Captain Bear "did not seem to recognize me as an officer at all." According to Bear's testimony, Robinson regularly interrupted them and kept coming to the guard room door-gate; Bear cautioned and requested Robinson on several occasions to remain at ease. He claimed that "in an effort to try to be facetious, Lieutenant Robinson bowed with several sloppy salutes, repeating several times, 'OK, sir, OK, sir,' on each occasion." Bear felt Robinson's attitude was "disrespectful and impertinent to his superior officers, and very unbecoming to an officer in the presence of enlisted men."

When Bear finally summoned a stenographer to record Robinson's testimony on the bus incident, the stenographer, a white civilian woman, did not simply write down Robinson's answers to Bear's questions, but instead continually interrupted him, saying, among other things, "Don't you know you've got no right sitting up there in the white part of the bus?" Robinson questioned whether she was objective enough to record his words accurately. According to Robinson, Bear then said that he was an "uppity nigger" and had no right to speak to a white woman in that manner. Some time after this abortive interview, Captain Bear ordered military police to escort Robinson back to the hospital in Temple. When Robinson asked if this meant he was under arrest, Bear refused to answer. Robinson stated that he had a pass until 8 A.M. the next morning; unless he was under arrest, he should be allowed to go where he pleased. Bear finally told Robinson he was under "arrest in quarters," which meant that he would not be detained at the base but was ordered not to leave the hospital. When he arrived back at McCloskey General, a colonel there told him "that he had been alerted to expect a black officer who had been drunk and disorderly and had been trying to start a riot"; he advised Robinson to take the blood test that proved there was no alcohol in his system.

Captain Bear initiated a court-martial. Such charges, however, required the permission of the commanding officer of the accused's battalion. Lieutenant Colonel Bates, who had nothing but the highest regard for Robinson's character, refused to give such consent. The top brass at Camp Hood responded by transferring Robinson to the 758th Tank Battalion; the commander of the 758th immediately signed the court-martial order. On July 24, Robinson was officially arrested.

A court-martial trial in the United States Army consists of two phases: In the first, charges are presented to a panel of officers, which then votes on their merit; in the second, those charges approved by the panel are tried before a jury of officers. In the first phase of the court-martial of Jackie Robinson, all charges involving Robinson's altercations with the bus driver were dismissed. Several white passengers testified that Robinson had cursed not only at the bus driver but also at them. These allegations were disproven and were also dismissed. Lt. Col. Paul Bates, who put his career on the line to defend Jackie Robinson on several different occasions in the weeks that followed, brought eight members of the 761st before the panel to testify to the rough and unfair treatment they regularly received on buses at Camp Hood. The Army could not afford the outcry and close scrutiny of bus policy that trying these charges against Robinson—already nationally known owing to his football career at UCLA—would bring. Instead, the court-martial trial of Robinson would turn on what happened after the MPs arrived at the scene. He was charged with behaving disrespectfully toward Captain Bear in the guard room, and with disobeying Bear's order to remain in the receiving area. Conviction would result at the very least in a dishonorable discharge.

On August 1, an advance detachment that included Maj. Charles Wingo was sent from the 761st to Camp Kilmer, New Jersey, to prepare for the unit's imminent departure overseas; the rest of the battalion was soon to follow. Lieutenant Colonel Bates remained behind at Camp Hood to testify at Robinson's trial, which began on August 2. Bates stated under oath that Robinson had performed with excellence throughout his time with the battalion, and was well-respected by all officers and enlisted men of the unit; he further testified that he would have utter confidence in Robinson's ability to lead his men in combat.

Robinson's lawyer attacked the prosecution's case on two fronts: first, by arguing that Captain Bear had himself acted in an unbecoming manner, and second, by underscoring the provocation that had led

Robinson to act with what might be deemed disrespect. Bear admitted that he had told Robinson he was "at ease"; he therefore had no right to question the manner in which Robinson conducted himself in the receiving room. Robinson's attorney argued that Robinson was well within his rights to voice concern over the accuracy of Mucklerath and Wigginton's statements regarding his behavior, and fully within his rights, as well, to demand to know whether or not he was under arrest. Bear had violated strict procedure when he sent Robinson—whom he had not placed under arrest—back to the hospital under military guard.

Robinson's attorney further sought to attack Captain Bear's assertion that he and the other soldiers present had treated Robinson with the utmost respect. Private Mucklerath testified in support of Bear's claim. Robinson's lawyer skillfully cross-examined Mucklerath, asking him "if he had ever called Jackie Robinson a nigger. He said 'Under no circumstances.' 'Did you ever use that word?' He said, 'No, I never used it.' 'Did any of you ever use that word? . . .' He said, 'No, none of us ever did.' 'I want you to tell me—and this is very, very important so that we can punish this man properly—I want you to tell me the exact words he used when he threatened you.' 'If you ever call me a nigger again, I'll break you in two.'" The jury found Robinson not guilty on all counts.

Robinson returned to the 758th, the battalion to which he had been hastily transferred by the brass at Hood. He requested that he be reassigned to the 761st. However, by the time this order was approved, on August 24, the 761st Tank Battalion had already departed. Robinson was transferred to Camp Breckinridge, Texas, and later to Camp Wheeler, Georgia. In November 1944—as the 761st was experiencing fierce combat in the Saar Basin of France— he was honorably discharged. A black baseball player Robinson had encountered at Camp Breckinridge had told him that the Kansas City Monarchs, a Negro League team, was looking for athletes. Robinson was looking for employment. In November, immediately following his discharge, Robinson wrote to the Monarchs and was hired; in August 1945, he was approached after a game the Monarchs played at Chicago's Comiskey Park by a scout for the Brooklyn Dodgers.

IN THE SUMMER OF 1944, as Jackie Robinson's court-martial began, the men of the 761st did not yet know that they were being sent to France. In June, July, and August, in the months between being put on alert and their departure, they didn't know whether they were heading to the Atlantic or the Pacific. Maj. Charles Wingo had made a speech to some of the men about walking over the dead bodies of Japanese soldiers like a carpet. If anything, the men thought they would be sent to the Pacific, where in August 1944, Gen. Douglas MacArthur and Adm. Chester Nimitz were preparing to attack Peleliu in the Palau Islands. Peleliu was needed to serve as a staging area for the upcoming invasion of the Philippines. The 761st would likely ship out, the men assumed, in support of that imminent attack, the Philippines being the last step in preparation for the climactic invasion of Japan itself.

WHEN LIEUTENANT COLONEL BATES first received the alert for deployment overseas, he had ordered the company commanders of his battalion to inform their men of their new status and, in preparation for what was to come, to read them the Articles of War. Among the articles the men heard recited that day were Article 56: "Whosoever shall relieve the enemy with money, victuals, or ammunition, or shall knowingly harbor or protect an enemy, shall suffer death, or such other punishment as shall be ordered by the sentence of a court-martial." They also heard Article 95: "When any non-commissioned officer or soldier shall die, or be killed in the service of the United States, the

then commanding officer of the troop or company shall, in the presence of two other commissioned officers, take an account of what
effects he died possessed of, above his arms and accoutrements, and
transmit the same to the office of the Department of War, which said
effects are to be accounted for, and paid to the representatives of such
deceased non-commissioned officer or soldier. . . ."

The reality of what was ahead began to sink in.

3

ETO

Everything was secret, secret, secret.

—William McBurney

On August 9, 1944, the 676 enlisted men and 36 officers of the 761st Tank Battalion boarded a United States Army troop train at Camp Hood. In a precaution taken by the Army with all American soldiers to guard against enemy spies, they had no idea where they were going. Many of them also couldn't help but wonder whether, on their arrival, they would be fighting as they had trained to fight—as an M-4 medium tank battalion—or instead be shifted into service and support roles. Their suspicions were not without reason. Despite the battalion's exceptional performance on maneuvers, white soldiers at

Camp Hood had openly continued to doubt that blacks would be allowed to fight in tanks. Moreover, while the men had been told on first being assigned their Sherman tanks that these were the vehicles they would be using if they went to combat, no preparations of any kind had been made for shipping them. Leonard Smith had reluctantly left behind "Cool Stud," the tank he had invested with so many dreams of blasting his way across enemy lines. Only personal equipment made it onto the troop train. Everything each soldier owned was crammed into a 24-by-18-inch duffel, or barracks, bag.

As the train jerked into motion, the men craned their necks looking out the windows for station signs. Several MPs walked through the troop cars pulling down the window shades. A few soldiers had time, however, to realize that they were moving north and east. The word spread like wildfire up and down the aisles. Despite what they had previously been led to think, it appeared Europe was their likely destination. When William McBurney complained to an MP about the lowering of the shades, he was told brusquely that in some of the Southern towns through which they were traveling, people would shoot at cars containing black troops. McBurney was quite happy to be getting out of the South.

Three days after their departure from Camp Hood, they arrived at Camp Shanks, in Orangeburg, New York. More than a million soldiers were to pass through Camp Shanks in the years between 1943 and 1945. Located twenty miles north of Manhattan on the west bank of the Hudson River, Camp Shanks was one of the principal ports of embarkation for troops headed to the European Theater of Operations, or ETO. Shanks was strictly a staging area, in which troops received last-minute inoculations, completed the paperwork for their wills, and waited for the arrangements for their transit overseas to be finalized.

To the New Yorkers in the group, Camp Shanks was paradise. Unit commanders tended to be liberal in handing out overnight passes while at Shanks. William McBurney and Preston McNeil spent time with friends and family in New York City with the Army's blessing. Leonard Smith, however, had gotten into trouble for returning late to Camp Hood from a furlough, and as a punishment was denied permission to leave the grounds. But Smith and several others who were not given passes tested the perimeter fence and found a place where they could slip out undetected. Smith sneaked out almost every night, traveling to Queens to see his family and getting back before roll call at 5:30 A.M.

In the battalion's first week at Camp Shanks, a large group took the bus across the George Washington Bridge into Harlem, to the legendary Savoy Ballroom. It was Thursday night, *the* night to be there. Thursdays, the women who worked as live-in cooks and maids—otherwise known as "pot-slingers"—had the evening off, and many of them would head straight to the club. Spanning a city block between 140th and 141st Streets on Lenox Avenue, the Savoy had hosted all the greats of the swing era: Louis Armstrong, Lionel Hampton, Duke Ellington, Ella Fitzgerald, Count Basie. There were bandstands at either end of the ballroom's vast 50-by-250-foot hardwood dance floor. When one orchestra took a break, a second would take over, allowing for uninterrupted dancing. At the club's peak in the 1930s and '40s, the floor was worn through every three years and had to be replaced. Whereas Smith, William McBurney, and Preston McNeil had been to the Savoy before they joined the service—Smith and McBurney had been going since they were fifteen—some of the men from small towns, like Willie Devore, had never seen anything like it. Devore was dazzled by the red and blue spotlights, the mirrors and chandeliers, and the hundreds of people pressed together and dancing like crazy.

Finally, on August 27, the 761st was put on "Alert" status, which meant they would be shipping out within the next twelve hours. The men were told to remove the armored unit patches from the shoulders of their uniforms (so that enemy spies could not assess troop movements); numbers were chalked on their helmets, giving them the order in which they were to march to and board the transport train. When asked where they were going, Captain Harrison told the men, "You'll know when you get there."

WERE IT NOT FOR THE hedgerow country of Normandy, the 761st might not have been called up from Camp Hood at all. In the weeks following the D-Day invasion of the northern coast of France, the Sherman tanks of the First U.S. Army had suffered tragic losses: By July 16, in its attempt to push inland, the 3rd Armored Division alone had lost more than a third of its 232 tanks. Scores of armored personnel were killed or seriously injured. So much planning had gone into the D-Day invasion itself that little time had been given to assessing the terrain beyond the beaches—terrain in which all the weaknesses of the vaunted M-4 General Sherman tank were thoroughly exposed.

The soil of Normandy's Cotentin Peninsula was loamy and contained few rocks; farmers there had for countless generations divided land among their sons by planting hedges. In hedgerow country, these bushes—bordering fields as small as one square acre—had developed into tangles of roots and trees that were three to six feet high and equally thick. The Germans could not have planned a better line of defense. Extending from ten to forty miles inland, the hedgerows acted as natural barriers against tanks and gave the Germans an abundance of places in which to conceal mines, tanks, and infantry carrying antitank weapons. When the nose of an American tank came up over the top of a hedge, the Germans on the other side would shoot through its exposed undercarriage. The few tanks that did make it over faced nightmarish obstacles ahead. The Panzerfaust, a German bazooka, fired a shaped charge that at close range blasted straight through the side of the Sherman tank with pulverizing effect. Still worse were the enemy tanks. American tank units learned in short order (as tankers had previously discovered in North Africa) that their 75mm shells bounced harmlessly off the sides of enemy tanks, while the Panzer tank's high-velocity 75mm and the Tiger tank's huge 88mm shells could rocket in one side of the M-4 and out the other.

In those first weeks in France, it was only because of the extraordinary courage of tank crews who would get out of damaged tanks and back into others that any ground was gained at all. Even so, as casualties mounted throughout July, the United States Armored Force began to run into manpower problems. Infantrymen who were pulled off the line, given a few hours of tank training, and sent out to fight in Shermans were invariably slaughtered, often within a matter of minutes. Tanks could be replaced; highly trained crews could not.

FROM CAMP SHANKS, the 761st rode the train a short distance south to the docks of New Jersey. From there they took a ferry across the Hudson River to New York Harbor. Lionel Hampton and his orchestra were on the midtown pier that day as part of the USO, playing a final farewell to the thousands of troops boarding the ships of the large convoy. Hampton's band played one of Leonard Smith's favorite tunes, "Flying Home." Though Smith was eager to get to Europe and join the battle, the song lent a bittersweet melancholy to the moment. As the men walked along the pier with their heavy barracks bags on their shoulders, they first caught sight of the ship that was to carry them to England, the HMS *Esperance Bay*. Like most members of the 761st, Smith had never been on a ship before. What he saw did not reassure him: The *Esperance Bay* was rickety in appearance, and was dwarfed by many of the transports around it.

Constructed in London in 1922 as a passenger ship, the *Esperance Bay* had been reoutfitted by the British navy on the outbreak of war and served a brief stint as an armed merchant cruiser before becoming a troop transport in 1941. Its odd, shaky appearance may have arisen in part from its layers of paint: from the bright colors of the cruise line, to dark gray with the white silhouette of a destroyer etched on it to scare off German battleships, to all gray. As on most troop transports in World War II, quarters on the *Esperance Bay* were extremely cramped: Its original capacity as a passenger ship was 1,500, but as a transport it housed thousands more. Bunks were stacked four and five high; soldiers slept in twelve-hour shifts and kept their bags with them at all times, because they never knew if they'd be going back to the same bunk. The food was terrible: William McBurney survived on a box of chocolate bars he took from the ship's post exchange. Leonard Smith ate next to nothing, as he was seasick from the moment the ship left port.

Like all military facilities at that time, the troop transports were segregated. White troops rode in the bow and midship areas, and blacks were quartered near the crew, in the hold at the bottom of the boat. Not many of the 761st's men ventured up to look around. They stayed belowdecks, reading, talking, playing cards, and shooting dice, often with the crew of the *Esperance Bay*, career merchant mariners who had enlisted en masse when the war broke out. They got along so well with the crew that Captain Jacoby, the transport commander, took the unusual step of giving Lieutenant Colonel Bates a letter of commendation before the ship reached port, complimenting the unit for its discipline, military courtesy, soldierly conduct, and high morale.

The ship reached port at Avonmouth, England, near Bristol, on September 8, 1944. As they gathered their gear and prepared to debark, Smith, McBurney, and the others had little sense of what lay ahead. At nineteen and twenty years of age, respectively, Smith and McBurney felt invincible. They had no idea what war was like. Moreover, they arrived in England under the impression (shared by most of their fellow Americans at that point) that the war was almost over.

The bloody fighting in Normandy had come to an end in August: In Operation Cobra, Gen. Omar Bradley's First Army and George S.

Patton's Third Army broke out of the hedgerow country after a massive air and artillery bombardment of enemy positions. The armored units in the battle were aided by a novel invention of Sgt. Curtis G. Culin of the 2nd Armored Division—steel prongs welded to the front of the Sherman tank that cut right through the hedgerows, a device known as the "rhinoceros." The prongs didn't allow the front of the Sherman to rise up, and the tank had power enough to push its way through, carrying roots and branches with it. The Americans quickly moved inland on the flat, open countryside beyond the hedgerows, taking St. Lo, Avranches, Chartres, and Rennes in rapid succession. On August 25, two days before the 761st sailed on the *Esperance Bay*, the Allies liberated Paris. As the men of the 761st stepped off the boat and onto the pier at Avonmouth, England, they had no way of knowing that some of the bloodiest fighting of the war was yet to come.

THE FEELING THAT THE WAR would soon be over was not limited to the general public. After the breakout from Normandy, there developed within the Allied high command a dangerous optimism. Gen. Dwight D. Eisenhower, now the Supreme Commander of the Allied forces in Europe, had an ongoing wager that the war would be over before Christmas. Gen. Omar Bradley was heard to comment that "the German army was no longer a factor with which we need reckon." Allied intelligence had learned that Hitler's own generals had tried to assassinate him on July 20; though that attempt had failed, Hitler seemed to have disappeared after the Battle of Normandy and there was speculation that another attempt had succeeded. For the first time since the German blitzkrieg had galvanized the United States Armed Forces into action in the summer of 1940, factory production of tanks and ammunition was allowed to slow.

Even George Patton, usually not one to underestimate his opponent, believed that the war would soon be over. On August 8, when in a single day his Third Army took St. Malo, Le Mans, and Angers, he wrote to his wife Beatrice about "how little the enemy can do—he is finished we may end this in ten days." On August 21, pressing rapidly eastward, the Third Army took more than seventy miles of ground, gaining Sens, Melun, and Montereau. Patton again asserted that, if he was allowed to continue his drive, "we can be in Germany in ten days. . . . It can be done with three armored and six infantry divisions. . . . It is such a sure thing."

The 761st Tank Battalion was ultimately bound for combat in the European Theater of Operations because Patton's Third Army needed tanks—and, more than tanks, trained Sherman crews. Patton himself specifically requested the unit: The battalion's future was to be linked directly with that of the man whose thirty-year career in the military had spanned perhaps more highs and lows than that of any other U.S. general.

Born in 1895 to a prominent Virginia family, Patton had a profound sense of personal destiny from his earliest childhood: At the age of five, he announced to his parents that he intended to become "a great general." He graduated from West Point in 1909 and rose from a young lieutenant to the rank of captain in World War I. On the creation of the Armored Force in 1940, he was appointed to command and train the "Hell on Wheels" 2nd Armored Division. Promoted to general, he led an initially disorganized U.S. Seventh Army in 1942 and '43 to victory in Tunisia and Sicily. But despite his undisputed tactical brilliance, his fierce, mercurial temperament landed him in trouble with his superiors as often as not. On New Year's Day 1944, command of the Seventh Army was taken away from him. He had—on two occasions that made world headlines the previous fall—slapped young soldiers suffering from battle fatigue; he considered the malady to be cowardice. Striking a subordinate was a court-martial offense. Only the intervention of his longtime supporters Dwight Eisenhower and George Marshall saved Patton from having to resign—and perhaps the stockade.

Patton intended to make the Third Army his redemption, the linchpin and consolidation of his role in history: When he was assigned command of the army in January, he wrote in his diary, "As far as I can remember this is my twenty-seventh start from zero since entering the U.S. Army. Each time I have made a success of it, and this must be the biggest." Though he was not directly involved in the planning of D-Day (he was used as the decoy commander of a phantom invasion force in order to dupe the Germans), his Third Army staff kept him abreast of the details. According to intelligence liaison Oscar Koch, when Patton was first shown an operational map of France early in 1944, he said the map was fine, then smiled. "But it only goes as far east as Paris. I'm going to Berlin." Patton's lightning-fast advance toward this objective in August was soon to be halted: He was to be stalled throughout the fall in the Lorraine region, outside of Metz, in the Saar Basin. This was the northeasternmost corner of France, forty short miles from the Siegfried Line, a series of massive fortifications designed to protect Germany from land invasion. The Third Army was there to encounter its bloodiest fighting of the war; and the 761st Tank Battalion was to play a key role in Patton's attempt to seal his reputation and make history.

ON SEPTEMBER 8. the members of the 761st boarded the train at Avonmouth that would take them on to Wimborne, twenty miles from the southern coast of England. Located amid the jewel-green hills of Dorset County, Wimborne had been a sleepy market town before World War II; during the war, houses, estates, and hotels were taken over to billet soldiers bound for France. As per Army policy, the battalion's six white officers were quartered apart from its thirty black officers in the rooms of an estate. The enlisted men stayed in a barn and series of outbuildings on the estate grounds.

They had finally been told that France was their ultimate destination. Couriers were sent to Southampton to make final preparations for their Channel crossing, which they were informed would take place on or shortly after September 30. The men were also told that they would indeed be fighting in tanks, though they hadn't yet received the new equipment. Leonard Smith couldn't believe his good fortune. He had been afraid he'd never get the chance to fight, much less in a tank. He couldn't wait to see his new Sherman. Pop Gates, who had always looked out for Smith, tried to calm him down. War wasn't a game, he told him, they'd be going up against real bullets. But Smith was too excited to listen. William McBurney, though more reserved and cautious by nature, couldn't help but be equally excited at the chance to prove himself.

One of the officers, however, was less than enthusiastic: Maj. Charles Wingo, the battalion's executive officer. Despite the battalion's excellent record throughout training, Wingo had told Able Company's Capt. David Williams that he didn't believe the men would perform well under fire. "What in the world is the War Department thinking about? These folks aren't fit for combat." Williams, too, had his doubts. Fair-minded but strict, he had continued to be a bit wary of the men (and they of him), at times erring in interpreting the humorous vein in which some of his soldiers took what would otherwise have been an untenable situation—training to fight in an army that viewed them as less than fully able—as a lack of discipline. While Lt. Col. Paul Bates had no doubts whatsoever about the abilities of the men, ever thoughtful and sober-minded, he couldn't keep himself from reflecting that some of them would not be coming home.

Warren Crecy and the quiet, serious Horatio Scott spent most of their free time at Wimborne writing letters home. Leonard Smith, William McBurney, and Preston McNeil took whatever opportunity they could to head to the nearby towns.

By the fall of 1944, more than 100,000 African American soldiers were stationed in or had passed through England on their way to war, most of them in quartermaster and service units. Young English women seemed to enjoy dancing and socializing with both white and black American soldiers. But many white American soldiers resented any contact between black troops and English women, and tried to impose American—particularly Southern—social mores, like forcing blacks to get off sidewalks to let white soldiers pass, and regulating which pubs and theaters blacks could attend. This may have contributed to the Army's decision to billet the 761st in Wimborne, far from any large towns.

In the unsegregated cities of England, clashes between white and black American soldiers had been frequent. In Launceston, in September 1943, black ordnance soldiers who were ordered to leave a pub by white soldiers returned, armed with guns; two MPs were wounded, and fourteen of the blacks were court-martialed. In Leicester, also in September 1943, white soldiers harassed mixed couples in the city's streets, with one incident escalating to a riot in which a white MP was killed. In Bristol, in July 1944, white soldiers attacked and badly beat several members of a black truck battalion; the incident escalated to a riot in which a black GI was shot and killed by MPs. One African American private stationed in England went so far as to cable First Lady Eleanor Roosevelt, who had pushed hard to integrate the Armed Forces: "This is a rather hard thing for me to do since it is my first time but I am very much sure that you have read many similar. We are, my unit, in a very tense situation and I am hoping you can help us in some way. We were told there was no segregation here in England, it isn't from the people, they are fine, only from our officers. . . . We are forbidden any recreation that might cause us to mix as a whole with the people. We are a Negro unit, I do hope you can help us in some way."

The letter underlined a contradiction faced by every black soldier, draftee or volunteer, in the U.S. Armed Forces at that time. They considered themselves first and foremost Americans, and were honored to fight in the nation's service. But they also had to internalize and transcend the knowledge that they were viewed, at best, as second-class citizens by the brass and many of their fellow soldiers—and often, far worse, as incompetent and cowardly. It was one of the tragic ironies that African Americans had come to understand as something they just had to live with.

The men of the 761st found the citizens of Wimborne and the surrounding towns wary of them at first. Over time, they got along well, dancing and drinking in the local pubs. They discovered that the townspeople weren't prejudiced themselves, but that some of the white American soldiers stationed nearby had warned the British townspeople that they were violent and untrustworthy.

Preston McNeil resented this. He had hoped such behavior had been left behind in Louisiana and Texas. It hurt to be seen as dangerous, as less than human, simply because of the color of his skin. But it didn't change the reasons for which he had originally volunteered. America was his country; he wanted to help defend it. He also hoped—as did many of the battalion's members—that in doing his part and proving himself on the battlefield, he would help make life better in America for himself and other African Americans when he returned. As they prepared to enter combat, McNeil and the other men of the 761st put aside the feelings of anger and confusion engendered by the ignorance and ill-will they faced; they put themselves into positive frames of mind that would allow them to perform to the capability of their training, a capability that perhaps only they themselves were truly aware of and confident in. Their ability to act as an effective fighting force, and their own survival as individuals, depended on it.

ON OCTOBER 5, the 761st Tank Battalion was officially assigned to Gen. George S. Patton's Third Army. Patton's injunction to his lieutenants—the same message Patton sent to all corps, division, and battalion commanders in his army—was clear: "Each, in his appropriate sphere, will lead in person. Any commander who fails to obtain his objective, and who is not dead or seriously wounded, has not done his full duty!" Patton's fiery rhetoric, and the fact that he himself was known to lead in person on the battlefield, helped to inspire strong loyalty among his troops. The men of the 761st, who had seen news clips celebrating Patton's victories, were inspired by the force of his personality, high standards, and example. They would have followed him into hell. And against the entrenched German resistance in the Saar Basin, the members of the 761st would in fact encounter what one war correspondent termed "a living nightmare of bloody hell." The 761st had been called up to join the Third Army as part of a massive new offensive, Patton's plan to break through the Siegfried Line and push toward Berlin.

From the end of August to the beginning of October 1944, Patton's Third Army had moved forward less than fifty miles. Patton's lightning-fast drive across France and toward the Rhine had been halted near the Saar Basin at the end of August—not by any German resistance but rather by the Allied high command. The stunning success of Patton's breakout from Normandy had created a logistical nightmare: The Allies had advanced, by mid-September 1944, to positions the Allied planners had not expected them to reach until May 1945. British Field Marshal Bernard Montgomery's 21st Army Group was positioned north of Paris, with Montgomery hoping to push north through Belgium and Holland, across the Rhine, and into Germany's crucial Ruhr industrial region, thus ending the war quickly. The general who forced the Germans to capitulate would be remembered forever in the annals of history; Montgomery wanted very badly to be that man. Patton, too, considered himself the man to end the war.

But there were not enough supplies and not enough of a transportation infrastructure to keep both Patton's and Montgomery's armies in motion. The French railroads had been all but decimated by

Allied and German bombs. A special one-way trucking system was created to carry rations, ammunition, and gasoline inland from Normandy; the most intrepid and highly effective of the supply units was the "Red Ball Express," an African American quartermaster regiment that often crossed territory that had not been fully secured under heavy fire to reach the front. But the combined Allied armies in Europe consumed more than 800,000 gallons of gasoline per day, and supply lines had simply been stretched too far—over three hundred miles from the Normandy beachheads. The trucks could not carry enough supplies to support offensives by two full army groups. Montgomery's offensive was given priority. Throughout September and October, though the lack of supplies precluded any major assault, Patton was determined to make periodic forays to "straighten out" his front and secure a better line of departure for his own massive offensive. He furiously advocated that he be given the men and equipment necessary to move forward in November.

Patton's successes thus far in Europe had rested on the highly coordinated deployment of infantry, artillery, airpower, and the divisions with which Patton's name was later to be considered synonymous—crack Sherman units. The one advantage the Sherman tanks held over the more heavily armored and more powerful Panzer and Tiger tanks was their greater maneuverability; to this end, highly trained crews were essential. Patton described a tank fight in the simplest terms, as "just like a barroom fight—the fellow who gets the hit wins. Our men . . . are magnificent shots. . . . The whole thing in tank fighting is to train crews not as individuals but as crews."

Patton's Third Army had sustained heavy tank losses even amid the relative ease of its push across France in August: By August 26, the 4th and 6th Armored Divisions, in spearheading for Patton's forces, had lost a total of 269 tanks. In September and October, though Patton's operations were limited in scope, both infantry and armored units took high casualties: A special truckload of supplies had to be sent from Normandy to the Third Army's graves registration squad, including 3,000 personal-effects bags. Patton desperately needed replacements—and, more than anything, trained Sherman crews.

Patton had no great regard for African Americans; his letters and private journals abound with racist stereotypes and rhetoric. He was, however, perhaps above all else a consummate pragmatist. When manpower later grew short in Europe in the winter of 1945, he was one of the first American generals to integrate his rifle units. And in October 1944, when he needed all available skilled Sherman crews to spearhead his planned assault on the Siegfried Line, he called for the 761st. He was fully aware that this would make them the first African American armored unit to be deployed in battle: Most of the Army's brain trust believed their deployment would be a waste of equipment. But Patton was running out of options. Had anyone of less than his stature called for the battalion, they might never have been allowed to see action.

As the men of the 761st spent their final days in Wimborne, they had no idea they were about to make Army history. All they knew was that they were black Americans trained to fight. They wanted to prove themselves in battle, just as they had at Camp Claiborne and Camp Hood. They were also unaware of the import of the offensive they were about to join—Patton's push into Germany to end the war. In the Army, as with most organizations, the farther down one goes in the structure of command, the less one knows. At the level of the enlisteds, as GIs everywhere were fond of saying, "you don't know shit." All they knew as soldiers was that the brass would tell them to go in a certain direction and that's where they went; told to take a hill without knowledge of the why or wherefore, they'd give everything they had to try to take it.

On October 7, the unit's full battery of fifty-six M-4 Sherman and seventeen M-5 Stuart tanks was delivered to the battalion. They immediately felt reassured. Wherever they were going, they'd be fighting in tanks. They'd be doing what they were trained to do. The majority of the medium tanks they received were the most recent model of the Sherman, the M4A3E8, known by tank crews as the "Easy Eight" because of its improved suspension and smoother ride. The Easy Eight, in addition to a better suspension system, had slightly thicker armor, safer stowage racks for ammunition, and—most important of all—a higher-velocity cannon. They were still "iron coffins," far outgunned by the Panzers, which could cut right through them, but at least they had more firepower. The original 75mm of the M-4s had a muzzle velocity of 2,050 feet per second; the longer-barreled 76mm of the M4A3E8 had a muzzle velocity of 2,900 fps, an improvement of almost 50 percent. Leonard Smith and the rest of his crew dubbed their new tank "Cool Stud," after their first Sherman at Camp Hood.

The battalion was notified that it would be moving out that afternoon. The men drove the tanks twenty miles south to the small fishing port of Weymouth, all five crew members of each tank standing up and looking out the hatches. When they passed some white soldiers along the way, one of them called out in a friendly tone of voice, "Who are you boys taking them to?" The soldiers had never seen blacks operating tanks, and assumed the crews were delivering them to another unit. Leonard Smith smiled and called back, "These are ours." He and the other members of the battalion were justly proud of their tanks. On October 9, at Weymouth, the battalion loaded their tanks, assault guns, and mortars onto the LSTs (for Landing Ship, Tank) that were to take them across the Channel.

4

BLOOD BROTHERS

Men are true comrades only when each is ready to

give up his life for the other, without reflection

and without thought of personal loss.

—J. GLENN GRAY

The Channel crossing took the better part of a day and night, as the LST's cruising speed was only ten miles an hour. LSTs were 328 feet long by 50 feet wide; each ship could carry twenty Shermans below in its hull or tank deck, chained in place to guard against rough seas. Navy crews had given LSTs the grim nickname of "Large Slow Targets"—but by the time of the 761st's crossing, the German guns at Normandy had long been cleared, and the most troubling obstacle was rough weather. The LSTs had flat bottoms to enable them to pull right up on the beach, but that meant they didn't plow through the waves as most boats did—they rolled. Leonard Smith was violently seasick.

Early on the morning of October 10, a weak-legged Smith, William McBurney, Preston McNeil, and most of the 761st crowded onto the upper decks of their LSTs to catch their first sight of the coast of France. Typically, it was raining and foggy. They were facing that section of the Normandy coast known by the code name it was given for D-Day—Omaha Beach. The men of the battalion knew, in a general sense, about the Allied invasion, but it was something else entirely for them to view the coast's sheer cliffs. The five-mile-long strip of sand below those cliffs had witnessed the highest casualties on D-Day: 55,000 American soldiers had landed in successive waves beginning at 6 A.M.; within the space of a few short hours, 3,000 had been killed or seriously wounded.

As the 761st drove their tanks down the ramps of the LSTs onto the sand, they stood up in the hatches, looking around them. Though the casualties from D-Day had quickly been cleared, damaged equipment had not—the beach was littered with tangles of barbed wire and burned-out vehicles. What struck William McBurney most were the Sherman tanks. Very few of the specially modified Shermans of the 741st and 743rd Tank Battalions, equipped for the invasion with canvas floats and propellers, had made it onto land. The majority of those that did had been devastated by mines and artillery fire, overturned like so many toys.

McBurney and the others weren't given much time to contemplate these ruins. The beach around them was a hub of activity: Ships were coming in and cargoes being unloaded on all sides. In the four months since the June 6 invasion, the Allies had converted the beaches of Normandy into highly efficient ports, processing the supplies, equipment, and replacement troops for the British and American armies in Europe—handling more cargo per day than did the port of New York City. The 761st was quickly guided off the beach by MPs to make room for the next round of landing craft.

They drove thirty miles west to a temporary camp in a field near the village of Les Pieux. The roads they traveled had been hotly contested in the fighting from D-Day through the August breakout. They passed ruined buildings, broken walls, trees demolished by high explosives. Even Leonard Smith found himself sobered by such sights. It was one thing to be a soldier far from the front in training, and another to be crossing recent battlefields and viewing the aftermath. But the damage was at one remove from him, like the setting of a movie. He was, he thought, exactly where he wanted to be. He was the hero of the war movie he'd been playing in his mind ever since America first joined the fight.

IN THE FIELD AT LES PIEUX, Lt. Col. Paul Bates received the 761st's final assignment for combat. The battalion was ordered to fight beside the 26th Infantry Division of the XII Corps of Patton's Third Army. The Third Army consisted of a quarter of a million men, a massive striking force divided—as per Army rules of organization—into two "corps," XII and XX Corps. A corps was a tactical headquarters responsible for positioning troops in the field: Patton's XII and XX Corps at the time supervised the placement of five "divisions" apiece, each division containing approximately 15,000 soldiers.

Most American GIs in World War II served in divisions. The 761st did not: It was part of a smaller manpower pool consisting of battalion-sized (500- to 1,000-man) units, including engineer, field artillery, tank destroyer, and tank battalions. These separate battalions were floating entities designed to be assigned to an Army corps; the corps, in turn, would attach them to whichever of its component divisions most needed their specialized services at a given moment. The separate battalions were rotated from corps to corps and division to division, and came to refer to themselves—in typical GI-speak—as "bastard battalions." In theory, the separate battalion pool provided for greater flexibility and adaptability to changing battlefield conditions; in practice, particularly for armored units, it often proved disastrous.

The separate tank battalions consisted, as did the 761st, of 700 men, 56 medium tanks, and 17 light tanks. The corps headquarters (in their case, XII Corps) would assign the battalion to the headquarters of an infantry division (the 26th Infantry), which would deploy the tanks as it saw fit to aid infantrymen in blasting through enemy lines. The most devastating flaw in this deployment of tank battalions was the marked inferiority of the M-4 Sherman: The U.S. tanks simply lacked sufficient armor for frontal attacks against fixed defensive positions. A second grave flaw was placing tank battalions under the direct command of officers who had no training with, and knew very little about the strengths and weaknesses of, the M-4 General Sherman tank.

Two types of American armored units fought in World War II: the separate tank battalion and the armored division. Armored divisions were vast organizations containing between 250 and 400 tanks; between 10,000 and 15,000 men; sizable artillery, engineer, ordnance, and quartermaster contingents; and their own highly trained squads of infantrymen (known as "armored infantry"). Armored division commanders were thoroughly versed in the uses of Sherman tanks; armored infantry had usually trained for more than a year to fight in close concert with the vehicles. By contrast, most infantry division commanders—the officers put in direct command of the separate tank battalions—knew nothing about tanks. Separate tank battalions had very little training in fighting with infantrymen, and infantrymen had even less training in fighting with tanks. Infantrymen and tankers had to learn—or fail to learn—to work together in the hardest way possible, under fire.

ON OCTOBER 22, the 761st left camp at Les Pieux to begin their four-hundred-mile drive to the battlefront. The division to which they'd been assigned, the 26th Infantry, was already engaged in tough fighting there. The 761st traveled due east for six days, moving through cities and towns liberated from the Germans back in August by the tanks of Patton's 4th and 6th Armored Divisions. The battalion's road march had the feeling more of a victory parade than of a journey into the heart of war. The weather was mild. The men leaned out of their hatches, taking in the sights. When local citizens heard that American tanks were passing through, they crowded into the streets and cried out from upper-story windows, cheering wildly, tossing flowers, waving flags. One town even set up a brass band. The tankers heartily waved back— in particular, of course, at the pretty young women—having a grand old time. Though they hadn't yet fired a single shot, they felt like heroes.

Pop Gates always made time to talk to Leonard Smith when the battalion camped at night. Gates didn't know why it was, exactly, that he continued bothering with Smith: After Smith's troubles throughout training, he should long since have written him off. There was something about Smith, however, that got to him, something he liked and even admired—a stubborn willfulness, naïveté, and a rare spark of life. He was convinced that Smith was going to do something foolish and get himself killed, and convinced, too, that this was one of the last things he wanted to see happen. Every night he lectured Smith with variations on a single theme: "What we're going into, this isn't a movie. They'll be shooting live bullets at you." Smith had always keenly felt the lack of a father and appreciated Pop's concern. But no amount of talk or concern, however well-meaning, could dissipate the grand adventure tales that had been his principal solace from the age of eight, looking up at the dime-store model planes hanging by strings from his bedroom ceiling.

The 761st reached their final destination, the town of St. Nicholas-de-Port in the French province of Lorraine, on October 28. The battalion had been instructed to wait there indefinitely. The weather had turned to rain and sleet. The field that was their designated bivouac (or camp) area was a mud hole reminiscent of Camp Claiborne. They were less than twenty miles from the Third Army's front lines, and they could hear the sound of heavy artillery like the rumble of thunder in the distance. Even to the group's more sober-minded members, however, like Preston McNeil and Warren Crecy, the war seemed remote; it was a hypothetical test the young men fully believed they'd pass. Some of the soldiers wasted no time in checking out St. Nicholas—where, like many young American GIs away from home for the first time, they visited the local brothel. Leonard Smith went along with his friend Willie Devore, entranced by the rich chocolate candy that was served, as well as by the women.

THE MAJOR AMERICAN OFFENSIVE for which the 761st unwittingly was waiting—Patton's upcoming attack on the Siegfried Line—was the biggest show going in the European Theater of Operations in late October 1944. Allied forces throughout Europe were at a standstill. Montgomery's British troops were still regrouping after the large-scale failure, in mid-September, of the attempted land and airborne invasion of Germany through Holland known as Operation Market Garden. The Ninth U.S. Army was meeting intense resistance in its drive to breach Holland's southern border. The First French and Seventh U.S. Armies had landed on the Mediterranean coast of France in August and fought their way north, only to be halted by the Vosges Mountains. The First U.S. Army had crossed the Belgian border and captured the German city of Aachen, but had since become mired in a disastrous campaign to clear the Hurtgen Forest. Patton's Third Army, starved of supplies in Lorraine, had thus far made only limited advances toward Germany.

Eisenhower had finally agreed to send the Third Army the supplies and reinforcements Patton had been demanding (first impatiently, then irascibly, then furiously) for two months. The 761st numbered among these reinforcements. Patton intended for his major attack on the German border to begin, depending on weather conditions, between November 5 and 8. The attack was originally supposed to take place in conjunction with renewed assaults by the First and Ninth U.S. Armies—but due to troop-resupply problems they would be delayed in their part until at least mid-November. Patton was only too happy to go it alone. He saw himself as a man of destiny; he was fiercely determined that the Third Army's early-November drive "make real history" and end the war.

In its simplest terms, Patton's campaign would entail a push by the ten divisions of his XII and XX Corps in an east-northeast direction across the German border (approximately forty miles distant) into the Saar industrial region. The Saar, historically a coal-mining district, stood as one of Germany's most important industrial centers. With his combined force of tanks, infantry, artillery, and fighter-bombers, Patton intended to swiftly crack the Siegfried Line (just miles beyond the border) in the Saar, then to continue on to establish a bridgehead over the Rhine River and seize the key cities of Mainz, Frankfurt, and Darmstadt. From there he hoped to drive across the open Rhine plains as far as possible, even to Berlin.

The obstacles facing this grand plan (known as the "Saar Campaign") were manifold. In its earliest phase—the drive across Lorraine to reach the German border—they were, in fact, formidable. The Lorraine province was composed of rolling farm country, with a gradual slope upward from east to west: Patton's troops would generally be attacking uphill. The terrain was further punctuated by a number of densely wooded ridges providing wide vantage points and ample cover to entrenched defenders. The Germans, determined to defend their homeland to the death, had massively fortified the area during the Third Army's enforced stall from September to early November with roadblocks and demolitions, minefields, pillboxes and machine-gun nests, and tank traps covered with artillery and Panzerfausts. But by far the greatest obstacle was the weather. The Lorraine province had experienced heavy rains throughout the fall. American air support was grounded. As October turned to November, near-constant rain produced the greatest flooding the region had witnessed in a generation. The fields became an ocean of mud, reducing off-road travel to a minimum—and rendering tanks more vulnerable to fire-covered roadblocks, tank traps, and artillery.

AT ST. NICHOLAS-DE-PORT, the men fell into a routine, each day preparing their tanks for battle as they had trained to do at Claiborne and Hood, oiling and re-oiling the guns. The Sherman tank held a massive amount of material in its cramped interior—fire extinguishers, blackout lamps, goggles, safety belts, helmets, a canvas bucket, a tarpaulin, a crank, an ax, a crowbar, a pick, a shovel, a sledgehammer, a track wrench, a track jack and fixtures, a radio, six periscopes, flexible nozzles, and more—and the men were constantly testing equipment and making minor repairs as needed. The maintenance teams of each company worked to attach newly issued "Duckbills" to the Shermans—metal track-extenders designed to distribute the tanks' weight more evenly to prevent them from bogging down in the mud. Drivers went on practice runs in the fields to get used to the feel of them. Despite the cold, driving rain, the men were in good spirits.

This routine was suddenly interrupted on November 2, when the entire battalion was called to assemble in the field in a semicircle formation. A grave-faced Lt. Col. Paul Bates directed the men to stand at attention. Several jeeps full of MPs armed with .50-caliber machine guns pulled up. A three-star general jumped out of one of the vehicles, and Bates gave him a hand in stepping up onto the hood of a half-track. Looking out over the assembled battalion stood George Patton, the Third Army's commanding general.

Though the men wore raincoats against the light drizzle, Patton was without a coat. He was shorter than William McBurney had imagined him to be from newsreel footage, and his voice had a higher pitch. He directed the men to stand at ease. His words were recorded by Trezzvant Anderson, a reporter assigned to the 761st: "Men, you are the first Negro tankers to ever fight in the American Army. I would never have asked for you if you weren't good. I have nothing but the best in my Army. I don't care what color you are, so long as you go up there and kill those kraut sonsabitches. Everyone has their eyes on you and is expecting great things from you. Most of all, your race is looking forward to your success. Don't let them down, and, damn you, don't let me down!"

Patton then stepped down and more quietly addressed the group closest to him. (He had gotten in trouble for giving similar exhortations to his men in Sicily, but continued doing so.) He told them, "This is war. I want you to start shooting and keep shooting. Shoot everything you see. Whenever you see a German, if it's male or female, eight to eighty years old, you kill them, because they'll kill you."

Despite Patton's rousing speech to the men, his views about the limited capabilities of black soldiers remained unchanged. That afternoon, he noted in his diary that the 761st "gave a very good first impression, but I have no faith in the inherent fighting ability of the race."

The men of the battalion were unaware of Patton's sentiments. In fact, they were proud that the legendary general had taken time to address their relatively small group, and his words made them proud to be part of his army. The phrase they repeated most among themselves was "nothing but the best": After the varied hardships of their training, he had acknowledged them, had specifically requested them, and they were there—as they had for so long wanted to be—to fight. November 2 happened to be the date of Preston McNeil's twenty-second and Leonard Smith's twentieth birthdays, and the impressionable Smith took Patton's sudden visitation as a confirmation of his boyhood notions of glory.

William McBurney started paying closer attention to the rumble of guns to the east. The sound, though faint, seemed abruptly to have taken on a life and personality of its own: He noted very precisely when it started and when it stopped, as did all of the battalion's members. They knew that soon they would be in the thick of it.

AS ONE OF THE STRONGEST proponents of the value of armor in combat, Patton had assigned separate tank battalions to lead and support each of his seven infantry divisions; the Third Army additionally contained three armored divisions. In preparation for the upcoming Saar Campaign, all ten divisions of Patton's XX and XII Corps were arranged along a front—in this case, a vertical north-south line—measuring approximately sixty miles. The five divisions of XX Corps were spread out along the northern portion of the front, running south from the vicinity of the city of Thionville to Pont-à-Mousson: These divisions were the 90th, 9th, 95th, and 5th Infantry Divisions and the 10th Armored Division. The five divisions of XII Corps held the southern portion of the front, extending south from Pont-à-Mousson to Moncourt Woods: These divisions, numbered from north to south, were the 80th, 35th, and 26th Infantry Divisions, with the crack 4th and 6th Armored Divisions waiting in the wings to strike on the battle's second day.

With no sign yet of a break in the weather, the campaign would most likely begin November 8. Patton's plan called for XII Corps to lead off the Third Army's assault (XX Corps would be held back until the ninth). The 80th, 35th, and 26th Infantry Divisions of XII Corps were to start their forward attacks against enemy positions simultaneously on November 8 at 6:00 A.M. The 26th Division and 761st Tank Battalion were specifically instructed to push northeast through terrain marked by wooded hills toward the cities of Rodalbe and Benestroff, key rail and communications centers.

AS THE DATE OF PATTON'S great offensive approached, Able Company's Capt. David Williams became the first to realize just what the

761st's separate, "bastard" battalion status meant. On November 6, Lieutenant Colonel Bates told Williams he was to lead Able Company's seventeen Sherman tanks northeast from St. Nicholas-de-Port to the village of Bezange-la-Grande—less than two miles behind the front line—and there report to an officer of the 26th Infantry Division. Able Company would be under the command of that officer for the duration of the unit's first combat action. Williams had come to rely on Bates's kindly, sober presence and judgment—and was more than a little anxious to be leading an entire company forward on his own, to report to an officer he had never before seen.

Though the 761st had trained to work together as a single unit, the 26th Infantry Division intended to break the battalion up in the coming assault to provide firepower and fill in holes wherever it deemed necessary. This was entirely in keeping with the Armored Force's guidelines for the deployment of separate tank battalions. But it made the tankers of the separate battalions themselves feel like bastards—illegitimate, at sea, ignored—as they were shifted from unit to unit within the 15,000-man divisions.

American infantry divisions in World War II contained three "regiments" of 3,000 men apiece; these regiments were further divided into three 500-man rifle battalions; battalions were further divided into three 189-man rifle companies; each company was further divided into three platoons. Separate tank battalions would be broken up along company (15-tank), platoon (5-tank), and even individual tank lines to support infantry regiments, battalions, companies, platoons—wherever a tank or group of tanks was requested. This could be a dizzying and—depending on how much the infantry officers to whom they reported did and did not know about tanks—profoundly unsettling experience for the tankers.

The three regiments of the 26th Infantry Division were the 101st, 104th, and 328th Infantry Regiments. Able Company had been sent to the 104th Infantry Regiment. Capt. David Williams was in for a rude shock when he reported to the 104th, and was told that one of his three platoons would be taken away from him, to fight alongside a battalion of the 101st Regiment. He felt nauseated: He had gotten his mind around fighting apart from the rest of the 761st but had not counted on losing one of his platoons. He accompanied Able Company's best platoon leader, 1st Lt. Samuel Barbour, to the 101st Regiment's nearby headquarters, where he was shaken still further. The 101st Regiment's commander told Barbour that he intended to send the platoon's Shermans to attack single-file straight down a road—where, as both Williams and Barbour knew from their training at Camp Hood, one well-positioned antitank gun could annihilate all five tanks. But such was the structure of command that they had no choice.

EARLY ON THE MORNING of November 7, the 761st's remaining four companies—Baker, Charlie, Dog, and Headquarters—were ordered to leave the bivouac area at St. Nicholas as well. They were to fight as part of a task force including the 328th Regiment, one company of the 101st Regiment, and the 691st Tank Destroyer Battalion. The company commanders informed their men that they would be attacking at dawn on the eighth. They had little time to worry. Before leaving camp, they had to make sure they had their full supply of 75mm or 76mm, .30- and .50-caliber ammunition, and were gassed up. Gunners had to zero in the tank gun, put a cross on it, and line up the sight. The crews checked over every piece of equipment before lining up in column formation and rolling east toward the village of Athainville. They traveled slowly, at four miles an hour, to save fuel. By the time they arrived, the weather had turned to freezing rain. They stopped for the night in a sodden field. The mud got inside their boots and somehow found its way into their C rations. They were less than five miles from the front. They had yet to meet the infantrymen beside whom they would be fighting.

Captain Williams's two platoons of Able Company, closer to the front at Bezange-la-Grande, were camped directly beside a detachment of soldiers of the 104th Infantry Regiment. Floyd Dade, the diligent, eager young recruit from Arkansas who had joined the 761st at Camp Hood, was the first to introduce himself. He did so not without some trepidation, after the battalion's experiences with white soldiers in training and in England. Some of the troops with whom the 761st was later to fight—green recruits facing battle for the first time—resented the fact that their armored support consisted of African Americans, felt cheated, betrayed, even set up to die, and voiced these sentiments within earshot. But the 761st was fortunate in its first assignment. The 26th Infantry Division had originally been created from several New England national guard units (hence its nickname, the "Yankee Division"). Most of its members were northeasterners, and while not all of them had risen above the prevailing prejudices of the time, the division had been fighting in Lorraine without tanks since early October, and the vast majority were simply so glad—as the major offensive approached—to have tank support that it made little difference to them who was at the helm. A few of the soldiers asked Floyd Dade where he was from, and he did the same; they traded C rations and talked about their hometowns, about sports, in particular a shared love of football. They talked well into the night, as most of them knew they wouldn't sleep anyway, talking about anything but what they were fully aware was coming within a matter of hours.

EATING FROM THEIR C RATIONS near Athainville, the men of Headquarters, Baker, Charlie, and Dog Companies talked in small groups. William McBurney checked and rechecked his "grease gun"—an odd-shaped, compact, .45-caliber submachine gun that was standard issue for tankers. Several of the men prayed together: Preston McNeil found that he wasn't the only one raised by a Holy Roller. Many were past the pretense of youthful bravado and were frankly scared. The impression some of the men had formed was that they, a battalion, were being sent to take a hill an entire division had been unable to take. The 761st had in fact been told by an officer of XII Corps that one of the positions they were to attack was a "big hill," Hill 253; the GI rumor mill had it that the crack 4th Armored Division had previously tried but failed to capture 253, and some of the men believed they were being set up to fail. (What the 761st had no way of knowing was that only a small group from the 4th had been involved, and had been starved at the time of ammunition and supplies.)

Lieutenant Colonel Bates had gone ahead to the 328th Regiment's forward posts to make a personal reconnaissance on foot, slipping through the mud to scout for himself the exact terrain conditions his men would face. In Bates's absence, the men built one another up, just as they'd done throughout training. Smith walked around encouraging his more anxious friends, as if they were a sports team the night before a big game. They were determined to show the Army and the Germans that they could take whatever came their way, that as black soldiers they were as good as or better than any other unit. Some of the men couldn't get past the worry that they *weren't* going to make it, that their superiors might have been sending them to die. But that sort of pessimism only made the majority all the more determined to do the best fighting they could and to look out for one another.

THE HARSH WEATHER SHOWED no signs of abating. Maj. Gen. Manton S. Eddy, commander of XII Corps, and Maj. Gen. Robert Grow, commander of the 6th Armored Division, visited Patton that night at his headquarters. The two highly distinguished veterans of Tunisia, Sicily, and Normandy took what was for them an unprecedented step—begging Patton to call off the attack. They voiced their belief that the severe weather conditions would preclude success. Patton brusquely responded that the campaign would go forward as planned. If either man refused, he was invited to make recommendations for a replacement. Patton later wrote his wife that though he "declined" to call off the attack, "it took some doing, as the ground is a bog." As he prepared to go up to bed, he paused at the bottom of the stairs, telling his personal aide, Lt. Col. Charles R. Codman, "I think this has been the longest day of my life."

Patton woke at 3 o'clock the next morning, the morning that was to be the start of his great "Battle of Germany," to find it raining worse than ever. Questioning his earlier decision, he repeated to himself his motto: "Don't take council of your fears. Demand the impossible." At 5:15 he was awakened again, by the sound of the Third Army's heavy artillery. In preparation for the tank and infantry assaults of XII Corps, a massive force of more than five hundred guns had begun firing on enemy positions at 4:30. Patton described the sound, from his quarters twenty miles away, as "like the constant slamming of heavy doors in a large empty house."

UP CLOSE, JUST BEHIND THE FRONT, the bombardment was deafening. The exploding shells sounded to Leonard Smith like the immediate crack of a lightning strike multiplied a thousand times. The force was unimaginable, ramming every nerve. The men knew that's what they were heading into. They had slept (those who were able to) in uniform inside their tanks, hatches closed against the driving rain. The turrets reeked of fuel and sweat. In the predawn darkness, company commanders gave the order to turn the tanks over. The tanks of Baker, Charlie, Dog, and Headquarters Companies started all together, like the Indianapolis 500. Colonel Bates led the way forward in his jeep. They rolled directly east in a column. Tank destroyers and trucked infantry of the 101st and 328th Regiments soon joined them.

Two miles down the road, near the town of Arracourt, they came to a sudden halt. A French farmer had blocked the crossroads with his herd of cattle. He was almost certainly a collaborator sent to disrupt American troop movements. Lorraine had passed repeatedly between French and German hands in the past two centuries: The Germans had deliberately maneuvered to increase their influence and create loyalty whenever they had control, shaping a populace split between pro-French and pro-German factions. Lieutenant Colonel Bates personally placed the farmer under arrest, then ordered several of the infantrymen accompanying the tanks to clear the road.

Just shy of the front, Bates left his jeep to direct the tank crews. The tank commanders had been told which way to go the day before, but Bates had since learned of an impassable, flooded area and had shifted their axis of approach by thirty degrees. It was daybreak and the men, seeing Bates, waved, then buttoned up their hatches and kept going. The Germans had begun to return artillery fire. The road was targeted, and shells exploded all around Bates. He nonetheless continued to stand in place, directing vehicles until the entire column had passed. Before he could make his way back to his jeep, a German patrol that had infiltrated behind American lines opened fire.

Bleeding heavily, Bates told medics who came to administer aid that he intended to remain with the battalion. His bullet wounds were severe enough, however, that the medics gave him no choice but to be evacuated. Word spread anxiously from tank to tank along the column that Lieutenant Colonel Bates was gone.

Maj. Charles Wingo—who had never had faith in the men—was second in command. Wingo left Headquarters Company and drove off in his jeep toward the front. Not long afterward, the tank crews sighted him heading back the other way. He kept on going. (Though he could have been court-martialed, Doc Adamson took pity on the terrified major and diagnosed him with "battle fatigue.") The men were on their own.

The column consisting—from front to back—of Baker, Charlie,

Dog, and Headquarters Companies continued its move toward the battlefront. The enemy shelling had stopped for the moment, and some of the men ventured to look out their hatches. William McBurney spotted a dead horse just off the road. It had been hit by an artillery shell with such force that it was essentially turned inside out, the strange pale lines of its intestines fully exposed. Though in the unit's trek across France he had seen various marks of devastation—buildings reduced to rubble, bombed-out tanks and half-tracks, ruined fields—for some reason this sight disturbed him more than anything and brought home to him with utter clarity where he was and what he was facing.

Preston McNeil and the five M-5 Stuart tanks of his platoon were just ahead of Headquarters. McNeil kept in radio contact with his company commander, careful to speak in code; he could switch off that network to speak more freely to his crew via intercom. Dog Company's platoon leaders received orders to stop on the road at 6 A.M.: They were to stand back in reserve while Baker and Charlie proceeded into battle. McNeil took the opportunity to step out from his tank and personally check on his platoon. He had to shout to be heard: The roar of the combat ahead was intense. McNeil went from tank to tank, reassuring his men and nodding encouragement to the infantrymen grouped around them, some of whom had pulled out cigarettes. Suddenly McNeil saw the infantrymen falling on all sides. There had been no warning. He didn't understand what was happening until he heard some of them screaming. Artillery shells were raining on them from out of nowhere. McNeil rushed back to his tank and buttoned up, pressing his face against his periscope. The Germans—once Baker and Charlie rolled out to battle—must have targeted the ridge to disrupt supply lines.

Leonard Smith's "Cool Stud" was the last tank in the column, still moving forward toward the stopping point. Smith and the rest of his crew could hear the enemy shelling up ahead. An American jeep swerved up from behind them and screeched to a halt. A young, thin-faced white officer jumped out and signaled for them to stop. He climbed atop the Sherman and informed them that he was an artillery observer, assigned to their vehicle. He took the tank commander's position, ordering Smith's tank to pull out and move forward to the edge of the ridge, to provide him with a view of the battlefield so he could report on enemy positions to American artillery teams.

As the Sherman started moving up, the young officer—standing with his head and shoulders protruding from the turret—was struck with shrapnel from an exploding shell. Smith, below in the loader's position, didn't realize what had happened until a fountain of blood started pouring down on him.

The hit had put a hole in the artillery observer's jaw. Smith tried ineffectually to staunch the wound and reassure the stunned officer, while the gunner closed the hatch, called for the driver to stop, and radioed back for medics.

NEAR BEZANGE-LA-GRANDE, the separate combat team consisting of the 104th Infantry Regiment and Captain Williams's two platoons of Able Company entered battle. The platoon led by 1st Lt. Joseph Kahoe, and that led by 2nd Lt. Robert Hammond, moved up the narrow muddy road from the outskirts of Bezange-la-Grande to a ridge overlooking the village of Vic-sur-Seille. At 5:15, Williams and his reserve tank led them down to the bottom of the hill. Infantrymen beginning to cross the mile-long meadow between the ridge and Vic-sur-Seille were already under fire, diving down in the mud then getting up to dart forward again. Williams stopped as he had been trained to do, taking up a command position concealed by brush at the edge of the meadow. The five tanks of Kahoe's platoon moved past Williams to the left, heading forward defilade—like a football blocking line—to cover the infantrymen with machine-gun and cannon fire. Hammond's platoon continued straight toward Vic-sur-Seille, intending to fire high-explosive ammunition on the town to clear the way for infantry.

The overriding impression of the tank crews heading into combat was a chaos of noise. With limited vision, all eyes pressed anxiously to the narrow periscopes, sound was the tanker's best ally and worst nightmare—constant radio traffic, the engine, the thudding and recoil of their own cannons, and the earsplitting crashes of incoming shells. Gunners and bow gunners followed the tank commander's orders. Loaders yanked HE and AP shells from racks on the turret walls and rammed them into the breech. Drivers struggled to keep moving forward, finding the Duckbills little help against the torrents of mud.

The ridge from which Able's tanks had departed was quickly zeroed by German artillery. Supply, medical, and headquarters detachments beyond the hill were in turmoil under heavy shelling. Captain Williams, in radio contact with his assistant above at the 104th Regiment's 1st Battalion headquarters, learned that the 1st Battalion's commander was so unnerved by the intensity of the fire that he had to be relieved from duty. Clifford Adams, a young private from Waco, Texas, in the 761st's medical detachment, was struck and killed by fragments from an exploding shell.

Nineteen-year-old Floyd Dade was among those moving forward in the first tank. Straining to see what little he could out of his periscope, he was astonished by the courage of the infantrymen they supported. The infantry took countless hits in the open field but kept going. The foot soldiers had never fought with tanks before and initially stayed too close beside the vehicles—working on the natural assumption that thirty-two tons of steel would provide them with cover more effectively to fire from. But the Sherman was essentially a big, wide, high-silhouetted target, drawing enemy small-arms, automatic, mortar, and artillery fire. The infantrymen quickly learned to spread out. Lieutenant Kahoe radioed the tank commanders to remind their gunners to aim high, to avoid hitting the American infantry charging on all sides through the field.

Dade, acting as loader, could hear machine-gun bullets ricocheting off his tank's turret. The bullets did not penetrate and he started thinking maybe they'd be okay. But the bullets proved to be tracer fire. A German antitank crew had them zeroed in. The Sherman happened to hit a dip in the field at the exact moment the shot came in. The armor-piercing 88 would have gone directly through the turret, immediately killing Dade and the gunner—but because of that dip it sheared off the .50-caliber machine-gun mount instead. The force of the blast rocked the tank. The cut to the gun mount was smooth and precise, as though someone had burned it off with a blowtorch. But the 76mm cannon and .30-caliber machine guns were still intact, and the crew kept fighting forward.

The fields and roads Able Company's tanks were crossing had been thickly sewn with mines. Two tanks were soon disabled by explosions, their tracks blown off; fortunately, no crew members were killed. Hammond's platoon closed in on Vic-sur-Seille, with twenty-six-year-old S. Sgt. Ruben Rivers, from Holtulka, Oklahoma, commanding the lead tank. Two hundred yards outside of town, the narrow road was blocked by a large felled tree that the Germans had mined and covered with small-arms fire. The road was the only route into town: The 104th Regiment's advance could have been halted for several hours. Standard military procedure dictated that Rivers's tank should stay back, shooting high-explosive shells for effect while the infantry attempted—at great cost—to clear the surrounding area so that the tree could safely be removed. Rivers saw enemy mortar and rifle fire devastating the American infantrymen stationed in the ditches beside the road.

Sergeant Rivers ordered his driver to roll forward. Watching through his field glasses, Captain Williams was stunned to see Rivers jump out of the turret of his tank, crawling ahead carrying his tank's tow cable. The Germans had attached a number of antipersonnel and antitank mines to the tree. Rivers moved carefully to fasten his cable to the tree trunk, exposed to small-arms fire. A brace of mortars exploded less than twenty yards away, sending up sheets of mud and shrapnel. But Rivers continued painstakingly to encircle the trunk. He then calmly remounted his tank and ordered the crew to back up, pulling the tree off the road—and exploding several mines in the process. Rivers had cleared the way for the attack to continue.

Rivers's tank and the rest of Robert Hammond's platoon moved ahead into Vic-sur-Seille, firing high-explosive shells into upper-level windows to take out German sniper and machine-gun posts while the infantry began battling house to house. Joseph Kahoe's platoon had crossed the meadow and opened fire on the opposite side of town.

AMONG THE ENEMY FORCES entrenched in the 26th Infantry Division's battle zone were the 361st and 559th Volksgrenadier Divisions— lightly trained units that nonetheless had the advantages of terrain and superior position—as well as one of Germany's finest military outfits, the 11th Panzer Division. The crack 11th Panzers had won victories throughout North Africa and on the Russian front, and were reinforced in Lorraine by 12,000 reserve troops and several dozen tanks and assault guns.

Charlie Company and the 328th Regiment were hit with a hail of mortar and artillery fire immediately as they moved down the ridge. Second Lieutenant Jay E. Johnson, commanding the first platoon of Charlie, was severely injured and temporarily blinded when a shell exploded near his tank. Charlie Company's remaining tanks gave covering machine-gun and cannon fire to infantrymen entering their first objective, the village of Bezange-la-Petite. One of the 328th Regiment's medics, Corp. Alfred L. Wilson, was hit while administering aid to a fallen infantrymen. Though in great pain and losing blood, he continued to crawl from one patient to another to give aid, well aware that there weren't enough medics to handle the high number of casualties. Even when he was too weak to move Wilson refused to be evacuated, verbally directing unskilled soldiers in treating their comrades' wounds until he lost consciousness. He was posthumously awarded the Medal of Honor.

The battle spread north toward the "big hill," Hill 253. A German HE 88 exploded just above the lead tank of one of Charlie Company's three platoons, commanded by S. Sgt. Harvey Woodard. The tank did not appear to have been hit, but soon came to a stop in the middle of the field as the fighting continued around it. The tank's hatches remained closed and no crew members emerged. Other tank commanders in the platoon attempted repeatedly to contact Woodard by radio and received no answer. Two other tanks were soon disabled by mines and enemy shells: Corp. James Edwards and S. Sgt. Samuel F. Saunders were critically injured and had to be evacuated by medics.

Dog and Headquarters Companies waited back on the ridge. Wingo's departure and the injuries to Lt. Colonel Bates and the artillery observer had forced a change in plans for Headquarters. Captain Harrison ordered the company's three Sherman tanks to stand back and guard the supply train, which had just arrived and was unloading. The tank commanders kept track of the unfolding combat as best they could over their radios. Leonard Smith's crew had shifted positions after the artillery observer was evacuated (they never learned what became of him). Gunner Daniel Cardell became Smith's tank commander, and Smith moved up to his dream position, the gunner's seat. The bow gunner had taken Smith's place as loader. Cardell, hearing the shouts and carnage below, told his crew, "They're tearing up C Company." Cardell decided, on his own, that they should go forward to try to help.

Smith's Sherman rolled east, when suddenly it hit either a natural dip in the ground or a tank trap. Driver Hollis Clark kept gunning it, trying to move forward or back out, but was unable to free the tank. Among the many vulnerabilities of the M-4 Sherman was a tendency for its exhaust to become blocked, allowing deadly carbon monoxide gas to back up inside the turret. Smith, with his slight frame, was the canary in the coal mine. He immediately passed out—and the others, realizing what had happened, switched off the engine and jumped out. Cardell pulled Smith up onto the turret to see if fresh air would revive him. It didn't: The crew couldn't see Smith breathing, could not feel a pulse, and assumed that he was dead.

They left Smith's body atop the turret, running back toward the supply train to inform the battalion's ordnance team—responsible for reclaiming damaged vehicles—of the tank's position.

LATE THAT AFTERNOON, Baker and Charlie Companies along with the 26th Infantry finally captured Bezange-la-Petite and Hill 253. But the cost had been high for all units involved. The infantry suffered casualties numbering in the hundreds. Members of the 761st had continued to try to contact Charlie Company's S. Sgt. Harvey Woodard. The ordnance crew went out to Woodard's tank when the field had cleared. The hatches were locked and had to be cracked open one at a time. Inside the turret, Woodard, gunner Carlton Chapman, and loader L. C. Byrd were sitting in position with their eyes open: All three of the men were dead. When they opened the front two hatches, the team discovered driver Claude Mann and bow gunner Nathaniel Simmons dead as well. There were no visible signs of trauma. The precise cause of death remained a mystery. The men may have sustained internal injuries from the high-explosive blast; it was more likely they died as a result of carbon monoxide poisoning.

Able Company had also captured its initial objective, the town of Vic-sur-Seille, after heavy fighting. Rolling through the town at the end of the day, Walter Lewis, the gunner in Lieutenant Kahoe's tank, was told by Kahoe to stick his head out of the turret. They were slowly approaching a dead German soldier lying in a gutter, blood streaming from his mangled body and pooling in the street. It was a man Lewis himself had killed. Gunners didn't often see the men they shot. Lewis never forgot it.

Floyd Dade, stepping out of his tank when the fighting had ended, asked after the infantrymen he'd talked with late into the previous night. Each time he asked a foot soldier, "Have you seen Private So-and-so?" he was told, "He got hit a while back."

THE BATTALION'S ORDNANCE UNIT had been too busy to recover Leonard Smith's "Cool Stud" tank. Smith woke late on the afternoon of the eighth to find himself draped across the turret. He heard the voices of German soldiers. An enemy patrol was approaching. Smith quickly decided his best bet was to lie there as though he'd been killed—a deception in which he could only pray he'd be helped by the artillery observer's caked blood on his uniform.

With the guttural voices drawing closer, Smith tried to remember the sequence of events that had brought him to this point. It was an odd, inglorious introduction to war. The voices approached within yards, but none of the patrol stopped to check if he was still alive. Smith's seemingly boundless luck held true. The voices faded into the distance. Smith wasn't taking any chances. He stayed there, not moving, until dark. Then he climbed down into the turret, locked the hatch, and went to sleep.

AT HIS HEADQUARTERS IN NANCY on the evening of the eighth, General Patton was pleased with the slow but sure progress made by the 80th, 35th, and 26th Divisions along the XII Corps front. The 80th Division had taken the towns of Aulnois-sur-Seille and Mailly-sur-Seille, and the 35th had captured Malaucourt-sur-Seille and Jallaucourt, advances equal in distance with the 26th's capture of Vic-sur-Seille and Bezange-la-Petite. At 10 A.M., the skies had cleared and the XIX

Air Tactical Command had been able to make several strategic runs against enemy headquarters. It was a rare stroke of good fortune; the rain soon returned and remained for the rest of the month. But that evening, Patton was in good spirits.

Baker, Charlie, Dog, and Headquarters Companies of the 761st set up defensive perimeters outside Bezange-la-Petite and bivouacked for the night. William McBurney and Willie Devore had learned of Leonard Smith's apparent death. The news hit Smith's buddy, Willie Devore, the hardest. It was difficult for all the men, particularly because their sorrow was mixed with the feelings of relief and even joy that they themselves had survived. Pop Gates had to put his grief aside as he checked and prepared the assault guns for what was likely to be a worse day of fighting to come.

ALONE IN THE WOODS, Leonard Smith woke just before dawn. He climbed out of the tank, unarmed. He didn't see a living soul anywhere. He was trying to decide just what to do when a grizzled German soldier appeared, walking toward him, holding a rifle up in the air.

Smith couldn't understand what the man was saying. The soldier wasn't shooting, he was holding the rifle with both hands above his head. It took Smith a moment to realize that the man intended to surrender. He took the rifle from him. He had no idea where he was or where the rest of his unit had gone. He figured the German would know the way. Smith signaled for the soldier to start walking, and followed him. They reached a road and walked for a while before they heard the sound of tanks approaching. Smith felt a moment's panic— then excitement as he realized the tanks were American. They were, in fact, a column of the 761st. The crews were so glad to see the resurrected Smith that they stood up, waving and cheering. He was a hero after all.

Smith turned his "prisoner" over to MPs at the rear of the column. He then ran and jumped up to rejoin his crew, who had been given another tank on which they'd already taken the time to paint the words "Cool Stud."

NOVEMBER 9 WOULD BE ONE OF the few days of the war when all four letter companies of the 761st were assigned to fight toward the same objective, the heavily fortified town of Morville-les-Vic. The town itself was less than a mile square, but of critical strategic value: It was situated along the main road to the 26th Division's first goals for the Saar Campaign (ten miles distant), Rodalbe and Benestroff. Able Company was to cover the west flank of the attack, taking the neighboring city of Château-Salins with the 101st Infantry Regiment quickly after dawn. Baker Company was to enter Morville-les-Vic from the southwest via the main road, covering elements of the 26th Infantry Division in what was likely to be very bitter house-to-house fighting. Dog Company was to guard the east flank, supporting the infantry in taking the town of Salival and then screening the nearby woods to keep German relief forces from reaching Morville. Charlie Company would push ahead through the woods, approaching Morville from the east and north and thus completing the encirclement of the town. Headquarters Company—with its three Sherman tanks, and mortar and artillery platoons—was instructed to stand by as needed.

The 761st's company commanders had been briefed by infantry intelligence on terrain and antitank obstacles. They had been trained to rely on infantry reconnaissance. Even the most accomplished of infantry scouts, however—having no experience with Shermans—had little understanding of what constituted a threat for the tanks. Charlie Company's captain, Irvin McHenry, was assured that the approach for his unit from the northeast side of Morville was clear.

Just after dawn, Captain Williams's two platoons of Able Company waited on the hill to the southeast of Château-Salins while eight

P-40-series fighter-bombers strafed the town. The infantrymen and tankers stood up to cheer them on. The poor weather had returned, a cold rain that soon turned to light snow, but the planes of the XIX Air Tactical Command continued to fly whenever possible in support of the ground forces. (They took such high risks in doing so that though their operations were grounded completely on twelve days in November, and limited on the remaining eighteen, they took as many casualties as they had during the previous three months combined.) After the bombardment of Château-Salins, Able Company's tanks rolled forward. They encountered only sporadic machine-gun and mortar fire. The tanks fanned out through streets filled with smoking rubble, covering the infantry as they cleared what was left of the town's buildings one at a time. To Captain Williams, the attack was working as it should, precisely as per their training in the States. Château-Salins was the first rail and communications center east of Nancy to be claimed by the 26th Division, and XII Corps would use the town as its headquarters for the next few weeks of the Saar Campaign.

BAKER, DOG, AND CHARLIE COMPANIES would not be so fortunate. A young driver in a Charlie Company tank was terrified and literally shaking that morning at the prospect of another day under fire. Sam Turley, the company's first sergeant—known throughout the 761st as the best first sergeant in the battalion—was supposed to stay back and supervise the company's progress by radio from a command post. Instead, he willingly volunteered to take the frightened driver's place. This would prove to be Charlie's one piece of good luck.

In its approach on Morville-les-Vic from the south, Baker Company was slowed by a series of roadblocks covered with machine and antitank guns. The Shermans worked for several hours in close concert with infantrymen of the 26th Division to clear the obstacles, firing their .30- and .50-caliber machine guns to cover the infantry while the infantry fanned out to spot and eliminate Panzerfaust and other antitank teams. When Baker and the foot soldiers finally reached the outskirts of town, the Shermans fired high-explosive shells to clear a path—but, as it turned out, with only limited effect. Realizing the importance of Morville as a passageway to the east, the Germans had manned the vast majority of buildings. German machine-gun and bazooka teams were strategically placed overlooking every intersection, and carefully positioned in cellars and upper-level windows throughout the town. The infantrymen fanned out with Baker's tanks in close support, firing their cannons to eliminate positions as the German teams opened fire and revealed themselves.

At an intersection two-thirds of the way through Morville, while taking up position to fire on a building containing several gun posts, the tank commanded by Sgt. Roy King took a direct hit from a Panzerfaust. Gunner Herbert Porter was wounded by metal fragments. The tank caught fire. When Roy King and loader Nathaniel Ross opened the top hatch to escape, King was struck and killed by machine-gun fire. Ross was also hit but managed to jump down and take shelter. The two remaining crewmen, James Whitby and John McNeil, exited through the bottom escape hatch, carrying their grease guns. Herbert Porter, severely injured, also managed to climb out.

Germans continued firing on the tank. Several infantrymen rushing to the aid of the Sherman crew were struck and killed. From under the tank, John McNeil began firing his grease gun at German positions in the windows above. Whitby reentered the burning tank to man the tank's .30-caliber machine gun, blasting out several German machine-gun posts and a Panzerfaust unit, clearing the way for the infantry finally to take the buildings around the intersection.

IN THE FOREST NEAR THE town of Salival, Dog Company's "screening" operation had quickly devolved into a pitched battle. Dog Company's light tanks had started by shelling Salival to clear the way for an infantry assault, then had taken up position in the hills and woods around the town. Lacking full armor, the light tanks weren't made for direct combat. But the situation dictated that they fight.

Warren Crecy's driver, Harry Tyree, manuevering in the forest, heard a BOOM! as a German 75mm shell hit the assistant driver's side. The blast tore out the right side of the tank's suspension system. Crecy shouted, "I'm going to get 'em" and jumped out of the turret. Tyree watched in wonderment through his periscope as Crecy ran forward, commandeering a nearby jeep that was armed with only a .30-caliber machine gun. Driving straight into a hail of bullets, Crecy routed the enemy antitank crew, then continued forward to provide covering fire for a squad of infantrymen who were moving up to take out several German artillery observers. Quiet and thoughtful in most situations, Crecy became a man possessed going into battle.

Crecy and his crew took over a second tank and pressed on. This tank soon became mired in the dense mud. Harry Tyree, hearing German machine-gun bullets striking the sides of the vehicle, told Crecy he intended to stay put inside the hull. But Crecy dismounted. He was trying to determine how to brace his tank's tracks when he heard a machine-gun barrage erupt nearby. American infantry units crossing an open stretch of terrain below were taking heavy casualties. Crecy climbed up on the rear of his immobilized tank, and, with no cover from incoming machine-gun fire, blasted at the enemy positions— allowing the American infantry to advance.

The Sherman tanks of Headquarters Company, along with the 105mm assault gun and mortar platoons, had moved up into the woods near Salival. In radio contact with the other companies, they could hear what was happening to Baker and Dog—and could hear that Charlie was being decimated. An American spotter plane sighted a relief column of two hundred German soldiers and thirty vehicles en route from the town of Hampont to the beleaguered Charlie Company's side of Morville. Pop Gates moved his five assault guns forward, trapping and destroying the enemy relief column with a well-executed indirect fire mission. This preemptive attack prevented a horrific situation from becoming even worse.

CHARLIE COMPANY HAD ENTERED BATTLE just after 9 A.M., pushing off ahead of Dog Company from the vicinity of Moyenvic toward the northern end of Morville. Charlie had such success in pressing through German-controlled terrain during this early part of the attack that it raced across a key bridge before the Germans had time to detonate it. The company began to be slowed, however, by a rain of carefully directed artillery fire from a German officer candidate school less than two miles away in the town of Marsal.

As 2nd Lt. Kenneth Coleman's platoon reached the outskirts of Morville, Coleman's tank took a direct hit from a nearby German anti-tank gun. His tank—the lead vehicle in the column—was immobilized. Though the five-man crew managed to evacuate safely, their tank now blocked the road, leaving the remainder of the platoon exposed. This was a common German tactic: When American tanks were in column formation, the Germans often waited until they drew close, then with pinpoint accuracy fired to disable the first and last tanks in the line. This left no exit for the other tanks—they were unable to move forward or back out—and the Germans could take their time picking them off one by one. Coleman reacted quickly, leading his crew on foot in an assault against the enemy artillery and small-arms positions overlooking the road. Though under fierce fire, armed with only grease guns on what should by all accounts have been a suicide mission, this crew succeeded in routing the German teams. Several of Coleman's men were hit in the attack and had to be evacuated. The damaged tank was pushed off the road. Coleman took command of the next tank in line and led the remainder of his platoon forward.

The advance was halted again by entrenched resistance. At this point, Captain Harrison's tank was called forward to the outskirts of town. A key bridge near Coleman's platoon had been damaged by German artillery; a platoon of American combat engineers was working furiously in the face of further shelling to repair it. Harrison backed his tank up against a nearby building to provide what covering fire he could. The German artillery barrage was so intense that the slates on the roofs were raining down, shattering over the streets and on the turret of his tank.

Through his periscope, Harrison saw Coleman's tank start across the partially repaired bridge, then abruptly come to a halt. He watched his friend's tank anxiously, hoping to see it start rolling again. He was struck by alarm quickly turning to rage as the Germans put a sudden, deadly accurate round of artillery on the tank, shooting it off the bridge—then continuing and blasting the bridge itself to bits. A young lieutenant directing the platoon of combat engineers had just seen most of his men blown apart. The lieutenant ran down the road in Harrison's direction, shell-shocked. He fell to his knees directly beside Harrison's tank and started praying. Captain Harrison felt real fear for the first time in his life.

THE TWO REMAINING PLATOONS of Charlie Company pushed through the forest to the northeast of Morville. They could see the town less than a mile ahead, down a steep wooded hill and across an open stretch of field and road. They had so far encountered only light opposition. They had been told by infantry scouts to expect unobstructed terrain from the edge of the woods across the field into town. The scouts had either not seen or had failed to mention a long ditch dug in precisely where the hill met level ground. The tanks planned to move ahead defilade (side by side), a tactic that would provide them with the widest possible field of fire. This formation meant, however, that there was no lead tank to act as a lightning rod for terrain and man-made obstacles. Fifty yards beyond the woods, the light snow helped to conceal German troops crouched in a series of concrete pillboxes. Charlie Company's Shermans moved as one body downhill into the trap.

The ditch had been dug deep and covered with brush. When the front ends of the thirty-two-ton Shermans pushed in, with the steep slope behind them they lacked sufficient traction to back out. The concealed German machine-gun, rocket-launcher, and antitank artillery teams opened fire. An 88 hit Corp. Raleigh Hill's tank and set it on fire. The bottom escape hatch wouldn't open. The tank's ammunition started exploding. The crew had to exit through the turret hatch—which the Germans quickly zeroed with a machine gun. As the men exited one by one, they were hit.

S. Sgt. Frank Cochrane's tank had also taken a direct strike. Tank commander George Collier and Earnest Chatmon were wounded in the blast; Frank Cochrane carried both men out. A third Sherman in which Dennis Osby held the position of bow gunner was hit and immediately caught fire. Osby's crew evacuated through the bottom escape hatch and scrambled for cover in the ditch. Only then did Osby realize one crew member was missing. He ran through machine-gun fire to reenter the burning tank. Autrey Fletcher, the gunner, was injured and his feet had become entangled in the .50-caliber ammunition belt. Osby freed Fletcher and carried him out into the ditch.

First Sergeant Sam Turley's tank was also struck by an antitank gun. Turley and his crew escaped, as did the crews of the three tanks closest to him. Seven tanks had now been knocked out. Turley directed the men to spread out through the ditch and give covering fire to the remaining crews as they tried to exit their vehicles. Turley removed the .50-caliber machine gun from his tank and ordered others to do the same, firing in teams over the edge of the ditch on the German positions.

Corp. Dwight Simpson, providing covering fire, saw Horatio Scott a short distance away beside his smoldering tank. Scott had managed to crawl out but had been unable to move himself any farther. He was lying exposed to continuous fire. Hugging the ground, Simpson wove his way through the incoming artillery to pull Scott away from the tank. Simpson then remained with Scott, doing what he could to stop the heavy bleeding.

There was no way for the surviving tank crews to escape the ditch. It would be suicide to advance toward the German guns and it would be suicide to retreat, as they would have to climb uphill fully exposed to enemy fire. Now the German artillery began "walking the ditch"—firing at evenly spaced intervals—attempting to finish off the remaining men. The smell of singed and burning flesh and the sound of shell fragments hissing and steaming as they struck water filled the air. Men hit by bullets and shrapnel were screaming for help. The Germans continued firing down the line. A high-explosive shell detonated near Dennis Osby and Autrey Fletcher. Both were grievously wounded.

Sergeant Turley realized that the situation was hopeless. He ordered the trapped men to begin to retreat up the ridge in teams. Those waiting for their turn to move out offered a semblance of covering fire. Turley himself stood before the ditch firing the .50-caliber machine gun from his hip. The men sprinted a few at a time up the hill to the trees, carrying their wounded comrades with them. Turley's heroic effort allowed most of his men to escape. Moments later, a high-explosive shell struck and killed Turley where he stood.

Dwight Simpson had been unable to carry the severely wounded Horatio Scott far when the German machine guns again erupted around them. He remained crouched beside Scott in a fairly open position. Across the field in Morville, the infantry, going house to house, were able to clear the town by the middle of the afternoon. The 761st received orders to fall back for the night.

Simpson had remained at Scott's side, exposed to continued enemy fire. As darkness fell, the Germans began dropping flares. Figuring the odds were as good as they were going to get, Simpson lifted Horatio Scott—barely conscious—over his shoulders and scrambled the three hundred remaining yards back to American lines.

SEVEN MEMBERS OF CHARLIE COMPANY had been killed on November 9: Kenneth Coleman, Samuel Turley, Emile Armstrong, Robert Briscoe, Alexander Anderson, Theodore Cooper, and Willie Lofton. Many more had been severely wounded. The toll on the 761st would have been much higher were it not for the courageous actions of Lieutenant Coleman and Sergeant Turley. The three Sherman tanks of Headquarters, including those of Leonard Smith and William McBurney, were shifted over as replacements the next day to become part of Charlie Company.

When Warren Crecy learned of Horatio Scott's injuries, he was devastated. Scott sent word to him from the aid station that he was fine and would be back in action soon. Reassured, Crecy distinguished himself as he had done previously in the bitter fighting that continued around Morville-les-Vic, firing the .30-caliber weapon on his light tank's turret to neutralize enemy machine-gun positions.

On the evening of the tenth, Crecy volunteered for a reconnaissance mission. The rest of Dog Company set up bivouac. Shortly afterward, they received word that Horatio Scott had died of his wounds. Crecy returned an hour later from patrol. Preston McNeil didn't know how to break the news to him. Nobody wanted to be the one to tell him that his friend was gone.

5

FIELD OF FIRE

You knew the kinds of ways people got hit. If there was

any chance at all, you went back for them.

Nobody wanted to die inside that tank.

—LEONARD SMITH

There was to be no break for the 761st. Able Company rolled east from Morville in a column, and bivouacked near the town of Wuisse. At dawn on the eleventh they were to attack Wuisse and the high ground that overlooked it, Hill 309, key to controlling one of the region's major roads to the east. Baker and Charlie Companies bivouacked nearby.

Leonard Smith found himself the only member of the battered C Company anticipating the next round of fighting with anything but dread. He was grieved by Charlie Company's heavy losses, but he had to this point been confined to a supporting role in Headquarters and had yet to fire his cannon in combat. He kept checking and rechecking his equipment and supply of shells, imagining every potential target, until his crewmates finally asked him to stop so they could sleep. Smith, who had no intention of sleeping, was the natural choice to stand guard. As he stood watch, the scattered flares and flashes of artillery over the trees only heightened his sense of expectation.

At dawn, Baker, Dog, and Charlie Companies were to join with elements of the 101st and 328th Infantry Regiments to clear the area around the towns of Marsal and Haraucourt as well as the dense Bride and Koecking Forest, objectives critical to securing several east-west roads.

When Warren Crecy finally learned of Horatio Scott's death, he went berserk. Early on the morning of November 11, he approached Capt. Richard English to request permission to transfer out of Dog Company to C Company, to Horatio's tank. Charlie Company had already gained a reputation for invariably catching the worst hell in combat. But Crecy wanted to be part of it—he said he intended to kill ten Germans for every dead and wounded member of the 761st.

PATTON HAD HOPED WITH GRAND OPTIMISM to crack the Siegfried Line by the eleventh, "as it was my birthday and my lucky day in North Africa." But it was not to be. Progress had been slow all along the Third Army's front. In the XII Corps sector, the 80th, 35th, and 26th Infantry Divisions had each advanced less than seven miles. Sherman tanks of the 4th Armored Division—held back until the 26th Infantry and 761st broke the tight German hold on Morville-les-Vic and environs—swung into action on November 10. The 4th Armored had become adept at operating deep behind enemy lines, creating devastation even when outnumbered and outgunned. A 4th Armored lieutenant colonel voiced the fierce division's ethos when he said, in the midst of a German counterattack, "They've got us surrounded again, the poor bastards!" But the severe weather and entrenched German positions in Lorraine proved too much even for the veteran outfit, which took heavy casualties and gained little ground.

XX Corps had begun its massive attack as planned on November 9. Its initial goal was to capture the fortified city of Metz, roughly seven miles distant. However, a sudden flooding of the Moselle River brought the entire corps almost to a standstill. Near Thionville, troops of the 90th Infantry Division found themselves in a dire and unprecedented situation. Three regiments of infantrymen crossed the Moselle River, transporting several 57mm antitank guns. But they were cut off from their ammunition and from communication with their main artillery and tank support on the west bank by flash flooding. They ran short of medicine and rations. They had no blankets or protective clothing against the cold. Some of the soldiers waded through water almost five feet deep to transport supplies to their comrades, hauling cables tied to motorless boats.

Patton's Saar Campaign, which had made such a promising start November 8, was beginning to look more and more like a disaster. But the ten armored and infantry divisions of the Third Army's XII and XX Corps continued at high cost to grind their way forward.

SHORTLY AFTER DAYBREAK ON NOVEMBER 11, the platoon of Able Company commanded by Lt. Charles Barbour attacked Hill 309 with elements of the 26th Infantry Division. Barbour's platoon had been operating on its own since November 8, split off from the other two platoons of Able. They had so far suffered few casualties—despite the commander of the 101st Regiment's lack of experience with tanks.

But that was about to change. The infantry's reconnaissance unit explicitly told Barbour's team that there were no antitank obstacles on Hill 309.

Working in close concert with infantrymen, the platoon advanced some distance against what seemed to be light resistance. All of a sudden, machine-gun and artillery fire erupted from concealed positions all around them. The tank commanded by Sgt. George Shivers of Bainbridge, Georgia, was hit. Shivers was killed and his four crewmen wounded. When a German shell penetrated a Sherman tank, fiery particles rained throughout the interior compartments. Anyone under this initial shower of fire died instantaneously. Pieces of shrapnel ricocheting through the compartments could also cause mortal wounds. Fires were common, as electrical cables, oil and gasoline vapors, and a hundred other items fed the flames and made them very difficult to extinguish.

Soon after S. Sgt. Johnnie Stevens saw his friend George Shivers's tank explode, his own tank took an artillery hit. The initial blast killed loader Walter Campbell. Stevens and the other three members of the crew managed to crawl out, but all suffered serious injuries. Eleven pieces of shrapnel were embedded in Stevens's legs. He was lying in an exposed position when the Germans started targeting the area with mortar fire. Stevens was stunned and unable to move. A tall sergeant from the 26th Division shouted out from behind an embankment to ask if he'd been hit. Stevens called back, "I'm hit hard as hell." The sergeant jumped up over the rise, put his arms under Stevens, and shoved him to safety. Before he could duck back down himself, a German stood from a concealed post fifteen yards away and killed the sergeant with machine-gun fire. Stevens would try for years, in vain, to learn the sergeant's name.

WHATEVER REMAINING NOTIONS William McBurney may have had about the glory of war had disappeared days before, when he saw the wounded from Morville (the ricochet effect inside the Sherman caused severed limbs, horrific wounds) carried back to the aid station. He was fully aware that this could happen just as easily to him. Setting out in the Bride and Koecking Forest, he executed his assignments as tank gunner with the same steady hand and stolid courage that had distinguished him throughout training. He was good at it. Each day became a series of zeroed targets, just trying to make it back to camp. Home—against his father's wishes the place he had been so eager to leave in order to prove himself—seemed not to be such an oppressive place in retrospect. But he accepted the motto repeated with varying degrees of irony throughout the ranks of Patton's GIs: "The quickest way home is through Berlin."

Leonard Smith, by contrast, was thoroughly enjoying the wild ride. He was utterly convinced that he and his close friends would not be killed or seriously wounded, a view that (with indomitable innocence) he actually took to be confirmed by his narrow brushes with death by artillery shelling, carbon monoxide poisoning, and a German patrol on November 8. He was in his element. Swinging his turret around, calling for ammunition, taking out whatever targets he was assigned—machine-gun nests, pillboxes, antitank positions—with the constant roar of the engine and the cannon blasting and incoming machine-gun fire, this was high adventure of the kind Smith had always dreamed about.

Warren Crecy, granted his request to move to C Company, had been made a tank commander. He fought with a vengeance. He had already been recommended for a Silver Star for valor in his first three days of combat, but those around Crecy noticed an increased intensity in his actions since Horatio Scott's death. Tank commanders were trained to wait until targets revealed themselves in order to conserve ammunition—but Patton advocated a tactic known as "reconnaissance by fire," raining shells anyplace where German teams might be hiding. Shermans contained storage space for roughly a hundred

75mm or 76mm shells (with tankers cramming extra rounds wherever possible): Crecy frequently ran out of ammo, racing back for resupply and rushing to return to the front. He seemed to be on a personal mission, attacking enemy positions with such ferocity and complete disregard for his own safety that he was given the nickname "Iron Man."

Preston McNeil, a platoon sergeant in Dog Company, kept in constant touch with the tank commanders in his platoon throughout the day, instructing and advising them. At night, in bivouac, he would lead in prayer the men who were willing to pray, and joke around with those who weren't, whatever it took to reassure them. They trusted him. This was what the war quickly boiled down to for him—trying to live up to his responsibility for their lives.

ON NOVEMBER 11, TWO PLATOONS of 761st Shermans had been assigned to clear the woods near Harraucourt before taking up positions to shell the town. Dog Company's light tanks spread out to screen their flank. The Shermans encountered fierce resistance from enemy infantry and concealed antitank teams. Several were hit at close range. Dog Company's Sgt. John Jennison, spotting a wounded crewman who had lost consciousness while trying to exit his burning tank, crawled through a barrage of antitank and small-arms fire to pull him out and carry him to the aid station.

A German reconnaissance patrol had located the 761st's main command post and bivouac area. The post suddenly came under an intense rain of fire. Fragments from an exploding shell severed the artery of a tanker who was standing at the post's perimeter, and crew members James Rollins and Austin Jackson dashed out in the middle of the barrage to carry him back for aid. Capt. Garland "Doc" Adamson saw another soldier who was wounded and could not safely be moved. Adamson ran out under the incoming 88mm shells to administer first aid, then quickly loaded the man onto a nearby truck so he could be taken out of the line of fire. Seconds later, a shell landed precisely where the wounded man had lain.

The bloody attack-and-counterattack on November 11 spread throughout the woods and hill towns northeast of Morville. A battalion of the 104th Infantry Regiment was sent several miles ahead without armored support to attack the fortified city of Rodalbe. A near-massacre followed: The Germans had an overwhelming number of tanks, forcing the American troops to find cover in cellars. German sympathizers directed the German teams to the cellars where the Americans were hiding, and the enemy tanks then aimed their gun muzzles down the cellar steps and fired 88mm shells point-blank at the Americans inside.

Infantrymen throughout Lorraine took by far the highest casualties of any units. With no protection against the cold, wet conditions—often leaving behind their packs, blankets, and even field jackets in the interest of making frontal assaults with all possible speed—they suffered the highest rates of disease as well. The tankers admired and felt pity for the vulnerable foot soldiers they saw falling on all sides and shivering at night in their perpetually damp foxholes. For their part, infantrymen usually envied the tankers—until they saw crewmen maimed and burned alive inside their vehicles.

The combat team of the 4th Armored Division assigned to the 26th Division's zone—"Combat Command A"—had been divided into two task forces. On November 11 and 12, Task Force Hunter was pushed back from Rodalbe by the Germans, suffering heavy losses. Several days later, Task Force Oden was similarly repelled from its assault on the cities of Guebling and Bourgaltroff.

ON NOVEMBER 12, SCOUTS FROM Lt. Joseph Kahoe's platoon of Able Company—which had faced tough combat around Wuisse—located the Germans' key antitank postions overlooking the town. On his own initiative, Kahoe staged a counterattack with elements of the 104th Infantry Regiment. Kahoe's tanks spread out and worked in teams to destroy the antitank guns, finally capturing Wuisse early in the afternoon of the thirteenth. They successfully defended it throughout the night against a series of German assaults.

Able Company's S. Sgt. Ruben Rivers—who had earlier removed the mined roadblock outside of Vic-sur-Seille—rolled east from Morville standing on his turret, firing his .50-caliber antiaircraft gun against German ground positions. The .50-caliber was highly effective against not only troops but also trucks and wooden structures, and it could rotate on its ring mount on a 360-degree axis. The only hitch was that in order to operate it, the tank commander had to stand fully exposed in the turret. When Rivers's platoon commander, Lt. Robert Hammond, radioed up to him not to go into one of the heavily defended towns east of Morville because reconnaissance reported it to be filled with German infantry and armored units, Rivers radioed back apologetically, "I'm already through."

There had been no change in the weather. It always seemed to be raining, turning fields and roads to the consistency of pudding. The tank drivers in the 761st had one advantage, they believed, over the drivers in other Sherman outfits. It was a skill hard-won in the swamplands of Louisiana: their unparalleled expertise with mud. They'd hated the mud they lived and breathed throughout their first months of training, but now counted that experience a blessing. Willie Devore had matured into one of the battalion's best drivers, with an ability to maneuver with coolness under fire. The Germans had been schooled to zero in on Shermans with three artillery shots, a first long, a second short, a third dead on. By that third shot, gunning the tank so as not to bog down, Devore would be out of sight.

Conditions in Lorraine soon became so terrible, however, that often there was nothing even the most skilled of drivers could do to avoid getting stuck. Rain turned to heavier rain. And, when it seemed the rain could get no worse, the rain would turn to snow. The wet snow melted on contact with the tanks, offering little camouflage, but it helped to conceal clusters of German mines, booby traps, Panzer-faust positions, and antitank guns.

ON NOVEMBER 14, WHILE ELEMENTS OF the 26th Infantry continued to hold the front, the companies of the 761st were pulled back to Hampont to perform the required 100-hour maintenance checks on their vehicles. Though the Sherman tank was generally outgunned in battle, it was reliably engineered. Hundred-hour maintenance procedure required essentially pulling apart the engine and checking all major systems, including fluids, belts, and spark plugs, as well as checking the wear of the tracks.

The battalion's ordnance units worked furiously around the clock, as they had throughout the 761st's time in France, to recover and repair the more seriously damaged tanks; seven of the nine Charlie Company tanks lost in the tank trap northeast of Morville were eventually put back in service. Though soldiers in ordnance did not participate directly in combat, they confronted the nightmare results of war each day. They were the ones who had to clean the insides of the tanks, washing out the blood and gore and repainting the walls, ceilings, and floors. They were responsible for collecting all body parts, however shattered, and keeping them together before turning them over for burial. The tank would then be sent back into action, but would often (so the tankers said) still carry the smell and presence of death.

Captain Williams of Able Company met the 761st's new commander, Lt. Col. Hollis Hunt, in the bullet-scarred house on the western edge of Hampont that served as the unit's temporary command post. Hunt had been assigned to the battalion after Lieutenant Colonel Bates was injured. Williams's first meeting with Hunt was not a pleasant one. Lieutenant Barbour, whom Williams considered his best first lieutenant, had been suffering from battle fatigue and shock since seeing his misdeployed platoon virtually slaughtered on Hill 309. When Barbour was unable to return to the front, Hunt wanted him court-martialed. Williams refused to sign off on the court-martial. How, he asked, could Major Wingo's abandonment of the unit go unpunished, yet Barbour be court-martialed after personally leading his men through four brutal days of close-in fighting? What Williams felt but did not directly argue was that Hunt's reaction had to do with the fact that Lieutenant Barbour was black. When Hunt persisted, Williams became defiant, refusing to betray the courageous officer who served under him, saying, "What the fuck can you do to me? Send me to the rear? Go ahead." As a compromise, Hunt temporarily transferred Barbour out to Headquarters.

Williams had felt some doubts himself, during training, about how the 761st would perform under fire—but he'd been amazed by the courage of his men from the outset of combat. This feeling was shared by most of the infantrymen who had initially felt cheated that their tank support consisted of a black outfit. Incoming barrages of 88, mortar, and machine-gun fire tended—for the duration of combat, at least—to reduce things to the barest essentials of life and death. All that mattered was how well you were protected by the tank crews beside you and how well you carried out your part in turn. The 761st performed with the highest distinction.

The battalion's members had learned to live with the wariness some of the officers and enlisted men displayed toward them. But this attitude came as a shock and revelation to Williams—whose innate sense of fairness was most outraged by a certain class of officers (in which he placed Hunt) who stayed far from the battlefront and never saw or acknowledged what the men did, how hard they fought, and the punishment they endured to gain territory yard by yard in the endless morass of mud and blood that was Lorraine.

Most of the enlisted men of the battalion never saw or spoke with Hunt. After Lieutenant Colonel Bates had been wounded, the men never again felt the sense of security and trust in the battalion's commander that Bates had provided. But the sergeants and company leaders stepped up wherever they could. Pop Gates took responsibility for men beyond his Headquarters Company platoon, checking in on Leonard Smith and others in Charlie whenever he was able to. Russell C. Geist, who became the 761st's executive officer after Wingo left, did everything he could for the battalion, regularly putting himself at risk to talk with the men in the field. Above all else, the men came increasingly to rely on one another.

Preston McNeil picked his way through the rubble-strewn streets of Hampont searching for Charlie Company's maintenance area. Tank companies—often spread out over miles, assigned to different regiments and objectives—had no idea in combat how other companies were faring. On rare occasions when they stopped in the same town, battalion members sought out friends in other companies like survivors of a shipwreck. They didn't talk about what they'd just been through—such recounting would only bring home the stark reality of their situation—instead expressing their concern for each other through good-natured gibes. Humor proved as important a survival skill for the tankers as any military tactic. Leonard Smith was often teased about and happily recounted the various scrapes that had led him to spend most of his time during training at KP.

ABLE COMPANY, THE FIRST TO ROTATE OUT for maintenance, was the first to push back into battle. Able had been assigned to support the 2nd Battalion of the 101st Infantry Regiment in attacking Guebling and Bougaltroff—cities from which the 4th Armored Division's Combat Command A had just been driven back with heavy tank losses. On November 15, Captain Williams, Lieutenants Kahoe and Hammond, and Platoon Sergeants Ruben Rivers and Teddy Weston traveled to a ridge above the city to scout the area with the 2nd Battalion's commander, Lieutenant Colonel Lyons. Guebling lay at the bottom of a valley approximately four miles long, surrounded on all sides by wooded hills: To enter, infantry and tanks would have to cross a stretch of open and exposed terrain. The bridge into the city had been detonated by the Germans and was now smoldering brick and metal. The steep slopes along the sole road into town would force the tanks to travel in column formation.

While some infantry commanders showed a marked lack of concern for the Sherman tanks attached to their units, Williams came to greatly respect a few of the commanders with whom he worked, Lieutenant Colonel Lyons most of all. Looking down from the ridge toward Guebling, Lieutenant Hammond voiced his concern over the extreme vulnerability of the tanks in their approach across the valley. Lieutenant Colonel Lyons agreed, saying he had expressed the same misgivings to his superiors and had recommended instead a pincer manuever encircling Guebling and Bourgaltroff. Lyons had, however, been overruled. The attack was set to begin at sunrise on the sixteenth.

Able bivouacked outside of Wuisse that evening and started rolling toward Guebling shortly before dawn. Cascades of orange streamers exploded across the dark sky: American heavy artillery was already pounding the city. The Third Army's field artillery units performed superbly, moving their heavy guns through what had essentially become marshland, taking on even more work when the fighter-bombers of the XIX Air Tactical Command were grounded due to the miserable weather. The Germans had begun, however, to develop strategies to counter Patton's reliance on artillery preparation to "soften" enemy lines. They had learned that troops waiting in forward positions were bound to be devastated by air and artillery fire: German commanders had therefore been instructed that whenever an attack was coming, they should pull the main body of their forces to positions several miles back, conserving them for the close-in ground battle to follow.

Just as the sky grew light, Able's tanks reached the bottom of the hill to the west of Guebling. Lyons's infantry had been sent ahead of them. Williams ordered Kahoe's platoon to peel off to the right. Kahoe's tanks would spread out as much as possible, screening the right flank of Hammond's platoon, which was to race down the road across the valley in a fully exposed column. Hammond's tanks would then conceal themselves just west of the city, amid the cluster of buildings around the railroad station. The ruins of the bridge they would have to cross in order to reach Guebling proper lay just beyond the station; the tanks had been instructed to wait as engineers rebuilt the bridge that would allow the main assault on the city to continue.

Floyd Dade, in the lead tank of Kahoe's platoon, rolled down for over a hundred yards from the shelter of the trees, certain despite the apparent lack of resistance that the Germans would counterstrike. He kept repeating to himself the Twenty-third Psalm: "The Lord is my Shepherd, I shall not want . . ." Able's tanks had a stroke of good fortune: The ground had frozen during the night. Thus, despite deep ruts and chewed-up earth everywhere from yesterday's sea of mud, the vehicles had ample traction. The two platoons moved some distance across the valley amid an unsettling quiet. The calm caused Captain Williams to think that perhaps the Germans had abandoned the city. Suddenly a barrage of mortars came in, white phosphorus shells intended to stop them and mark their positions. Williams tried to reach the others over the microphone, but his throat was blocked with burning smoke. His eyes watering, he began to choke and cough. He felt his gunner next to him begin to shake and realized that his crew and the other tankers were suffering also. With zero visibility, Able's tanks could do nothing but wait in place until the mortar barrage had ended. It lasted a full twenty minutes, although the mortars had only been tracer fire for artillery positioned in the hills above. What followed next was a rain of high-caliber German fire.

Within moments, Lieutenant Kahoe's tank took a direct hit. Four of its five crew members escaped and started running, falling across the frozen, rutted ground. When an artillery shell scored a direct hit, another shell was sure to follow. Kahoe's gunner, Walter Lewis, stopped a short distance away from the tank, realizing that loader Harold McIntyre was still trapped inside. Lewis ran back, jumped onto the turret, and reached through the hatch to pull out McIntyre. The two men dove off the tank together into the partial shelter of a nearby shell crater. A second later, another shell hit the tank with such force that it spun the thirty-two-ton vehicle over on its side.

Robert Hammond's platoon, in the meantime, raced toward the train station just west of Guebling. Ruben Rivers's tank started across the railroad tracks when a deafening explosion from its undercarriage sent up a fiery black plume of smoke; it had struck a German Teller-mine. Mines that detonated outside of the tank's tracks could have limited impact, damaging the tracks or suspension. Mines exploding betweeen the tracks, as Rivers's had, were devastating, their explosive force blowing straight upward into the turret. A piece of metal knocked loose by the blast cut Rivers's leg to the bone.

Captain Williams rushed up to find Rivers and his crew beside their disabled Sherman. Rivers allowed medic Ray Roberson to clean and disinfect his wound—which ran from knee to thigh—but refused morphine and refused to be evacuated. He knew the opposition his platoon was likely to face as they pushed farther into the city and toward Bourgaltroff. He took over a second tank, ordering the tank commander, Henry Conway, out. Rivers's initial crew took up rifles and joined the nearby infantry.

Able's tanks assumed positions concealed by the buildings around the tracks, and combat engineers started rebuilding the crucial bridge to Guebling. Their work would continue throughout the next day, with the engineers continually taking casualties from German fire.

The 2nd Battalion's commander, Lieutenant Colonel Lyons, visited Captain Williams near the railroad station on the afternoon of the seventeenth. Lyons's voice broke as he told Williams that the 2nd Battalion's F Company, which had been ordered to cross a flat field on the right side of Guebling to dig in around Bourgaltroff, had been surrounded by enemy tanks. The Germans defending Bourgaltroff were the same Panzer group the 4th Armored's Combat Command A had battled two days before—an entire battalion from the crack German 11th Panzer Division.

Unable to cross into Guebling until the bridge was completed, Able's tanks could do little but wait. Williams visited the men of his company. A medic had again inspected Rivers's wound and discovered that infection was setting in. Rivers was clearly in great pain. Told that the infection was likely to cost Rivers his leg and become life-threatening, Captain Williams ordered Rivers to the rear. But Rivers shook his head, telling him, "This is one order, the only order I'll ever disobey." Williams had been informed by Lieutenant Colonel Lyons that the bridge into Guebling was close to completion; he instructed Able's two platoons to prepare for a massive assault through Guebling and toward Bourgaltroff with the remainder of the 101st Infantry Regiment the next day.

Up to this point, although the 761st Tank Battalion had faced the whole spectrum of German antitank weapons, from Panzerfausts and rocket launchers to high-velocity 75s and 88s, they had yet to encounter German Panzer and Tiger tanks in force. German armor had been depleted in the region by the battles with Patton's troops between August and October. As a consequence, German generals had sent only small numbers of tanks forward to meet the initial thrust of Patton's November 8 assault—keeping their main force back to hold a firm north-south line running through the cities of Rodalbe,

Benestroff, Guebling, Bourgaltroff, and Dieuze. This was the line that all five companies of the 761st were about to challenge.

BAKER, CHARLIE, DOG, AND HEADQUARTERS left Hampont to take up positions in the woods directly southwest of Guebling, preparing to support the 328th Infantry Regiment in its assault on the crossroads city of Dieuze. Leonard Smith's "Cool Stud" crew found one bright spot as they set up camp—the addition of a mascot, a rooster they aptly dubbed "Cool Stud." Cardell had spotted the rooster pecking around the streets of a small ruined town and placed him on the side of the tank. He was an odd, scrappy, bedraggled-looking bird. He wasn't tied down—but for whatever reason or quirk of nature (probably the bits of food they fed him), the rooster chose to stay even amid the shelling of the woods by enemy artillery.

Patton had planned the 761st's attacks on the cities of Dieuze, Guebling, and Bourgaltroff after the slow progress of the Saar Campaign's first few days, as part of his revised strategy for cracking the Siegfried Line. On November 18, a series of renewed attacks all along the Third Army's front were to mark the beginning of this second campaign phase.

In the XX Corps' zone, the 5th, 95th, and 90th Infantry Divisions were to complete their encirclement of Metz. These units had faced bloody resistance throughout the previous eight days of battle. A rare clearing in the weather on November 17 allowed the XIX Air Tactical Command to fly a number of key bombing runs; by the end of the day, the American divisions around the city had advanced to positions just four miles apart from one another, and were ready to break through the outer approaches of the city's defense.

In the XII Corps sector, Patton planned a renewed push by the 26th Infantry in conjunction with the 80th and 35th, and the 4th and 6th Armored Divisions, moving north and east to converge on the cities of Sarreguemines and Saarbrucken. These cities—located just beyond the German border, thirty miles east of the Corps' current positions—controlled the approaches to major strongholds in the Siegfried Line. The 26th Division and 761st were specifically instructed to attack through Rodalbe, Benestroff, Guebling, Bourgaltroff, and Dieuze, then to push northeast through a series of fortified woods and hill towns including Honskirch and Sarre-Union. The assaults were to begin just after dawn on the eighteenth.

Popular histories of the Second World War have tended to bypass both the Saar Campaign and the First Army's concomitant attack through the Hurtgen Forest (which had started in September and was joined with renewed force on November 16)—rushing instead from the costly yet triumphant invasion of Normandy straight to the bitter yet also unquestionably successful Battle of the Bulge. The Saar Campaign, like the Battle of the Hurtgen Forest, was in the end to prove a victory—but it numbered among the bloodiest and least successful victories of the war. Patton's Saar offensive had deteriorated, by mid-November, into a series of disjointed and not always well-advised drives. Patton had lost sight of his larger objectives and the costs, and instead seemed concerned, as the official U.S. Army campaign historian would note, "simply with driving steadily forward, going as far as his strength and supplies would permit."

BAKER, CHARLIE, AND DOG'S OBJECTIVE—Dieuze—was a vital communications and rail center. The Germans had been convinced the November attack coming in the 26th Division zone would drive toward that city, and had been surprised by the initial thrust on the eighth toward Rodalbe instead. Dieuze, a point of convergence for several rivers, bordered on a large marshland and lake. It was terrain upon which tanks had not been designed to fight. The ground-bearing pressure of the M-4 Sherman was approximately seven pounds per square inch, equivalent to that of a man walking—making it all too easy for tanks to bog down.

Late on the 17th and 18th, the XIX Air Tactical Command passed over Charlie's waiting positions, flying a series of bombing missions against Dieuze. Leonard Smith looked up through the trees to catch the glorious sight of the fugitive sun glinting off the wings of the Allied P-38 Lightnings and P-47 Thunderbolts. It further heightened his perpetual adrenaline rush. William McBurney had a reaction of a different sort, remembering his conversation of years before with the Army recruiter, wondering why he couldn't be soaring up there instead of stuck down below inside the type of vehicle that Sherman crews everywhere nicknamed "Iron Coffins" or, alternately, with gallows humor, "Ronsons" (after a brand of cigarette lighter whose motto was "Lights up every time").

Baker, Charlie, and Dog Companies, along with the 328th Infantry Regiment, began rolling forward shortly after dawn on the nineteenth—immediately encountering minefields and a hail of antitank weapons.

A typical M4 firing sequence, as engine noise and crashes from enemy fire engulfed the cramped interior of the tank, went like this:

> Commander to driver: "Driver . . . STOP"
> Commander to gunner: "Gunner . . . TANK" [naming the type of target]
> Commander to loader: "AP" [calling for armor-piercing shells]
> Commander to gunner: "Traverse left . . . Steady-on . . . One thousand."
> Gunner to commander: "Ready!"
> Commander to gunner: "FIRE!"

Leonard Smith's excitement over the adrenaline rush of battle never diminished: He kept a running tally in his head of his hits on enemy infantry and antitank positions. William McBurney, on the other hand, quickly lost all sense of numbers, time, and location.

Tank gunners were restricted in vision to a narrow periscope and a horizontal rectangle in the turret: McBurney often didn't know the names of the towns they entered, how many buildings or machine-gun nests they destroyed, or how many miles they crossed. All he knew was that they were moving forward. And all he focused on was the mechanical process of calling to his loader for rounds, steadily firing and repeating. He found that church steeples—which, because they often housed German snipers and artillery observers, Patton instructed all tankers to blow apart—were one target he never had any trouble seeing.

The 761st and the 328th Infantry successfully drove the Germans back in two days of fierce fighting from the towns of Val-de-Bride and Guebestroff. As they approached the flooded outskirts of Dieuze, Pop Gates's Assault Gun Platoon was ordered forward to fire on the city. Under heavy German fire, Gates's guns carefully took up position. His platoon destroyed its designated targets with such a high degree of accuracy that Maj. Gen. Willard Paul, the commander of the 26th Infantry Division, praised the unit, claiming he had "never seen a better demonstration of firing by weapons of that type before."

In the action on the twentieth, Charlie Company's captain, Irvin McHenry, weary from two continuous days of fighting, failed to move away from his cannon's recoil and broke his hand. McHenry was evacuated to the aid station, and Gates was transferred over to head Charlie. Gates was now directly responsible for the lives and well-being of many of the young men, including Leonard Smith, with whom he had formed such a close attachment.

The 761st's determined advance through the rubble and morass of Dieuze's outskirts, and its successful firing mission—eliminating critical perimeter defenses—helped make possible the capture of that city by the 328th Infantry Regiment and elements of the 4th Armored Division on the afternoon of the twentieth.

AS BAKER, CHARLIE, AND DOG COMPANIES of the 761st prepared to drive toward Dieuze on November 18th, Able Company launched its assault through the city of Guebling and toward Bourgaltroff. It was a two-day battle that proved to be the company's costliest of the war. The 101st Infantry Regiment had been battling house to house for several days in Guebling. Enemy troops in the area had largely fallen back in order to make a final stand at heavily fortified Bourgaltroff, but the Germans had left behind harrassing forces and Guebling was still subject to shelling. Captain Williams ordered his Shermans to cross the just-completed bridge into Guebling. He divided his tanks into three groups, with one group moving straight through town and the other two going around the northern and southern perimeters to take up positions in the field on the far side of the city, overlooking Bourgaltroff to the east.

Williams's tank reached the center of Guebling without opposition, although the young captain saw a number of burned-out half-tracks and overturned Sherman tanks, disturbing evidence of the 4th Armored's recent bitter battle with the 11th Panzers.

Floyd Dade's tank rolled past the center of Guebling and came under German fire. The Sherman took up position, unable to move in any direction, behind a disabled tank of the 4th Armored Division. German soldiers, aware of their predicament, continued directing fire at them but were unable to target them firmly because of the other tank. Dade and his crew, assigned to guard a crossroads five hundred yards away, stayed in position amid the barrage to keep it sighted.

Ruben Rivers, moving around the perimeter of Guebling toward a low hill that gave him a line of fire on Bourgaltroff, encountered two enemy tanks. Despite his life-threatening injuries from two days before, Rivers calmly targeted the tanks for gunner Everett Robinson, shooting an intense round of armor-piercing and high-explosive shells until both German tanks withdrew.

The 101st Infantry Regiment battled toward Bourgaltroff against entrenched German forces. The tanks of Able Company were ordered to stand by and hold their stations throughout the night of the eighteenth. The sound of burp guns and M-1s was constant, and the Germans sent up a series of flares. Ruben Rivers reported to Captain Williams a sound that was equally ominous. Throughout the night, the staff sergeant noted the distinctive rattle of large numbers of German tanks taking up position in the field.

Williams, coming by Rivers's tank just before sunrise on the nineteenth, asked Rivers one last time to evacuate so that his injured leg could be saved. Rivers refused, telling him, "How in the hell can I go back and leave you all here?" The assault on Bourgaltroff was set to begin in earnest at dawn.

Lieutenant Colonel Lyons, commanding the 101st Regiment's 2nd Battalion, continued to believe that the direct attack on Bourgaltroff was a mistake. He felt that the 26th Division should instead encircle and close off the city, telling Captain Williams, "Division should pinch out this sector and be done with it." He would be proved correct; the attack would become a slaughter. Nonetheless, Lyons was again overruled by his superiors.

Lyons was concerned in particular with the German antitank guns, which were well-positioned throughout the vast meadow, as well as with the Panther and Tiger tanks. The enemy tanks could penetrate the sides of a Sherman from 1,200 meters; to penetrate the thicker German armor, American tanks had to close to a range of 400 meters, hardly an equal match. The turret on the Tiger was slow, not fully electric like the Sherman's. But the German crew could rapidly stop one track and essentially jump the entire tank around: The 761st called it pouncing "quick like a cat." One well-placed Tiger could cover a great deal of ground.

Able Company's plan of action was for Ruben Rivers and a companion tank, commanded by Sgt. Walter James, to cross the field toward Bourgaltroff and fire on the western edge of the city with high-explosive shells. Second Lt. Robert Hammond and an additional tank would move across the field more slowly, spreading out to destroy as many enemy infantry and machine-gun positions as possible. Captain Williams's tank, Floyd Dade's tank, and the rest of the company would in the meantime head down the road toward Bourgaltroff in column formation.

The assault was preceded by a heavy American artillery barrage. Dade's tank, commanded by Teddy Weston, rolled forward just as dawn broke to lead the column on the road to Bourgaltroff. The 101st Infantry was already filtering past them into the meadow. As they did, they were mowed down by machine-gun fire. German antitank tracers started raining in. Rivers's tank advanced some distance across the field and was the first to spot and open fire on German positions.

Back along the road, Dade's tank took an artillery hit on its turret. Miraculously, none of the crew was injured and the tank was still mobile. But the tank's 76mm gun had been disabled. The Germans slowly zeroed in on the tank column. Artillery crashed in around the exposed vehicles, striking a second tank. Dade's tank backed up behind the shelter of a ruined house. Captain Williams, seeing that the situation was hopeless, ordered the others in the column to do the same.

Ruben Rivers sighted several Mark IV Panther tanks and enemy tank destroyers concealed behind a slope in the meadow. These vehicles had a wide field of fire and were devastating the American tanks and infantry. Rivers advanced, firing off tracers and armor-piercing shells. Captain Williams, from his position on the road, spotted enemy tracers flying in across the field toward where he knew Hammond's and Rivers's tanks were advancing. Williams, unable to keep the fear from his voice, radioed both tank commanders to pull back. Hammond attempted to fall back behind a clump of trees. Rivers, instead of retreating, pushed ahead to provide cover for the retreating infantry and other tanks in the field. He radioed Williams, "I see them. We'll fight them."

Williams rolled his tank forward from its sheltered position to provide some kind of covering fire for Hammond and Rivers. Dade's tank, armed with nothing but machine guns, followed. Rivers and Hammond had moved beyond a crest in the meadow, out of their line of sight.

The infantry was everywhere taking casualties. Antitank tracers continued raining in. An infantryman jumped up on Williams's tank with orders from Lieutenant Col. Lyons to the American troops to fall back to defensive positions. Williams radioed both Rivers and Hammond again to take cover. This time he received no answer.

IN HIS POSTWAR STUDY of the Lorraine Campaign, military historian Christopher Gabel criticizes the American generals for their part in its high casualty count, stating that Eisenhower, Bradley, and Patton were so intently focused on cracking the Siegfried Line that they grossly underestimated the terrain and man-made obstacles in the way. In essence, a growing gap in perception arose between the high commanders "who drew large arrows on maps and the tactical units fighting for yards of muddy ground." At 1300 hours on November 19, Able Company and the 101st Infantry Regiment received word that the sector including Bourgaltroff had been pinched out—as Lieutenant Colonel Lyons had argued all along that it should be. The deadly attack across the open field had been for nothing.

Lyons, leading from the front, had been struck by mortar fire early in the afternoon; he survived, but lost an eye and a leg. The 101st Infantry Regiment was devastated with heavy losses, as was the 761st. Able Company's 2nd Lt. Robert Hammond was killed by a direct strike from a Tiger tank. Technician Roderick Ewing was also killed. S. Sgt. Ruben Rivers, who had refused to leave his men and fought on for several days though badly wounded, died when two German high-explosive shells ruptured the turret of his tank as it rolled forward, fully exposed, toward enemy positions across the field.

Rivers's loader, Ivory Hilliard, was gravely wounded by ricocheting fragments. Hilliard escaped the tank, but in shock ran toward the German lines. Hilliard's body—missing for two days—was eventually discovered curled up in fetal position in an abandoned enemy trench.

Captain Hart, commander of the distinguished tank destroyer unit assigned to protect the rear and flank of the 761st at Guebling, was amazed by the courage of Able's lead tanks. He formally addressed the battalion's acting commander, Lt. Col. Hollis Hunt, saying, "I've never seen a tank company stand in there like this one."

On the nineteenth, Captain Williams and several other members of Able Company, including Henry Conway and Mose Bryant, crawled forward through the open meadow with stretchers—endangering themselves under enemy machine-gun fire—to remove the severely wounded crew members Vinton Hudson and Roderick Ewing from their tanks. American tankers, subject daily to the extreme vulnerabilities and terrible injuries afflicting Sherman tanks and crews, had a firmly held code that if there was any chance to save someone, you risked your own life in the attempt. You knew beyond doubt that if it were you out there, trapped and unable to move, others would do the same.

The remainder of Able Company moved ahead to the town of Marimont, performing maintenance and repairs on their vehicles in advance of their next assault. On the morning of November 21, the company held a memorial service in the town's weather-beaten church for those killed and wounded, sitting together in the pews without benefit of a chaplain present. According to Captain Williams, "There were no sounds except for quiet weeping."

6

THE SAAR

Our helmet was our home.

—WILLIAM McBURNEY

After the capture of Dieuze on November 20, the 761st's Dog Company was ordered six miles north to support the 26th Infantry Division's reconnaissance and field artillery units attacking the hill town of Benestroff. Benestroff had been one of the 26th Division's initial objectives for the Saar Campaign. The American artillery briefly shelled the town. Preston McNeil saw a French woman emerge from a building at the outskirts, desperately waving a white flag.

Dog Company was the first unit into Benestroff. It appeared to have been abandoned. Nonetheless, McNeil cautioned his men to be careful as they fanned out through the gutted streets. Mines and booby traps left by the Germans in abandoned buildings, under rubble, even under corpses, wired to detonate days or even weeks later, took a high toll both physically and psychologically on American troops. In the action around Morville, McNeil had seen an infantryman severely injured by such a device while trying to pull a Luger pistol off a dead German soldier, and was determined the same thing not happen to any of his men. It could be exhausting trying to keep his platoon together. He was just twenty-two and scared himself. He prayed constantly for the safety of his men, and prayed more than anything he wouldn't let them down.

While Dog Company rolled through the streets of the near-deserted town, Baker and Charlie Companies fought their way northeast from Dieuze toward the town of Torcheville with the 328th Infantry Regiment. Pop Gates stayed close to the front, regularly conferring with the foot soldiers on potential hazards and frequently going himself or sending his tankers on foot to scout ahead. If there was one thing Gates had learned in the battalion's first two weeks of combat, it was that anything could happen to anyone at any time. Like McNeil, his first concern was his responsibility—seventeen M-4 Shermans and eighty-five men.

He'd given up on trying to talk Leonard Smith down from his perpetual combat high, but always checked in on him and was always encouraged, at the end of another day's slogging through the mud, to see Smith still alive and in good spirits. They pressed rapidly through a series of small towns. The limited vision that defined the tanker's world in combat was restricted still further on entering a village: In open terrain, they'd been trained to know where enemy teams might hide, but in a town any window, cellar, or alleyway might hold a Panzerfaust or rocket launcher team. Smith moved his periscope in all directions, searching for any sudden movement.

On the roads between towns, the tankers fired on virtually everything, from buildings to haystacks to the tops of clusters of trees, that might house a sniper. Smith never tired of the hunt for targets.

The rooster "Cool Stud" had remained atop Smith's tank despite the near-continuous combat. It would get off to forage when they bivouacked at night, and get back on again before they headed out in the morning. The rooster became a legend, treasured pet, and welcome source of humor for all of Charlie's crews, not so much begging for as huffily demanding scraps of food.

ON NOVEMBER 16 AND 17, while traversing the Bride and Koecking Forest in their approaches on Guebling and Dieuze, the 761st unwittingly crossed an unmarked but politically crucial boundary within the French province of Lorraine: They had entered into the region known as the Saarland, or Saar. The Saar spans the border of France and Germany, with approximately half of its area on either side. Though measuring just 992 square miles—considerably smaller than the state of Rhode Island—the Saar, a coal-mining and industrial district studded with breathtaking valleys and woods, nonetheless has been one of the most contested regions in history. Romans and Celts fought for control of the Saar and Alsace-Lorraine as early as 54 B.C.; Attila the Hun crossed the region in A.D. 451 during his invasion of Gaul; Emperor Charlemagne's grandsons declared the territory part of Germany when they divided his kingdom in A.D. 870. The Saar was reclaimed for France in 1680 by Louis XIV, and again in 1801 by Napolean Bonaparte; it was seized by the Germans in the Franco-Prussian War of 1870. The area had been for centuries "the traditional invasion route between east and west"—a fact of which the history-minded George Patton was not unaware when he planned his own Saar Campaign.

The Saar was declared an independent territory by the Treaty of Versailles, which ended World War I. But the Germans had deliberately colonized the realm, and in 1935, more than 90 percent of its citizens voted by plebiscite to become part of Hitler's Third Reich. This bias on the part of civilians became clear to the 761st as they moved ever further into the Saar, ever closer to the German border. Leonard Smith, who had enjoyed more than anyone else the grand victory parade of the road march from Normandy across central France, felt the shift strongly. It was apparent in the way the citizens avoided acknowledging them but shot sidelong glimpses or glares from upper-level windows. William McBurney noted that this guardedness and outright hostility wasn't directed solely at the black men of the 761st, but at the 328th's infantrymen as well; it seemed an equal hatred of all things American.

Not only the populace but the weather, too, had changed, growing colder at night. The tankers began collecting and hoarding blankets, the only means of warmth they had against the brutal conditions. The biting cold of the steel interior of the tank was the bane of tankers throughout Europe. The walls of his tank would get so cold at night that Preston McNeil chose to dig a little hole beside the vehicle, grab as many blankets as he could, and sleep there instead—finding the dampness that soaked through from the mud or melting snow preferable to that searing cold. Several of Charlie Company's tankers slept on the rear engine compartments of their Shermans, drawing the last remnants of heat from the motors as they cooled. Leonard Smith and his crewmate, Hollis Clark, preferred to stay inside "Cool Stud." They had managed through various elaborate barters with other tankers and infantrymen to collect ten blankets apiece, ten of which they'd put on the turret floor and ten on top of them. No matter how many blankets they used, the cold still came through. They slept turned away from each other in the turret, but close enough to share the warmth from each other's bodies. As fired up as he was throughout the action of the day, Smith slept like a baby at night, even when the sounds of artillery came close.

A rare treat and welcome harbor was the chance to bivouac in or near an American-held town. One lonely crew member was assigned to guard each tank, while the others competed for floor space in abandoned houses and beds of straw in barns. Smith had chosen, despite the limited room for personal effects in his barracks bag, to pack his favorite pair of pajamas. Anytime he stayed in a town, however tenuously held, he would change into his pj's. The other tankers, ever-wary of shelling, slept ready to roll in uniform and had to laugh at Smith's blithe unconcern.

Food was always on the minds of American GIs. Their staples of C and K rations provided them with basic nutrition, but were about as flavorful as cardboard. C rations contained three cans of greasy meat and vegetables and three of crackers, sugar, and coffee; K rations contained a small tin of meat spread, hard cheese, crackers, and instant coffee or powdered lemonade. When rapidly spearheading, the lighter K rations were the more common fare for tankers. They foraged through American-held towns to supplement their rations whenever possible, feeling more at liberty to do so the more hostile the local populace became.

In one farmyard, Smith watched in amusement as his tank's driver, Hollis Clark, emptied an entire clip from his grease gun trying in vain to shoot a clucking, madly zigzagging yardbird. Finally, a fellow tanker who'd grown up on a farm stepped in, grabbed the bird, and broke its neck with one smooth motion. On another occasion, the crew of Isiah Parks's C Company tank captured a barnyard hen, stripped and cleaned the bird, and started a small fire to cook it— despite their sergeant's admonition that German artillery observers were scattered throughout the surrounding hills. Parks's crew dove away just in time as an enemy shell whistled in, landing square in the center of and extinguishing their fire. They ate the bird raw, deciding that cold K rations weren't always the worst of options.

Warren Crecy seemed never to eat or sleep, regularly volunteering for night patrols. He would go off by himself, stealthily approaching a German-held town on foot with an M-1 Garand rifle he'd taken from an infantryman killed in action and carried strapped to his Sherman. Night after night Crecy would go off alone, coming back with invaluable information on enemy positions and also—so the men suspected, though he never directly said it—killing as many Germans as he could in the process. Some nights, when he intended simply to slip behind the lines and scout out antitank posts, he'd ask for volunteers to accompany him—but he had fewer and fewer takers as the days wore on. Most of the men had come to realize that serious injury or death was a distinct possibility on such missions. While they intended to do their jobs, they weren't about to seek death out. Leonard Smith was one of the few who enjoyed going off on the scouting forays. Willie Devore always did his utmost to dissuade his best friend, telling him—as Pop Gates had tried before him—that this was war, not an adventure novel.

Some of the men took the opportunity of whatever brief stops they made to attach anything available to the front and side armor of their tanks to buffer the devastating effect of a direct strike—logs, spare tracks, and most often sandbags. Nothing was going to stop a well-aimed high-velocity 75mm or armor-piercing 88mm shell—but the motley assortment of barriers did provide some protection against oblique shots and gave them a necessary illusion (they knew on some level it was an illusion) of security.

THE MEN HAD SPOTTED ENEMY GUNS and expected heavy resistance at Torcheville, but they rolled though that city unopposed. By now, they knew enough to be distrustful of any mission that was too quietly or easily accomplished. They were just eight miles west of the Sarre River, which roughly bisected the Saarland and figured prominently in Patton's battle maps of the region. The Germans had strategically fallen back to fortify the towns to their east, among them Munster and Honskirch. On November 22, Charlie Company was ordered to attack Munster.

KAREEM ABDUL-JABBAR'S father, F. L. "Al" Alcindor, in uniform in the 16th Battalion, Field Artillery Replacement Center, Fort Bragg, North Carolina. (AUTHOR'S COLLECTION)

KAREEM'S PARENTS, 1943. Al Alcindor always said that meeting Cora was the high point of his time in the army. (AUTHOR'S COLLECTION)

LEONARD SMITH

LEONARD "SMITTY" SMITH, wearing the uniform and insignia of the 761st Battalion. (COURTESY LEONARD SMITH)

2nd LIEUTENANT JOHN Roosevelt "Jackie" Robinson, while serving in the 9th Cavalry, the famed "Buffalo Soldiers," before his transfer to the 761st. (COURTESY RACHEL ROBINSON)

LEONARD SMITH AND comrades in the 761st training in the U.S.
(COURTESY LEONARD SMITH)

HEADQUARTERS COMPANY, 761st Tank
Battalion, Camp Claiborne, 1943.
(COURTESY LEONARD SMITH)

DOG COMPANY, 761st Tank Battalion, checking equipment before leaving England to go into combat. (U.S. Army photo courtesy of the Patton Museum, Fort Knox, KY)

TANK COMMANDER Harvey Woodard assessing terrain, Nancy, France, November 1944. (U.S. Army photo courtesy of the Patton Museum, Fort Knox, KY)

761st FIELD OFFICERS (from left to right) Captain Ivan Harrison, Headquarters Company commanding officer; Captain Irvin McHenry, Charlie Company commanding officer; and 2nd Lieutenant James Lightfoot, the 81 MM Mortar Platoon Leader. (U.S. ARMY PHOTO COURTESY OF THE PATTON MUSEUM, FORT KNOX, KY)

A TANK FROM Able Company of the 761st Tank Battalion, crossing the Seille River on November 9, 1944. (U.S. ARMY PHOTO COURTESY OF THE PATTON MUSEUM, FORT KNOX, KY)

THE REMAINS OF four German Panzers and two 761st Sherman tanks after fierce fighting on November 19, 1944, in an open field between Guebling and Bourgaltroff. (COURTESY OF THE NATIONAL ARCHIVES)

CAPTAIN GARLAND "DOC" Adamson, M.D. (COURTESY OF THE NATIONAL ARCHIVES)

GENERAL GEORGE PATTON awarding a Silver Star to Private Ernest A. Jenkins. (U.S. ARMY PHOTO COURTESY OF THE PATTON MUSEUM, FORT KNOX, KY)

PRIVATE EUGENE HAMILTON guarding the tank park of the 761st Battalion following the war, January 1946. (U.S. ARMY PHOTO COURTESY OF THE PATTON MUSEUM, FORT KNOX, KY)

LEONARD SMITH AT a cemetery in the Netherlands, visiting the gravesite of a fallen comrade.

(COURTESY LEONARD SMITH)

LEONARD SMITH, TODAY.

(COURTESY LEONARD SMITH)

Charlie Company moved two miles due east through the Hessling Forest with elements of the 328th Infantry Regiment, stopping at the outskirts of Munster. The 761st's Assault Gun Platoon rolled ahead to shell the town. The infantry and Charlie's tanks then pushed forward, encountering a range of concealed enemy sniper and mortar positions. The tanks spread out to provide cover and fire on upper-level positions in the town as the infantry waged a house-by-house battle. Smith's "Cool Stud" tank and McBurney's "Taffy" moved up ahead of the rest. As they passed through Munster, well-hidden Germans strafed the tanks with abandon. The tracks of both vehicles were disabled, unable to move. The American infantrymen around them, taking insupportably high casualties, were forced to fall back.

By nightfall the Americans controlled most of the town, but the Germans controlled the area to the east. Smith's and McBurney's tanks were immobilized just inside the German zone. Whenever one of the crewmen would make a move to open a hatch, a sniper would fire. The men—including, for once, Leonard Smith—were too frightened to sleep. The only reason they were still alive was that the tanks' cannons were still working and no Germans were foolhardy enough to run up within range and toss a grenade. It was, for the time being, a standoff. But the tankers were well aware that the Germans had Panzerfaust and antitank guns in the vicinity, and that eliminating Sherman tanks was a priority. They were sitting ducks. A direct hit could come at any moment, without warning. There was nothing they could do about it. To keep their minds off their plight, they talked.

Sherman crews talked to each other via their intercoms all throughout battle. Though strictly forbidden from saying anything that would reveal their objectives or position to Germans who might be listening, tank units developed their own codes, carrying themselves through the day with ongoing banter. The 761st made use of slang from the streets of New York, including, of course, with typical GI profanity, a frequent use of the word "mother," "that mother this," "that mother that." It had to confuse the hell out of any Germans listening. The voices of crewmates in their headsets were the one familiar sound in all the chaos that kept them sane.

Stuck in the vicinity of Munster—fully exposed, their location no grand state secret—they could simply, freely talk. The two crews talked among themselves, and talked by way of their tank commanders' two-way radios back and forth. At times the artillery crashed in close enough around them, loudly enough that they had to fall silent and then at least to comment on it—wondering if it was German or American, and wondering whether it would make any difference in terms of the payouts to their families if friendly fire killed them. The artillery never let up, close then far then close again. None of the men directly voiced his fear. Smith's showed itself only in the fact that he was even more talkative and playful than usual, McBurney's in a greater irony and openness and willingness to laugh more than was his custom.

It was dawning on Smith, for the first time in his life, that there were no guarantees, that the glorious luck he had enjoyed so far might be in fact a precious, limited commodity and not a defining state of grace. Even if he somehow made it, there was no chance that all ten crewmen would. For every story Smith told about his nine lives and narrow scrapes thus far, he started seeing other alleys of possibility, other ways each situation might have gone.

They talked about their hometowns, about football and baseball, and of course about girls. McBurney, Smith, and Willie Devore talked about a girl all of them had noticed at the Savoy Ballroom in Harlem but none had worked up the nerve to talk to. Devore, they agreed, with his unerring charm, would have had the best chance. They survived by sharing a few C-ration cans of bacon and beans. Their stomachs gnawing with hunger, the cold, greasy fare had never tasted so good.

The 328th Infantry and the remainder of Charlie Company's

tanks finally cleared the area around them after fifty-one straight hours. The German guns had, miraculously, never zeroed in on either tank. Smith jumped out and hugged the first startled GI who reached them—a mud-soaked infantryman of the 328th who quickly grinned and offered him a cigarette.

But there was grim if not unexpected news. There was again to be no break. The tracks of both tanks were quickly repaired. The company was told to gear up and press on. Baker, Charlie, Dog, and the assault gun and mortar platoons had been ordered to attack three miles north toward Vittersbourg, and from there one mile east toward the crossroads city of Honskirch. Intelligence from the 26th Division had reported a heavy concentration of armor at Honskirch, their last major barrier before the Saar River.

THE TOWN OF VITTERSBOURG fell with brief if intense resistance from the Germans on the morning of the twenty-fifth. Charlie Company was then split up along platoon lines, with Smith and McBurney's platoon continuing to support the infantry in clearing the surrounding area. A second platoon of Charlie's tanks had been ordered to spearhead the assault on Honskirch. Pop Gates, however, delayed in executing this command.

Gates, who had learned well the lesson of Morville-les-Vic, had personally gone ahead to scout the approaches to the city and had spotted the formidable defenses of the Germans. The surrounding terrain was so sodden that Charlie's tanks would be forced to travel along the road in column formation. The Germans—fully aware of this—had placed antitank guns throughout the woods and hills that overlooked the route. Captain Gates informed the commanding infantry officer that the attack, as planned, would be a disaster. The officer ignored Gates's detailed enumeration of the entrenched enemy defenses and ordered the attack to proceed.

Gates allowed his tanks to move within half a mile of Honskirch, then called them back, despite the officer's command, to wait for artillery. Four guns from the 761st's assault gun platoon rolled forward as far as was possible over the marshy ground. They opened fire, though as Gates knew, the Germans were so well-entrenched that the 105mm howitzers would have only limited effect. Gates was playing for time—delaying the attack for four hours. Finally, the officer gave him a specific order to move the tanks straight down the road. Gates was certain it would be suicide for both the tankers and the infantry accompanying them. But in the military line of command he had no choice: If he refused, the determined officer would simply relieve him, going down the line until he found someone willing to carry out the order. Charlie's tanks and the infantry were going to be sent down that road no matter what, and Gates intended to be there with his men.

The six tanks along with the infantry began moving forward. The Germans immediately started barraging the formation, hitting every other tank, working their way down the column. The men in the tanks that had been hit cried out for help on the intercom. Smith, just a mile away, heard their fragmentary pleas relayed over Cardell's earphones. It was the worst moment of the war for him up to this point, to hear the voices of friends screaming for help and know that there was nothing he could do. In the space of less than five minutes, five of the platoon's six tanks were destroyed.

Pop Gates's tank driver, Lane Dunn, was killed by a shell. Gates, wounded by ricocheting shrapnel, managed with the rest of the men in his tank to escape before they were hit again. Gates half-ran, half-staggered along the length of the column, trying to order his crews to fall back. In the tank commanded by S. Sgt. Frank Cochrane, a direct artillery strike killed driver James Welborn. A second armor-piercing 88 blasted through one side of the turret and out the other, severing gunner Frank Greenwood's legs. Greenwood didn't feel any immediate pain—but looked down at a slight tickling sensation suddenly to see that both his feet were gone. In the driver's compartment, James Welborn's lifeless body slumped forward over the controls, causing the tank to back up until it slammed into a narrow stand of trees. Staff Sergeant Cochrane pulled Frank Greenwood out.

The mortar, artillery, and sniper fire on the tanks did not let up. Cochrane—stumbling and running—carried Greenwood in his arms, racing along with dozens of infantrymen for the shelter of a roadside ditch. Greenwood had lost consciousness from shock; upon reaching the ditch, Cochrane rested Greenwood's head on his boot to keep it from being submerged in the cold, muddy water.

Back on the road, Sgt. Moses Ballard's tank was hit; Ballard and all his crew were wounded by the blast. Ballard exited and went back three times under fire to carry members of his injured crew to safety. Sgt. James Stewart's tank was also struck. Stewart, like Ballard, pulled out his wounded crew one at a time, staying with the most severely injured beside the exposed tank until medics arrived.

Cpl. Buddie Branch's tank, of Baker Company, moved up behind Charlie's platoon on the road. Branch attempted to provide covering fire for the wounded Charlie crews. Pop Gates, though bleeding heavily, kept rushing from tank to tank—pulling out and tending to the platoon's wounded, refusing treatment for himself. Corporal Branch dismounted and, along with fellow tanker George Goines, despite the incoming hail of 88s and mortar, machine-gun, and sniper fire, made numerous trips to carry litters of casualties back some three hundred yards to shelter.

The battalion's executive officer, Russell Geist, ran forward from the command post to provide what help he could. He encountered Sgt. Robert Johnson's 105mm assault gun tank, mired in the swamp-like terrain. Johnson and his crew were working furiously to extricate the vehicle. Geist walked ahead, exposing himself to enemy artillery, to scout a route over which the tank could travel to provide cover for

Charlie's retreat. Johnson finished freeing his assault gun and ordered it forward, with gunner Elwood Hall firing everything they had.

German artillery observers spotted the ditch where Staff Sergeant Cochrane, Frank Greenwood, and the dozens of infantrymen had fled for cover. Mortar teams began "walking" the ditch at evenly spaced intervals, just as they had at Morville. They walked up the line to within thirty yards of Cochrane and Greenwood.

Johnson's assault gun tank was now pummeling the German positions in the high grounds. In their fury the crew had fired off such an intense barrage that they soon ran out of ammunition. They resorted to firing the only ammo they had left, white phosphorus shells. Johnson had not seen the American soldiers trapped in the roadside ditch below. But the white phosphorus shells served better than any artillery fire could have to cover their retreat. In fact, the smoke laid down by the phosphorus shells saved the men's lives, blocking them from view, buying them time to scramble out and carry their wounded comrades to safety.

FOUR OF THE 761ST—Lane Dunn, James Welborn, Coleman Simmons, Ardis Graham—and dozens of infantrymen were killed in the misguided attack on Honskirch. More than twenty tankers and scores of infantry were wounded, many of them, like Frank Greenwood, gravely. The 761st and the 26th Infantry ultimately pulled back toward Vittersbourg. Pop Gates, who made only the briefest of stops at the aid station for treatment of his shrapnel wounds, could not help but feel that something had snapped in him that day; he had acquired a bitterness over war's futility and waste that was to color the remainder of his experience in Europe. Men who were in his care had been slaughtered, and for nothing. But he didn't have the luxury of much time for existential musings: He still had what was left of a company to look after. All he could do was resolve—whatever it took—not to let the same thing happen again. The sole positive outcome of Honskirch, in his eyes, was a visit from Third Army commander George Patton. Patton, who was a frequent visitor to the front, wanted to know why the 761st lost five tanks in such a short period. Gates told him about the ill-conceived attack. Within two weeks, the officer who had refused to listen to Gates had been shipped back to the United States.

ABLE COMPANY HAD ADVANCED from Marimont to the town of Albe-stroff on November 23, four miles southwest of Honskirch, supporting the 104th Infantry Regiment in what proved for the tankers to be relatively light fighting. The Germans had pulled back the majority of their tanks and antitank guns to block the assault around Honskirch. Williams was saddened to hear that Charlie had been devastated yet again—and confirmed in his own bitter experience with certain infantry commanders who failed in the field test of armored tactics at a high and unnecessary cost in blood.

On the afternoon of the twenty-fifth, Able Company was ordered back to the town of Bidestroff, just outside of Guebling, for maintenance. Baker, Charlie, and Dog Companies soon followed. Since November 8, 34 of the 761st's tanks had been damaged or destroyed. The unit had suffered 125 casualties, 81 combat and 44 noncombat. Twenty-six men had been killed in action.

In Bidestroff, Pop Gates held a dinner for the tattered remnants of Company C in a farmhouse he had commandeered. He served chicken from a barn they had raided, and red wine one of the men had found in a basement. The men ate their meal crowded together in the dining room by candlelight. It was a vigil of sorts—but not entirely a grim one, with a curious, shifting admixture of sorrow beyond words and bittersweet laughter.

Gates, at the head of the table, looking around at the faces of the men he'd grown to love, made no speeches, as he was determined not to break down in front of them. The survivors told stories about their fallen comrades and friends, toasted and promised to remember them.

IN A LETTER TO HIS FRIEND Gilbert R. Cook, General Patton reported on the overall progress of the Saar Campaign to date: "The fight we are now having is less spectacular than the fight across France, but it is a damn sight harder. . . . However, I believe we are breaking through—at least we are doing our damdest." By the final days of November, Patton's Third Army had in fact attained several of its key objectives. In the XX Corps sector, on November 22, the fortress city of Metz had fallen to the 5th, 90th, and 95th Infantry and 10th Armored Divisions. In the XII Corps sector, the 80th, 35th, and 26th Infantry and 4th and 6th Armored Divisions had ground their way slowly forward, advancing an average of thirty miles from their starting points. The five divisions were positioned along a front roughly ten miles from their objectives of the Siegfried Line cities of Saarbrucken and Sarreguemines.

But these gains had come at extraordinary cost. In the hellish conditions of the Saar, sickness took a toll almost equal to that exacted by enemy guns: At one point, the flu and trench foot, among other maladies, incapacitated almost a tenth of Patton's quarter of a million troops. Trench foot, a circulatory disease stemming from prolonged exposure to cold and wet, was particularly costly. Virtually every member of the 761st suffered from it. To prevent trench foot, they had been instructed to change and dry their socks as often as they could—a lesson Patton called "more important for young officers to know than military tactics." But trying to follow these directives in the field was an exercise in futility. William McBurney, determined not to lose any of his toes to the malady, was particularly diligent in following this command. Every night he took off his socks to dry them out—but they were soaked through from the rain and mud, and the nights were so cold that the socks would simply freeze. In the morning, McBurney would wake to find them frozen solid, standing straight up at attention.

With such severe combat and noncombat losses, Patton's Third Army desperately needed replacements. But owing to high casualties throughout the European Theater—from Normandy to the bloody Hurtgen Forest—there were simply not enough available troops to bring the army up to combat strength. In mid-November, Patton called for volunteers from his corps and division headquarters units to replace killed and wounded tankers and riflemen. Two weeks later, he "drafted" an additional 5 percent, telling them, "We are not going to be stopped now by lack of replacements. We will lick that as we have other obstacles, by our own efforts."

Many of these volunteers and draftees—among them cooks and supply troops—had not fired a weapon in several years, since basic training. The tankers had to do what they could to train the newcomers at the front. Some of them hadn't even seen a tank before, but there they were, in the thick of it. Many of them didn't know enough to be afraid, to be careful. Only experience could teach them that.

James Jones, a twenty-one-year-old replacement from Laurel, Mississippi, who was sent to the 761st's Dog Company, took his training five miles behind the lines. It was exciting to him, and he looked forward to doing his part. But even more than the prospect of combat, what he enjoyed most was spending time with others in the battalion. What kept the men going day after day was their friendships with their buddies. At night, in bivouac, they'd sit back and joke and talk about things back home. Several black officers who had been to college took the time to encourage the men in their ambitions once the war was over. James Jones was amazed at the intellect of some of the other enlisted men. He learned more about Einstein at camp in the war zone than he had in school.

AT THE END OF NOVEMBER, into December 1 and 2, the 761st attacked from the vicinity of Munster toward the strategically crucial city of Sarre-Union. Sarre-Union lay just east of the Sarre River; it served as a junction point for several major highways as well as a railroad line. German troops—including the 11th Panzer Division—were determined to prevent a breakthrough past that city. The 761st fought to clear the area west and south of Sarre-Union, through the towns of Altwiller and Pisdorf.

Leonard Smith's "Cool Stud" tank was moving fast amid heavy shelling when their rooster mascot, which had been riding with them since mid-November—even staying on through the shelling near Munster—jumped off. Tank commander Daniel Cardell, grown perhaps too attached to the rooster, stopped the tank and ordered Smith out to retrieve the bird. When Smith refused, he was told, "That's an order!" He climbed down a hill, swearing to himself, looking everywhere. Fortunately, Smith was able to find the rooster before the Germans found Smith.

The Germans in the area were thoroughly dug in, continuing to hold outposts overlooking several of the 26th Division's main supply lines. American trucks were getting hit and couldn't get through. The 761st's intrepid supply officer, Philip Latimer, worked with Dog Company's captain, Richard English, to improvise a solution to the dire supply situation, drafting the light tanks into service. Preston McNeil organized the men of his platoon to work in shifts night and day, bringing gas and rations up to the front, aware how crucial they were to the advance of his friends. The fuel-hogging Shermans kept moving forward.

ELEMENTS OF THE 101ST AND 104TH Infantry Regiments had dug in and prepared in advance of the tanks to assault Sarre-Union. The foot soldiers fanned out through the streets, at first taking the town with relative ease, then being forced out in a vicious series of counterattacks. The infantry engaged in such close-in, house-to-house combat that it often became impossible to distinguish American from German-held buildings. The infantry finally succeeded in driving out the German troops on the afternoon of the second.

The tanks of the 761st, on reaching the city later that day, were ordered to stand in reserve to fend off a likely German counterattack. At 1100 hours on December 3, the 11th Panzer Division attacked in force from north and east of the city. Baker and Charlie Companies swung into action, attempting to drive the German armor back from a wooded area on the eastern edge of town. Several tanks were knocked out in the intense firefight. Five 761st members were seriously wounded, including Joseph Tates and James Stewart, both of whom had earlier earned Bronze Stars for risking their lives to help wounded comrades. Baker and Charlie's tanks continued battling for two hours before finally forcing the 11th Panzers back, with key support from 26th Division's artillery.

THE CITY AND ITS OUTSKIRTS weren't fully cleared until late on December 3, providing the Third Army with a crucial rail and communications junction east of the Sarre River. But for American ground troops, Sarre-Union offered a bounty even more concrete than its strategic value: The city was home to the legendary Pomeroi champagne factory. The GIs couldn't resist indulging themselves. After what they'd just endured, an all-out raid on the treasure trove seemed well within their rights. The 761st was ordered to push forward from Sarre-Union on the third with little rest. But before they did, the men tied cases of champagne to the tanks. Even the teetotalers like Leonard Smith drank champagne straight from bottles. After about an hour of feeling mighty fine, Smith quickly regretted it, becoming nauseated and dizzy.

The 761st pushed north and east toward the city of Oermingen. Battling constantly forward from town to town, the 761st's tank crews had long since mastered the rhythms of daily life inside their vehicles. But they never grew entirely used to them. The tankers weren't given replacement uniforms, and they wore the same gear for months. Their clothes literally disintegrated, rotting off of them. If they were in a town for more than a day, even a few hours, they would seize the opportunity to wash them in a creek. But they rarely had that chance. More often, in the field, they'd wash out their underwear and socks with gasoline. They'd wash their faces, chests, and underarms with water gathered from streams in their helmets when they could, using the helmet like a birdbath. If there wasn't any water available, they'd use gasoline, pouring it into their helmets and rubbing it on. The steel GI helmet served multiple purposes in the field. A helmet was a stove, a bathroom, a bathtub. In the morning, they'd cook breakfast in it. When they were rolling, they'd urinate in the helmet and empty it out the side or bottom of the tank. Then they'd clean the helmet and wash up in it, before using it to wash their clothes.

They heard some of the infantrymen beside whom they camped talking about the field showers they were given in their brief rotations out. The Red Cross moved mobile showers up just behind the front, trying every few weeks when possible to give front-line troops a brief but welcome cleansing and fresh gear. But the 761st never got such a break. Even the more naive and trusting of the battalion's members, like Leonard Smith, couldn't help but wonder whether this inequity had something to do with their race. This physical discomfort was the least of the hazards they faced—they were fortunate, they knew, simply to be alive—but the thought of it as an inequity was a bitter pill.

DAILY PRESSING NORTH AND EAST, the 761st was fast approaching the famed Maginot Line, located six miles north of Sarre-Union. The

Germans resisted fiercely, delaying the American forces with a screen of well-positioned forward troops to cover their strategic retreat behind the line. The Maginot Line had been constructed by the French in the years immediately following World War I to forestall German attacks. It ran for 150 miles, positioned five miles inside of and roughly paralleling the northeastern border between France and Germany. The line was composed of a series of complex defensive fortifications, including concrete pillboxes, machine-gun emplacements, underground bunkers, and triangular concrete antitank barriers known as "dragon's teeth." In the blitzkrieg of 1940, the Germans had simply circumvented the formidable barrier, rendering it useless by entering France through Belgium and the Ardennes Forest. But the fortifications proved extremely useful to the Germans in the fall of 1944 in hindering the Allied advance toward Germany.

As the 761st moved ever closer to the border, the fighting became heavier and more ferocious. On December 7 and 8, the tanks of the 761st first came within sight of the Maginot Line: Able Company near Achen, Baker Company near Etting, and Charlie Company near Oermingen. The tanks were ordered to roll forward to take out German machine-gun positions. But when they opened fire, their 76mm high-explosive shells simply bounced off the unusually thick pillbox walls. The company commanders called for support from the XIX Air Tactical Command.

The air bombing continued for more than two hours. As always, Leonard Smith found awe-inspiring the sight and combined power of the P-47s' strafing and bombing. The ground shook with the force of it. He took the slight risk of standing up in his turret just to observe it. The planes kept passing over, circling back to fire again. American engineers moved forward after this bombing run to clear a path for the 761st's tanks through the remaining antitank barriers and dragon's teeth. As the Shermans passed through the rubble of the Maginot fortifications, they received no return fire. The Germans had chosen to use the Maginot

Line along the Third Army's front simply as a delaying screen, concentrating their forces instead farther back toward the German border and at the Siegfried Line, the German equivalent to the Maginot.

Floyd Dade's tank commander in Able Company, S. Sgt. Teddy Weston, went forward on foot in advance of the infantry and his platoon to reconnoiter enemy positions in the town of Achen, allowing his company's tanks to pinpoint and eliminate machine-gun positions without a single American casualty. The infantry and tanks rapidly advanced.

Baker, Charlie, and Dog Companies assembled near the town of Woelfling-les-Sarreguemines, preparing again to push forward. The 761st's tanks were moving through territory more heavily mined and booby-trapped than any they had yet encountered. They were now just two miles from the German border and seven miles from the more formidable barrier of the Siegfried Line.

On December 9, Colonel Palladino of the 104th Infantry Regiment informed Captain Williams that the entire 26th Division was slated for rotation out for several days of R and R, rest and recuperation—not just the working maintenance period in which troops were still situated at the front and subject to shelling, but a bona fide rest behind the lines. The colonel told Williams to tell his men to "keep their heads down." Williams received the news with elation, as did Pop Gates and the other company captains, fully aware that their men and equipment had already been pushed beyond the limits of their endurance.

Williams caught a glimpse of the division that was to relieve the 26th Infantry, the 87th "Golden Acorn" Infantry, marching to take up positions along the front with a jauntiness and eagerness of purpose that could only be attributed to those who had never experienced combat. He reflected that ignorance is bliss. On December 11, the infantrymen of the 26th Division were pulled back thirty miles to the city of Metz.

But instead of its own well-deserved rest, the 761st at the last moment was switched over to the command of the 87th Division and ordered to continue pressing forward. After thirty-four unrelieved days on the front, Smith, McBurney, McNeil, and the others—who had heard of the promised upcoming rest and spent the past few days dreaming of hot baths, mattresses, and a clean change of clothes—were deeply disappointed.

Their frustration itself, however, was soon overwhelmed by what was, for most of them, a harsh and even tragic realization. Their accomplishments, bitter-fought miles, and horrific casualties meant nothing to the vast majority of the new white troops beside whom they'd been assigned to fight. They were seen not as soldiers but as black. Leonard Smith heard the phrase "nigger tankers" frequently repeated, in a tone that implied the very thought of it was absurd. Even William McBurney, who tended to be among the more watchful and reserved of the 761st's members, was cut to the quick.

It wasn't by any means all of the soldiers in the 87th who stirred up trouble, and it wasn't as if the tankers hadn't heard such slurs before. What had changed was that they'd seen so many of their friends killed; they'd seen Samuel Turley, Ruben Rivers, and Kenneth Coleman, among others, give their lives for their country, and had hoped—without consciously realizing they were doing so—that their valor and sacrifices were accomplishing gains beyond any measured in yards and miles.

They would hear much the same from other units beside which they'd later serve—an initial wariness and hostility that almost always changed under fire to respect and even admiration. The needle would be set again to zero every time they shifted divisions. By then they were prepared for it, prepared to wait it out. But in this first reassignment, they weren't prepared and had no defense. For most, those days numbered among the most painful of the war.

AT WOELFLING, NEAR THE CITY of Sarreguemines, American combat engineers, while under heavy mortar fire, constructed a bridge across the Blies River. The 761st's Baker and Charlie Companies rolled across, firing on the German positions. They continued battling their way forward, and on December 14, 1944, crossed the border into Germany for the first time. A communiqué from the Supreme Head-quarters for the Allied Forces reported that "Lt. General George S. Patton's Third Army infantry and armor slammed into German terri-tory at a new point . . . above Sarreguemines."

Able Company, several miles east of Baker and Charlie, was fast approaching the German border in the vicinity of Guiderkirchen and Erching. Captain Williams noted an odd quiet in the area. He was concerned, because the company had received no opposition, and no Germans came out of hiding to surrender. Floyd Dade, too, found the sudden lack of enemy presence disconcerting. At one town near the border, he asked a woman who knew some English what had hap-pened, and she told him, "The Boche [Germans] have gone." Due to the divided loyalties of the citizens of the Saar, he didn't know if he could trust what she said.

But the Germans had in fact departed; the 11th Panzers, unbe-knownst to the Americans, had been called up to Belgium's Ardennes Forest. On the afternoon of December 14, while the 87th Infantry continued holding the front, the companies of the 761st were pulled back to the city of Sarre-Union for a long-overdue 100-hour mainte-nance check.

Before rotating out to Metz with his 26th Infantry Division, Maj. Gen. Willard Paul had forwarded a commendation to the 761st Bat-talion from XII Corps commander Manton S. Eddy. Major General Paul wrote: "It is with extreme gratification that the Corps Comman-der's commendation is forwarded to you. Your battalion has supported this division with great bravery under the most adverse weather and terrain conditions. You have my sincere wish that success may con-tinue to follow your endeavors."

Major General Eddy's enclosed commendation read: "1. I consider the 761st Tank Battalion to have entered combat with such conspicuous courage and success as to warrant special commendation. 2. The speed with which they adapted themselves to the front line under the most adverse weather conditions, the gallantry with which they faced some of Germany's finest troops, and the confident spirit with which they emerged from their recent engagements in the vicinity of Dieuze, Morville les Vic, and Guebling entitle them surely to consider themselves the veteran 761st."

ON THE FIFTEENTH OF DECEMBER, after forty straight days of combat, George S. Patton's Saar Campaign had brought him, finally, to the point he had envisioned when he first assumed command of the Third Army almost a year before: His troops were poised to smash through the Siegfried Line and push northeast to the Rhine River. This sustained drive had cost more than Patton could possibly have imagined in the glory days of his August drive across France—certainly more than he acknowledged in his early, optimistic predictions for the campaign to higher headquarters. During the first three weeks in August, Patton's troops had advanced four hundred miles and liberated more than a third of France. By contrast, to capture the province of Lorraine, a stretch of territory with a width of only sixty miles, the Third Army had fought for more than three months, from September through mid-December, and suffered 50,000 casualties—which accounted for a third of the total number of casualties it would endure throughout all its operations in the European Theater (including the Battle of the Bulge). More than 25,000 of these casualties were sustained during the Saar Campaign.

Postwar military studies have criticized Patton for spreading his forces too thin in Lorraine. Historian Christopher Gabel writes, "The German defenders were critical of, but grateful for, Patton's decision to [sic] a broad front of nine divisions spread out over sixty miles. . . .

One rule of thumb for mechanized forces that emerged from World War II was to march dispersed but concentrate to fight. In Lorraine, Third Army fought dispersed." Military historians have also criticized Patton for overoptimism about the strength of the obstacles in his army's path, an overoptimism that translated from the highest levels down the chain of command into the sorts of impossible missions the enlisted men of the 26th Division and the 761st were all too often given: "The corps commanders were trapped between Patton, who continually urged aggressive action, and the grim realities of terrain, weather, and a determined enemy."

The Saar Campaign was in the end a victory, gaining Patton the jumping-off point he had so urgently wanted. But it was a victory gained at an appalling price. As biographer Stanley Hirshson wrote of the siege of Metz, the Saar was not one of Patton's finest moments, and "he preferred to forget it."

WHILE THE MEN CONTINUED CHECKING and repairing their engines, tanks, and guns at Sarre-Union, Captain Williams was visited by Colonel Sears of the 87th Infantry Division. Sears informed him that the battalion's rest would be short-lived. The 761st Tank Battalion was to play a large role in a massive new assault planned by General Patton. Sears told Williams that the 4th and 6th Armored and the 80th and 87th Infantry Divisions were going to go through the Siegfried Line to the Rhine, with the 761st spearheading for the 87th.

On December 10 and again on the thirteenth, Patton met with his staff to refine their plans for this attack, plans in which, according to biographer Robert Allen, "every defensive position and obstacle was meticulously pinpointed. Thousands of 1/25,000-scale multi-colored collated maps were compiled and distributed." Patton's XII and XX Corps were to drive east simultaneously from the vicinities of Sar-reguemines, Saarbrucken, and Saarlautern into Germany's Mainz–

Frankfurt–Darmstadt corridor. This ground assault was to be preceded by a bombing campaign more intense than any in the war thus far, with sorties by five to six hundred medium bombers and twelve hundred to fifteen hundred heavy bombers, all supported in turn by hundreds of fighter-bombers. The distinguished RAF would follow this initial thrust by sending one thousand of its bombers farther ahead into Germany. The air assault would continue for three days before any American infantry involvement.

After the final strategy meeting on the thirteenth, Patton's deputy chief of staff, Maj. Hobart R. Gay, summarized his opinion of the significance of this operation: "It is my belief that if this air attack is carried out as planned, and if the ground attack is carried out as planned, it will breach the Siegfried Line, which means the advance of American troops to the Rhine and might well terminate the war."

Had events unfolded differently in mid-December, and had the sacrifices of Lorraine indeed proven to be a jumping-off point for the road to final victory in Europe, the Saar Campaign may have come to be viewed as equal in significance with the invasion of Normandy. This was undoubtedly George Patton's intent. Instead, today the Saar Campaign has largely been forgotten. Twenty-six members of the 761st Tank Battalion, along with thousands of other members of Patton's Third U.S. Army, were buried in the northeasternmost corner of France, in the province of Lorraine and in the Saar.

The reason the Saar Campaign would fade in significance would soon become clear. On the night of December 15–16, as General Patton continued studying maps and planning his attack, he was disturbed by complete German radio silence in the area. He asked his intelligence liaison, Oscar Koch, what this might mean. Koch replied, "I don't know what it means when the *Germans* go on radio silence. But when we place one of our units in radio silence, it means they're going to move."

7

THE BLOODY FOREST

It just looked almost endless, like you were going

to be there the rest of your life.

—PRIVATE BART HAGERMAN, 17TH AIRBORNE DIVISION

At 5:30 A.M. on December 16, a massive attack was launched by 250,000 German troops in the forested region of Belgium and Luxembourg known as the Ardennes. The offensive took the Allied high command utterly by surprise. American generals had viewed the harsh, rugged woodland of the Ardennes as the least likely location for a German attack, and had defended the eighty-mile front with only four thinly spread divisions of the First U.S. Army. These troops were overwhelmed by the staggering force of the enemy artillery and armored assault, many of them falling back in a confused, disorderly retreat, leaving behind those too badly wounded to walk. By December 19, the German armored spearhead of Joachim Peiper's 1st SS Panzer Regiment had advanced thirty miles west. Outside the Belgian city of Schonberg, 7,000 American soldiers of the 106th Infantry Division—surrounded on all sides, under constant bombardment, and entirely out of ammunition—surrendered, the largest surrender of American troops since Bataan. The Germans continued pressing rapidly west, forcing a showdown that would enter military history as the single bloodiest struggle ever engaged in by American forces: the Battle of the Bulge.

On December 19, at Verdun, France, in what was to prove to be one of the most crucial meetings of the war, Eisenhower summoned George Patton, Omar Bradley, Lt. Gen. Jacob Devers, British Air Marshal Arthur Tedder, and Field Marshal Bernard Montgomery's chief of staff to discuss the Allied response to the German breakthrough. When Eisenhower entered the conference room at Verdun, in a cold, dimly lit French barracks, he found the faces of the Allied commanders around the table markedly grim. The notable exception was George Patton.

Eisenhower asked Patton how soon he could have his Third Army on the attack in Belgium. Patton answered that he could attack the morning of December 21, with three divisions. Eisenhower told him to launch his attack on the twenty-second. The effect of this exchange on the assembled officers was what one of them later described as "electric": the act of pulling three full divisions off the front line, pivoting them ninety degrees from their planned axis of attack, and sending them more than a hundred miles north across icy roads to Belgium to attack in strength in less than three days was unprecedented.

Patton expressed his concern, in strategizing the withdrawal of his troops, with guarding the hard-won Saar. The Germans could not be allowed any advances in the south. The 87th Division and the 761st were to hold the southernmost sector of the line while Patton's 4th Armored and 26th and 80th Infantry Divisions raced north, until elements of the Seventh Army could move up from Alsace to take their place. Then the 761st and the 87th Infantry would rush north-west to Reims, France. Their initial assignment—as the objectives of the German offensive were at this point unclear—was to guard against a repeat of Hitler's 1940 blitzkrieg through Sedan. But before the 761st had even arrived at Reims, Patton had changed their reserve status and committed them to battle near the Belgian town of Bastogne.

ON THE MORNING OF DECEMBER 19, as the men of the 761st readied their tanks at Sarre-Union for the assault on the Siegfried Line, the battalion was informed of a sudden change of plans. They had no knowledge of the bitter fighting in the Ardennes. To Leonard Smith, the news they received seemed like an early Christmas present, a welcome break: The American offensive had been postponed. Now Able, Baker, Charlie, and Dog Companies and the assault gun and mortar platoons were ordered to return to positions they had left five days before, to support the 87th Infantry Division in holding the front line.

The front to which they returned, just beyond the German border, was oddly quiet. There were no sounds of shelling or machine-gun fire. Over the next three days, the men maintained their posts against only scattered pockets of enemy activity. Stretches of territory that had been hotly contested now appeared, as Preston McNeil looked east through his field glasses, inexplicably to have been transformed into ghost towns. On December 23, the 87th Infantry Division was pulled off the line—an unusual order, as the unit had been in combat for less than two weeks. The tanks of the 761st covered their withdrawal as elements of a new unit, the 44th Infantry Division of the Seventh U.S. Army, took over their positions. The following day, the 761st itself was pulled out.

They drove to the south ten miles, spending Christmas Eve bivouacked in the small town of Weidesheim. On Christmas Day, they rolled southwest, past Honskirch, Bourgaltroff, and Guebling, to

Wuisse, where the company cooks had gone ahead to prepare Christmas dinner. Their mood was relaxed, even playful. William McBurney, Preston McNeil, and Leonard Smith were only too relieved to be moving out of the Saar. It had been the stuff of nightmare. Smith's unthinking zeal for combat had been tempered by the devastation he'd witnessed at Munster and Honskirch, difficult to reconcile with any of his comic book notions of war. But he still maintained on some fundamental level a belief in his own boundless hero's luck. Wherever it was they were off to, Smith was game for the new adventure.

He sought out Willie Devore, joking around and stamping his feet against the cold as they waited for their holiday dinner. Christmas was to be their first full hot meal in weeks.

But before the food was ready, the battalion was ordered to move out. Chunks of steaming, half-done turkey were ripped off the baking birds and tossed to the tankers as they mounted their Shermans.

THE 761ST'S ULTIMATE DESTINATION, Bastogne, was in many ways an unremarkable town. A sleepy market village with a population before the war of fewer than 4,000, it lay in a picturesque resort area that reminded most American visitors of nothing so much as upstate Vermont. But Bastogne was also a crossroads for seven hard-surfaced roads, crucial to the rapid movement and deployment of armored vehicles, infantry trucks, and supply vehicles. It was the hub of a transportation wheel that could greatly aid or hinder the German advance to the west. Realizing the scope of the German breakthrough on December 17, Eisenhower had dispatched his only available reserves, the 7th and 10th Armored and 82nd and 101st Airborne Divisions, to the Ardennes, with the 101st Airborne and Combat Command B of the 10th Armored moving directly to Bastogne. These units had begun arriving there on December 18—only to witness the sight of hundreds of civilians and American soldiers retreating on the remaining roads out to the west. Combat Command B, the 101st Air-borne, Combat Command R of the 9th Armored Division, the 705th Tank Destroyer battalion, and remnants of other miscellaneous units, such as the 969th Field Artillery—an African American battalion—were ordered to hold Bastogne at all costs.

In the face of intense enemy shelling and relentless infantry attacks, American forces at Bastogne held out amid dwindling food, ammunition, and medical supplies. By December 22, they were completely surrounded. German general Heinrich von Luttwitz delivered a surrender ultimatum that afternoon to the 101st Airborne's Gen. Anthony McAuliffe, to which McAuliffe answered dryly, "Nuts!"

Patton's three divisions were fast closing on the city. Between the nineteenth and the twenty-second, Patton had rushed back and forth between his divisions on the road, exhorting them to "drive like hell!" At 6 A.M. on December 22, as he had promised the high command—in a logistical feat never before accomplished in the history of war—Patton's 4th Armored and 80th and 26th Infantry Divisions began attacking south and southeast of Bastogne.

Elsewhere throughout the Ardennes, the German advance had been slowed as small numbers of valiant troops held firm as long as humanly possible against much larger German forces, from Elsen-born in the north to Echternach in the south. The Germans had hoped to press forward on a wide, eighty-mile front, but the northern and southern shoulders of the attack had been narrowed and stabilized by this defiant resistance. By December 23, at the center and farthest point of the "bulge" in the American lines, Joachim Peiper's SS spearhead had advanced to Dinant, less than six miles from their initial goal of the Meuse River. But on the twenty-third, the U.S. 2nd Armored Division and British 29th Brigade mounted a furious counterattack against them. Everywhere on the twenty-third, with the first clearing of the skies since the German offensive began, Allied troops received supplies and relief from the Ninth U.S. Air Force. Patton's

4th Armored and 80th and 26th Infantry Divisions waged a continued, close-in ground battle south of Bastogne against entrenched elements of the German Seventh and Fifth Panzer Armies.

On December 26, a combat command of the 4th Armored finally broke through the German lines. But the lifeline they established into the city was so tenuous that, in the words of one 4th Armored tanker, "you could spit across it." Historian John S. D. Eisenhower describes it as a string attached to a balloon. The section of the American lifeline to the southwest of Bastogne was particularly soft and lightly defended. Patton was aware of its vulnerability; as it turned out, so too were the Germans. This was the 761st's assigned sector.

THE 761ST ROLLED WEST throughout Christmas day and night, stopping for maintenance checks in the city of Bar-le-Duc, France, the following afternoon. The enlisted men had learned by this point that the Germans had mounted an enormous offensive, and that that was where they were headed. But in typical military fashion, they were told nothing more. Leonard Smith pestered Pop Gates with questions. Gates simply responded that he should try to get some sleep. Something about Gates's grave, intent expression made sleep a practical impossibility. William McBurney had noticed it, too.

On the twenty-seventh, they pivoted and began moving north, driving for two days. They stopped north of Reims, at Rethel, where they camped in the ruins of a World War I battlefield. The weather had turned bitter cold, with temperatures hovering around zero. Before dawn on the twenty-ninth, as the crews warmed up their engines, the men took turns standing behind them, grabbing a bit of heat from the exhaust fumes.

They took off again, advancing in a column through the following night. Drivers strained to keep sight of the taillights of the tank before them. William McBurney talked by headset to Willie Devore to help keep him focused. In the rush across the steep, narrow Ardennes roads made treacherous by snow and thick ice, ten of the battalion's tanks were lost to accidents and mechanical breakdowns. The tank commanded by Sgt. Robert Johnson slid off the road, and Johnson—who had fired the white phosphorus barrage that saved tankers and infantrymen in the ditch at Honskirch—died from injuries he sustained in the crash.

THE 761ST PRESSED ON to the northeast, arriving on the afternoon of December 30 at the village of Offagne, Belgium, located in the 87th Infantry Division's assembly area between Bertrix and Libramont. MPs directed the battalion's tanks to a wooded area two miles north of Offagne. It was so cold that the snow around their Shermans burned the men's hands if they were not wearing gloves. Leonard Smith tried to catch some sleep in his tank as they waited, but found he'd wake himself shivering, regardless of how tired he was. Captain Williams, Captain Gates, and the other company commanders could not find anyone to give them clear orders for their deployment. Unbeknownst to them, the headquarters of the 87th Division was in a turmoil: The faint guns the men of the 761st heard to their north were the sounds of a confused melee.

On Patton's orders, the untested 87th Infantry Division and 11th Armored Division had engaged the German forces in the southwest quadrant straight off the road at 7:30 A.M. with no time for reconnaissance or planning. Maj. Gen. Frank Culin of the 87th and Maj. Gen. Charles Kilburn of the 11th Armored had protested that their forces should wait a day; Patton insisted they attack immediately. He was to count this among the more fortunate decisions of his career.

Bastogne, though useful and important, was not an absolutely essential military objective for Hitler, whose initial plans had called for the town simply to be bypassed if resistance there was too stiff. Hitler wanted nothing to interfere with his lightning push west to reach the Meuse River within two days, and the Belgian port of Antwerp within four days. But the strict timetable of the German offensive had been thrown off already by fierce resistance from American forces. Enraged at the disruption of his plans, Hitler came to view Bastogne as a symbol of American defiance. He developed what can only be described as a personal vendetta against the troops holding the town. On December 26, he gave the order for his SS Panzer divisions and crack Fuhrer Begleit Brigade to turn back from their push to the Meuse to "lance this boil." The assault from the southwest to cut the Bastogne lifeline was set to begin on the thirtieth.

Patton knew the sector was vulnerable, but he had no specific knowledge of the German plans. He would say of his decision to rush the 87th Infantry and 11th Armored to battle, "Some call it luck, some genius. I call it determination." The 87th Infantry Division had stumbled off their trucks straight into the teeth of a massive German counterattack, a hail of mortar, artillery, and tank fire.

JUST BEFORE DAWN ON DECEMBER 31, the 761st's Charlie Company rolled northwest from Offagne to join the 87th Division's 345th Infantry Regiment. What Leonard Smith glimpsed in the white-shrouded woods along the road gave him pause: the remains of a desperately contested battlefield, blasted trees, upended jeeps, and terribly shattered bodies. These bodies, partly covered with snow, were casualties from the fighting ten days earlier, when the German Seventh Army broke through thinly spread elements of the 28th U.S. Infantry Division. Scattered among the ruins, farther on, were fresh shell craters and overturned, still-burning American vehicles. The inexperienced Americans had been badly defeated the day before. The 87th Infantry had taken severe casualties against an elite German Panzer division; directly to its east, Combat Command A of the 11th Armored Division, rushed to the front from training in England, had been virtually slaughtered, suffering more than a hundred killed and wounded in its first twenty minutes of battle outside the village of Remagne. Despite such hellish losses, their presence had succeeded, as Patton had hoped, in turning the flank of the German forces approaching Bastogne.

The 11th Armored's Combat Command A had withdrawn at midnight across the woods to the east; the 345th Infantry Regiment and Charlie Company of the 761st were ordered to take over its zone of advance. Their orders were to continue pushing the Germans back from Bastogne. Charlie's tanks were first to attack the German outposts at Nimbermont and Rondu. From there they intended to proceed north, supporting the 345th Regiment's assault on fortified Remagne itself.

The geography of this region of Belgium, known as the "High Ardennes," heavily favored the German defenders. Towns tended to be located in the low ground along the banks of countless streams, surrounded by thickly wooded hills where the Germans had clear views in every possible direction.

The weather in itself posed problems of a kind the tankers had never before experienced. Dense, shifting ground fog was a frequent occurrence, giving the terrain an unreal and spooky aspect. This fog acted, at times, in the Americans' favor, neutralizing the superior range of the German guns. More often, it simply helped to conceal the waiting German troops. The overcast of the day before had turned to snow. The Germans, issued gray-and-white uniforms, snow capes, and whitewashed tanks, were hard to see until they opened fire. The American soldiers and tanks, lacking such camouflage, stood out plain as day.

Rondu and Nimbermont proved to be lightly defended and were taken easily. The attack on Remagne, however, promised to be more difficult, involving a push across open ground heavily mined and covered by high-velocity guns. Charlie Company attempted to provide covering fire for the infantry before moving in to support their close-in fighting in the town. Warren Crecy, as had become his custom, stood on his turret directing a constant stream of .50-caliber ammunition against German ground positions. Smith and McBurney fired their 76mm cannons at suspected machine-gun nests and anti-tank posts.

The tankers saw the exposed, ragged line of American infantrymen stumbling and taking enemy hits on all sides. Although the foot soldiers were young, many of them seventeen and eighteen, somehow they kept getting up and pressing forward. While the anguish of the men of the 761st on their first meeting with the 87th Division—the racial remarks and distrust on the part of some of the infantry—had left a bitterness on both sides that never fully disappeared, the two groups came to fight with a grudging respect. Whatever their underlying attitudes, they had no choice but to work together and support each other.

The American team continued its advance. Charlie Company knocked out three machine-gun nests and killed fourteen German gunners. But the German resistance at Remagne, while heavy, was less intense than the men had expected. And though the tankers and infantry kept careful watch against a counterattack once they had cleared the town, no enemy troops emerged from the surrounding woods. The Germans seemed to have strategically fallen back. By evening, the infantry and Charlie had succeeded in capturing all three of their assigned towns.

For the weary enlisted men, however, these small gains hardly felt like victory. The territory in almost every direction around them was still held by entrenched enemy forces, and the dense woods and rugged terrain tended to compartmentalize combat to the extent that capturing one hill or town meant very little in terms of scouting and capturing the next. The ground troops often felt as though they were fighting in circles. The Battle of the Bulge was everywhere becoming a desperate yard-by-yard struggle with no clear lines of advance. It was occuring, moreover, in the midst of the worst European winter in thirty-five years.

On New Year's Eve, the tank crews of Charlie Company shivered in their tenuous forward positions in the interior compartments and beside their vehicles in the snow. Their eyes were red from lack of sleep, their combat fatigues and gloves threadbare, stained with motor oil and gunpowder. Leonard Smith and Hollis Clark had managed to add a few more blankets to their secret stash, but they felt so cold they might as well have had none. William McBurney, huddled against Willie Devore, wore two pairs of pants, two shirts, and every single piece of clothing he could find, but this did little to keep him warm.

The few tankers who did manage to fall asleep were awakened on the stroke of midnight by a tremendous series of explosions. At 12:00 A.M. on January 1, Patton ordered every piece of artillery under his command to fire "on a likely target as a New Year's salute from Third Army to the Wehrmacht." American forward artillery observers reported for hours afterward the sound of wounded German soldiers screaming in the woods.

AT DAWN, BAKER AND DOG COMPANIES of the 761st rolled forward from Offagne to join Charlie. The battered 345th Infantry Regiment marched along the road in the opposite direction. The unit, which had fought against veteran troops with considerable courage, had suffered so many killed and wounded in its first two days that it had been ordered back from the front, to be replaced by the 347th. The ill-fated 345th took further casualties during its withdrawal, triggering a series of antipersonnel mines and Tellermines concealed beneath the ice and snow.

The 761st's Charlie Company continued to press forward. Charlie, along with Baker Company, was ordered to spearhead a push by the 347th Infantry Regiment from Moircy and Remagne toward Jenneville, Pironpre, and Tillet. Although not so much towns as tiny hamlets, they were nonetheless of critical strategic importance, clustered around a major highway system running southwest from St. Vith through Houffalize, Bastogne, and St. Hubert to the Meuse River. In his December 22 surrender demand to Anthony McAuliffe, German General von Luttwitz had boasted of his capture of the "Hompre-Sibret-Tillet" section of this highway. The significance of such roads in the Ardennes fighting cannot be overstated: Control of the roads in the Ardennes, quite simply, equaled control of the war.

Success for the German offensive depended on the rapid movement of large armored forces over a region of dense second-growth woods and jagged terrain that, as the 761st quickly discovered, was just plain hell for tanks. Moreover, in order to neutralize American air superiority, Hitler had deliberately scheduled his attack for one of the worst weather periods of the year. Armored vehicles needed the hard-surfaced roads to move forward. Supply trucks needed these roads to reach them.

With the First U.S. Army blocking off the Germans in the north, and with elements of Patton's Third Army (including the 26th "Yankee" Infantry Division) fighting steadily forward across the extensive road system south and east of Bastogne, the Bastogne–St. Hubert highway assumed even greater importance. By December 27, it had in fact become one of only a handful of remaining supply routes for German forces west of Bastogne. By recapturing the towns and territory that overlooked it, the 87th and the 761st would help deprive the forward German units at the tip of the Bulge of supplies of gasoline and ammunition, as well as of a path back to the east.

The Germans, equally aware of the importance of this highway, had been ordered to hold it at all costs. The 87th Division's 347th Infantry Regiment had developed a two-pronged plan of attack in its sector, to advance on either side of the dense Haies de Tillet Forest.

The 761st's Baker Company was situated on the left (west) wing, supporting the 347th's 3rd Battalion in attacking north from Moircy to cut the highway at Pironpre and Bonnerue. Charlie Company was on the right (east) wing, supporting the 1st Battalion in pushing north from Remagne, with the goal of cutting the highway at Amberloup. Each branch of the 347th's planned advance held aspects of a suicide mission: Pironpre was situated across an open field where any movement was certain to be seen and met with fire; Amberloup was located across a valley overlooked by heavy artillery in German-held hills. Two Sherman tanks of the 761st were to attack in advance of each infantry company.

New Year's morning brought sleet, snow, and plummeting temperatures. The 761st and infantry struggled across high snowdrifts. Willie Devore found that the intense cold had one blessing to it, in that the ground was frozen rock solid, providing him with some room and traction to maneuver off the main roads. But the Germans, with ten days to fortify the area, had considered every axis of attack. Though they did not know it, the 761st's tanks were heading straight into waiting elements of the most prestigious German armored unit, the Panzer Lehr Division, created around a group of top instructors from the army's tank-training schools. The majority of these soldiers were decorated veterans of the Russian front who had a thorough (and hard-earned) understanding of winter warfare.

The attack on January 1 began with deceptive ease. Baker Company and the 3rd Battalion advanced north from Moircy successfully to claim the hamlet of Jenneville—the site of a previous failed attack by the 345th Regiment—by noon. They had, however, little time or cause for celebration: The 902nd Regiment of the Panzer Lehr had simply fallen back eight hundred yards to the village of Pironpre. Pironpre was the crossroads for two major spokes of the St. Hubert highway system and had been prepared by the German defenders as a "hornet's nest." As Baker's tanks rolled north from Jenneville, they were met with a hail of enemy machine-gun, mortar, and artillery fire. To this was added another, more ominous sound—the distinctive bark of German tank guns.

Six Panzer tanks had been carefully positioned at Pironpre to maximize their fields of fire. They were concealed behind the high wood piles of a local sawmill—impossible to spot from the road. The 3rd Battalion and Baker Company attempted repeatedly to cross the open terrain below Pironpre. Scores of infantry were killed, and armor-piercing rounds devastated the exposed Shermans. These attempts, coming at great cost, gained nothing. Unable to locate the source of this relentless fire, the Americans were forced to pull back for the night.

To their east, across the Haies de Tillet Forest, Charlie Company and the 1st Battalion advanced steadily throughout the early part of the day against only small-arms fire and scattered artillery. To Leonard Smith, taking out target after target, they seemed to have it made. Their objective seemed well within reach; in fact, forward patrols successfully crossed a stretch of highway north of Remagne. But the Panzer Lehr, with orders to defend the road at all costs, had been waiting for nightfall to provide its troops with cover from roving American fighter-bombers. Enemy tanks attacked at dusk and drove Charlie and the 1st Battalion back toward Remagne. They, too, bivouacked having made no appreciable gains.

The following morning, Baker Company and the 3rd Battalion regrouped and altered their plan of attack to circle around Pironpre. Their flanking maneuver successfully captured Pironpre and Bonnerue, temporarily cutting the highway there. But they were forced out in a furious series of counterattacks at the crossroads and in the surrounding forest. The undetected Panzers continued to inflict heavy damage. The 3rd Battalion of the 347th Infantry Regiment reported that by the afternoon of January 2, "three of the [761st] tanks were burning and one was damaged beyond use."

Charlie's tanks, spearheading for the 1st Battalion, fought their way over a mile north to claim the village of Gerimont. They peered through their periscopes and blasted out all the upper-level windows, taking no chances.

The intense cold and lack of sleep tended to reduce to the barest, most immediate essentials the goals of American GIs. Their first thought wasn't about winning the war, but rather about getting warm. The Bulge was becoming for Leonard Smith and William McBurney what GIs everywhere in the Ardennes termed "the bitter battle for the billets." They fought viciously to take the next town for the simple purpose of gaining access to whatever shelter and food it might afford. But Charlie's commanding officer, Pop Gates—who felt very acutely his responsibility for the deployment and well-being of his company—had larger concerns and was facing a grave decision.

Gerimont consisted of a small cluster of buildings atop a hill; down this hill, to the north, across a ridge-studded valley and atop the hill beyond, lay the 347th's objective of Amberloup. More than a dozen Sherman tanks of the 11th Armored Division were visible in that valley—wrecked and overturned, mute testimony to the presence of German antitank artillery in the surrounding woods and hills. At the center of the valley, at the center of the road Charlie Company would have to follow to reach Amberloup, lay the village of Tillet. Pop Gates had been ordered to make a frontal attack on Tillet.

The antitank guns in the woods to the north were not Gates's only problem. By the evening of the second, the German-controlled Haies de Tillet Forest stood as what the official U.S. historian terms a "dangerous gap" between the 347th's two battalions. The left (west) flank of Gates's company was fully exposed to this forest; Gates and his tanks had taken antitank fire from their left every time they tried to move north from the protection of the buildings at Gerimont. With numerous mechanical breakdowns from its rush to Belgium, Charlie was at a shadow of its full strength. Gates was on his own: The infantry officers seemed to have had no training with tanks, and he could not find a company commander when he needed to talk to one to address his concerns.

Gates stationed his tanks just beyond the monastery at Gerimont for the night, holding their positions against the cold and blowing snow. He posted a forward watch until daybreak, as the infantry, against standard procedure, had been ordered back by an inexperienced lieutenant, leaving the tanks exposed to potential infiltration by Panzerfaust teams. Enemy mortars and shells continued to fall at random intervals into the houses on the edge of town. Determined to avoid a repeat of the disaster at Honskirch, Gates had made a decision. He refused to send his tanks and accompanying infantry straight down the road into the valley, ordering them instead to keep their defensive positions in Gerimont. Over the next several days at Tillet, his decision would prove to be a wise one.

JANUARY 3 MARKED A TURNING POINT in the Ardennes fighting: the start of a coordinated counterattack by the Allied forces. Patton's Third Army continued its northern push around Bastogne; the First Army began a concomitant push toward the south. The two American armies, separated since December 16 by the "Bulge" created by the attacking Germans, intended to link up at the town of Houffalize. From there they would force the Germans back to the east. Patton objected bitterly to the strategy, arguing instead for the more aggressive approach of driving north and south along the initial start line of Hitler's attack (the eighty-mile line along the Belgium–Luxembourg border with Germany), which would have trapped the main body of Hitler's troops west of the Siegfried Line, within the Bulge. By doing so, Patton claimed that he "could win this war now." But Eisenhower, following the advice of Field Marshal Montgomery (whom the irascible Patton called "a tired little fart"), had opted on

December 28 for the more cautious strategy of attacking farther west on the broad axis around Houffalize. The 87th Division and the 761st had been released from strategic reserve to Patton on the date of Eisenhower's decision, the twenty-eighth, for the specific purpose of carrying out the westernmost edge of this attack.

The problem with Eisenhower's attack plan was that while it forestalled any further westward movement by the Germans, for the American troops involved it virtually guaranteed a bloodbath. Rather than moving north as he had hoped along the "narrow front" of the Germans' original line of attack, Patton, writes historian Peter Elstob, "had to try to push a twenty-five-mile-wide front some twenty miles through country which seemed to consist of natural defensive features." Patton's chief of staff, Hobart Gay, was troubled in particular by the problems this plan would pose for the 87th Infantry and 11th Armored Divisions, reflecting in his journal on December 30 that their assigned angle of attack evidenced "a complete misunderstanding of the problem involved." It "would drive the enemy back on this high ground rather than take it away from him." By January 3, both divisions had already suffered greatly from this fundamental flaw; in the coming weeks, it would cost the 87th Division and the 761st grievously.

The 11th Armored Division, directly to the east of the 87th, had taken casualties so severe in its attack against the Fuhrer Begleit Brigade that on the morning of the third, Patton, remarking that the unit was "badly disorganized," ordered it pulled off the line. In just four days of battle, the division had lost fifty-four tanks—almost a third of its armor—and 661 men wounded, missing, or killed in action. The 11th Armored was replaced by the 17th Airborne, which had also been rushed to the Ardennes with no combat experience. It was similarly savaged by the entrenched German troops, leading even the generally sanguine Patton to reflect that "we can still lose this war." At Tillet, the 761st Tank Battalion was soon to encounter this same brigade.

ON THE MORNING OF JANUARY 3, the temperature was falling, the snow blowing wildly in near-blizzard conditions. Supply trucks skidded and overturned on the icy roads. Dog Company, as it had been in the Saar, was temporarily removed from screening operations to take the supply trucks' place. Preston McNeil and the other members of Dog Company found themselves given an additional task of carrying back the bodies of the wounded and the dead. In the frigid cold, the injured died of exposure within a few minutes. McNeil found himself picking up bodies that were frozen solid and securing them with ropes to the tank hulls. The well-placed German artillery took a brutal toll throughout the Ardennes: 50 percent of all American combat casualties were the result of artillery hits. A large number of American soldiers simply disappeared, forever to be listed as MIA. McNeil found soldiers who were literally blown apart, the worst carnage he had witnessed so far. He tried not to think about the fact that those body parts had been men.

Able Company had been kept in reserve thus far in the woods outside of Offagne, listening to the rumble of artillery and wondering when they themselves would be called up. The men huddled miserably together around small fires they had built from twigs and branches. When an officer of the 87th Division told Captain Williams that he and his tankers were not permitted to cut wood for fires, as the surrounding trees were the property of the king of Belgium, Williams responded, "I'm going to speak for my whole company. . . . Fuck the king of Belgium." On the morning of January 3, Able Company was ordered forward to relieve the besieged Charlie Company.

Able's assignment was to attack simultaneously in two directions from Charlie's tenuous outpost at Gerimont: west through the Haies de Tillet Forest toward the hornet's nest at Pironpre, and north toward the village of Tillet. Williams was not satisfied with either the intelligence or the orders he was given by the infantry colonel, convinced he was dealing with yet another officer who knew nothing about the uses and vulnerabilities of tanks. Williams informed S. Sgt. Teddy Weston that once again it looked like they were on their own.

When Williams moved forward to relieve Charlie Company, a grim-faced Pop Gates warned him to be careful. The officers at the front had been of no help to the tankers. Charlie's remaining tanks rolled back over the slippery, tree-lined road to the assembly area for maintenance and repair. It was so cold that Leonard Smith found it nearly impossible to do the kind of maintenance work necessary. Smith and best friend Willie Devore huddled shivering around a small fire in the encroaching dark, as Devore talked about the long, hot summer days he'd known growing up in South Carolina, the light, swaying summer dresses of the girls offering tantalizing glimpses of their bare calves.

ABLE COMPANY TOOK UP Charlie's positions, preparing to attack down the road toward Tillet the following morning. In the monastery just outside of Gerimont, several of Able's enlisted men stumbled upon the pitiable sight of dozens of civilians, many of them wounded and half-starved, shivering against the searing cold. The bodies of other civilians lay among them, including those of several small children. Civilians paid a high toll throughout the Ardennes conflict. Some 2,500 had been killed by the battle's end, many in documented massacres by SS troops such as those at Stavelot, Ster, and Bande, but many more from the indiscriminate hail of German and American bombs and artillery shells.

Captain Williams informed the infantry battalion commander at Gerimont that the attack on Tillet would be suicide for the tankers and infantry alike. The colonel responded that their assault would be preceded by an artillery barrage directed at German positions, beginning just after dawn. Williams—who had seen at close hand in the Saar the limited effect of artillery against entrenched troops—continued to protest, but the colonel remained steadfast, ordering him to attack. Williams returned to his men and, his voice breaking, told them their mission. S. Sgt. Teddy Weston told him they were more than willing to go. In the company's two months of fighting, the men had grown to respect Williams as much as he had grown to admire them. They knew he wasn't sending them anyplace he wasn't intending to go himself.

Like Gates, Williams was determined not to send his tanks straight down the road in the open, telling the men that they would "go very damn slow and easy. We'll look for every bit of cover and wait to see if the infantry knows what they're doing." The situation—heading down a narrow, exposed road into a heavily fortified valley—seemed eerily similar to that at Guebling and Bourgaltroff.

Pvt. Thomas Bragg, the young driver of Sergeant James's tank, approached Captain Williams, telling Williams about a premonition he'd had that he would not survive the day. Williams, who had long been impressed with Bragg's dedication and willingness to volunteer for difficult duty, told him he had his permission to sit out the day's attack and head back to the assembly area. But Bragg refused, telling the captain simply, "There's no one to take my place. We're all together up here."

The American artillery barrage began on schedule. Williams, in a light tank, accompanied four of his Shermans two hundred yards down the road, where they stopped, partially sheltered from the Germans across the valley by a small rise. He had sent his two other Shermans just west of Gerimont to guard the troublesome left flank. The infantry soon marched north from Gerimont to join Williams's group of tanks behind the rise. Inexperienced in working with tanks, and sent forward without an officer to guide them, the young foot soldiers bunched up too close to the Shermans. No one, it seemed, had informed them that tanks draw fire. Williams sent his sergeant out to caution them away—just as a German mortar barrage came crashing in.

The Shermans loosed a return barrage of high-explosive shells to protect the infantry, and American artillery observers called in heavy shells to push the Germans off their firing positions. But the mortars had been devastating, leaving at least a dozen infantry wounded. Williams, "chilled thoroughly" by the suffering around him, watched as the remaining infantry ran back down the road to Gerimont (the barrage was so intense, they had little choice), leaving their weapons behind. More mortars fell among them as they ran, killing several. The Shermans could not advance without the infantry, so Williams ordered the tanks to back out one at a time, providing what cover they could for the wounded men until medics arrived.

As the tank commanded by S. Sgt. James Nelson began to back out, taking care to negotiate around the fallen soldiers on the road, heavy enemy artillery started coming in. The tankers knew the Germans had 105mm shells in the vicinity; Williams estimated that these were at least 150s. The wounded infantrymen near the tanks were literally torn apart, limbs and body parts flying in all directions. Nelson's tank had almost made it back to the relative shelter of Gerimont when it took a direct hit and exploded. The loader, gunner, and bow gunner exited, carrying the wounded driver toward the houses. Staff Sergeant Nelson had been killed in the initial hit.

THOSE INFANTRYMEN WHO HAD GONE ahead to Tillet were now taking heavy casualties. The two Able Company tanks to the west of Gerimont provided covering fire for their retreat. The remaining three Shermans of Able moved forward to fire additional covering rounds, spreading out to get the widest possible field of fire from the partial shelter of the slight ridge.

As they moved out, Sergeant Woodson's tank lost radio contact with command. Their transmission was scrambled by German interference. Gunner Walter Lewis heard the improbable and, in this deadly context, haunting sound of Louis Armstrong's version of "I Can't Give You Anything but Love, Baby" being played. The tanks fired high-explosive shells onto the houses at the edge of Tillet as the infantry struggled to make their way back along the icy road.

Artillery fire continued to come in. Woodson's tank took a hit in the driver's compartment from an 88mm antitank gun, sounding like plate glass shattering into a thousand pieces. The concussion blew Lewis out the top hatch, shredding his clothing. Bleeding profusely, he got up and ran back for the American lines in a state of near-hysteria. Crew members James Jordan and Charles Brooks were also severely wounded.

Woodson carried Brooks back to safety as enemy shells continued raining in. Jordan would lose his leg; Brooks, who had been hit in his lower spine, was paralyzed. As his premonition had warned him, Pvt. Thomas Bragg, whose wife was expecting their first child, had been killed in the explosion.

ABLE COMPANY'S REMAINING FOUR SHERMANS kept watch throughout the night on the outskirts of Gerimont, preparing for the German counterattack that would most likely come the following morning. For Williams and the men, it was impossible to keep warm. Their extremities were numb and hurt to use. A ground fog rolled in, shrouding the valley and the hills beyond. Shortly after dawn, Able Company's Herman Taylor spotted German infantry crossing the valley from Tillet. The Able Company tanks stayed back in their defensive positions; the German infantry advanced to within two hundred yards of the American tanks but came no farther. The tankers held their fire: They had learned that the Germans would use such tricks to lure them into revealing their positions.

Able Company had received no reinforcements. Several Able Company members who had been left without tanks carried their grease guns forward to join the thinly spread 87th Infantry, dug into shallow foxholes in the frozen ground. The front was deathly quiet for the next three hours, as the tankers scanned the ground fog that covered the valley below. Finally, the strange silence was broken by a German artillery barrage. Incoming shells shattered the ground around the Able Company tanks, which were hidden behind a row of houses. Williams spotted through his field glasses two German tanks concealed by a stone wall on the edge of Tillet. Mortar fire started coming in, and rifle fire sounded below. The American artillery reply was delayed.

In the ongoing German barrage, the Sherman tank commanded by Sergeant Murphy took a hit from an 88mm shell and Technician Jessie Bond was killed.

As the light faded, the Germans, as battered as the Americans, pulled back for the night. But for the Americans, the news was grim. The American relief column was still nowhere in sight.

8

TILLET

To introduce into a philosophy of war a principle of moderation

would be an absurdity. War is an act of violence

pushed to its utmost bounds.

—CARL VON CLAUSEWITZ

The German defense of the village of Tillet and its environs fell to the Fuhrer Begleit Brigade, commanded by Col. Otto Remer, who had been awarded this coveted post for his decisive role in thwarting the July 20, 1944, attempt on Hitler's life. The brigade once served as Hitler's personal palace guard. Like the Panzer Lehr Division, the unit had been created around some of the premier tank soldiers in the German army, members of the Grossdeutschland Panzer Division who had earned their reputation at the Russian front. While the villages of Bonnerue and Pironpre continued to be defended by the

Panzer Lehr, by January 3 control of the area around Gerimont and Tillet had shifted to the Fuhrer Begleit Brigade. It was the 761st Tank Battalion's misfortune to be straddled between these two crack armored teams.

The Fuhrer Begleit was an exceptionally large brigade, equipped with seventy-one tanks and assault guns and supported by a range of heavy artillery and self-propelled weapons. Its handpicked soldiers fought with a discipline and dedication military historians would come to term "fanatical." The 761st's enlisted men knew nothing at the time of their opponents' storied history; nor did they know the name of the tiny hamlet that happened to be situated, on military maps they were not privy to, between their line of departure at Gerimont and their objective of the St. Hubert-Houffalize Highway.

Able Company held on to its battered outpost at Gerimont throughout the morning of January 6. The Fuhrer Begleit Brigade's artillery shelled the hamlet with devastating accuracy, exploding an infantry supply truck moving just beyond the monastery and narrowly missing the 761st's medical jeep. Captain Williams and his men were by this point simply too weary and too cold to be scared. Infantry reinforcements did not arrive until that afternoon. Only then was Able sent back to Remagne for much-needed maintenance and reoutfitting. Elements of Charlie rolled forward to take their place, waving and nodding acknowledgment as they passed. But Able's rest was to be short-lived.

The Fuhrer Begleit Brigade had meticulously mapped out its defense of Tillet and the highway beyond. Tillet was overlooked by dozens of ridges, which were fully exploited in the Germans' complex fortifications, holding machine-gun nests covered by tanks and self-propelled guns, and further supported by Panzerfausts, mortar teams, and heavy artillery. The 87th Infantry Division's command had finally realized the depth of these defenses and was preparing to stage a massive assault in conjunction with the tanks of Able and Charlie Companies. Leonard Smith, looking down across the snow-covered valley at Tillet, had seen enough combat by this point to know the attack would not be easy. But there was little that stood out about the village that would come to haunt him and define the war for him more than any other.

TWO MILES WEST OF GERIMONT, at Pironpre and Bonnerue, the attack by elements of the 761st's Baker Company and the 347th Infantry Regiment against the Panzer Lehr Division continued without rest. Infantrymen were sent to clear the woods, fighting against combat engineers of the Panzer Lehr who had taken up rifles in a pitched, bloody battle reminiscent of the American Civil War. In the fields around Pironpre, the tankers and infantry shivered at night beside their vehicles and in their shallow foxholes. Each day they awoke to make another series of futile charges against the entrenched defenders.

Equally fierce fighting and grave losses were occurring throughout the whole of the Ardennes. "The Battle of the Bulge" is in many ways a misnomer, for due to the ragged, divided nature of the terrain, the campaign rapidly developed into a series of separate and distinct battles. Historian John Eisenhower describes these engagements as "difficult to follow because so much was happening in so many places at a given time. . . . [I]t is almost impossible to visualize the entire picture as it unfolded." The Bulge can perhaps best be understood as a jagged collage of numberless place-names like Pironpre, Pinsamont, Villers-la-Bonne-Eau, Kaundorf—meaningless to most people, except for the men who struggled, suffered, and died in these small hamlets in the relentless cold in the very heart of war.

The 761st's blood brothers of old, the 26th Yankee Infantry Division, had been fighting in isolation southeast of Bastogne since December 27, through the towns of Kaundorf, Bavigne, and Nothum. Separated from all other American divisions, with both its flanks wide open, the 26th Division's disastrously exposed position can best be conveyed by orders issued to the 101st Infantry Regiment for New Year's Eve: "Each Battalion will be prepared to meet counterattacks from the north, northwest and northeast."

The weather throughout the Ardennes continued to exact almost as dreadful a toll as the German artillery. Even the most experienced of American generals had not faced war in conditions like these. The Allied air force would be grounded due to the severe weather for all but a few days in January; when pilots did fly they took great risks, as in every direction around them all they could see was white. On January 3, the First U.S. Army's attack from the north was halted by deep snowdrifts, icy roads, and dense ground fog. Everywhere the Germans, ordered to hold their ground, viciously contested and counterattacked the Americans. Surveilling his exhausted troops, and the conditions and the carnage they daily endured, Patton reflected, "How men live, much less fight, is a marvel to me." Tillet was to stand among the bloodiest of the many battles within the Bulge.

THE 87TH INFANTRY DIVISION'S ATTACK on Tillet began in earnest on January 7. Captain Williams was not present for the assault: When Able Company arrived at Remagne on the sixth, Doc Adamson diagnosed him with severe trench foot and an infection in his leg requiring immediate treatment. On the morning of the seventh, the company gathered around the ambulance that was to carry Williams to Sedan, France, presenting him with a captured German flag that all the men had signed. Able, in its battle-scarred tanks, would soon be back at the front. The joint team consisting of Able and Charlie Companies was to be commanded by Pop Gates.

The rolling, exposed terrain around Tillet was a tactical nightmare for the Americans. The ice and deep snow made extraordinarily difficult manuevering for the Shermans, which were initially instructed to stand back and perform a supporting role. Dog Company continued its grim task of carrying supplies to the forward elements and carrying back the wounded. Preston McNeil had tried to say a prayer for each, but in the endless work he soon lost count.

The young infantrymen attacked with great heroism in a series of drives on entrenched positions across the open, snow-covered hills and fields. The 87th fought through surreal levels of bitter wind and enemy fire, waiting out whistling German artillery barrages, stumbling a few yards forward and firing their M-1 rifles before diving down to avoid more incoming shells, then struggling up and trudging forward again. S. Sgt. Curtis Shoup of the 346th Infantry Regiment led an uphill assault on one of the ridges near Tillet; when his company was pinned down by machine-gun fire, unable even to dig for protection in the frozen ground, Shoup exposed himself to German fire, moving forward while firing his own automatic weapon. Though hit several times, he pulled himself to his feet and staggered straight into the teeth of the withering enemy barrage until he was close enough to throw a grenade. His heroic, dying act destroyed the enemy emplacement.

Leonard Smith, standing by in reserve along with several other tank crews, felt the ground shaking from the heavy artillery of the Fuhrer Begleit Brigade. The men had grown used to the lighter artillery, but no one ever got used to the 150s (known as "Screaming Meemies") and 203s when they came that close. Despite the extraordinary sacrifices of the 87th Infantry, the battle around Tillet throughout January 7 and 8 was at best a bloody stalemate.

TEN MILES EAST OF TILLET, on the morning of the eighth, Patton was driving in an open, unmarked jeep. On the narrow highway he passed a convoy of trucks stretching for several miles, carrying the 90th Infantry Division forward into battle. Heading in the opposite direction was a convoy of ambulances bringing the wounded of other divisions back to the rear. When the men of the 90th recognized Patton, they broke into wild cheers, waving, leaning out of their trucks. Patton, well aware of what the ambulances on the other side held, and what would happen within a matter of hours to many of these same men who were his direct responsibility, described it as "the most moving experience" of his life.

THE NEXT DAY, THE 761ST received orders to take the lead in a renewed assault on Tillet. While the infantry had repeatedly reached the outskirts of town in the last few days, engaging in punishing house-to-house combat, on each attempt they had been pushed back by the suicidally determined Fuhrer Begleit Brigade. Today would prove a crucial turning point. Pop Gates was responsible for deploying the tanks of Able and Charlie companies in spearheading for the 87th throughout the woods, fields, and ridges of the valley.

Leonard Smith's "Cool Stud" tank, having logged well over a thousand miles, had finally joined the numerous ranks of the battalion's mechanical breakdowns. The other crew members enjoyed the rare chance for a rest while the overworked maintenance department struggled to repair their vehicle. But the irrepressible Smith, who, for all he had been through, was still eager to go out and engage the Germans, volunteered to act as loader in another Charlie Company tank—William McBurney's "Taffy." Pop Gates was simply too short of men by this point to caution him away.

The battalion had taken so many casualties with only limited replacements that most tanks were reduced to crews of four, operating without their bow gunners and the firepower of the .30-caliber ball-mounted machine guns. Without Smith, "Taffy" would have been forced to function with a crew of just three men (the tank commander doubling as loader). "Taffy"'s commander was a young sergeant from Cleveland, Ohio, named Teddy Windsor. McBurney had the gunner's seat. The driver was Smith's best friend, Willie Devore.

The temperature that day stood at −6 degrees Farenheit. As

McBurney checked over his equipment in the early-morning darkness, the steel of the tank was so cold that even wearing his gloves, he could hardly stand to touch it. Pop Gates had been ordered to cover as wide an area as possible with his two tattered, depleted companies of Shermans. He had no choice but to split up Able and Charlie along platoon lines, and further to split up these platoons. Gates would lead the largest force, consisting of ten tanks; his other teams on the ground were to be led by S. Sgts. Henry Conway, Johnnie Stevens (recovered from his November injuries), Frank Cochrane, and Moses Dade, as well as Sgt. Teddy Windsor and Sgt. William Kitt.

In the breaking dawn, all along the designated line of departure, infantrymen gathered around the M-4 Shermans. Though Leonard Smith had just recently turned twenty himself, as he prepared to mount "Taffy"'s turret he was struck by the foot soldiers' youth and their air of bewilderment and vulnerability; some of them had been pulled straight out of high school. One of the soldiers closest to his tank carried a bazooka so awkwardly that Smith realized he had likely never fired it before. Smith wondered, for the briefest of moments, just what it was that all of them were about to head into.

There were no clear military guidelines for their mission. So wide was the area they had to cover, and so divided was the terrain by ridges and thick stands of trees, that Gates was forced to disregard many fundamental tenets of his training. Advancing in a clear line was a practical impossibility. Radio communications were occasionally scrambled. As they buttoned up and started rolling forward, each one leading its own small group of infantry, the Shermans quickly lost sight of one another. At Tillet, more than in any other battle site they experienced, each individual tank fought its own war.

SHORTLY AFTER SUNRISE, American field artillery teams sent a thunderous advance round of fire on German positions. They were immediately met with pinpointed return artillery fire, taking heavy casualties. The Fuhrer Begleit Brigade had carefully concealed its forward artillery observers throughout the valley. As the 761st's tanks moved out, enemy fire came in from every direction.

Able Company's Johnnie Stevens, attacking on rising ground, saw only one advantage between this situation and what he'd faced at Hill 309 in France: Here he knew in advance and had warned his men of the hopelessly entrenched positions they were heading toward. As the Shermans spread out, they took numerous hits, but the crews continued to fire off their high-explosive and armor-piercing shells. Henry Conway, rolling in advance of a second platoon, quickly became cut off from the rest of his unit, surrounded on a ridge by German infantry and several Panzer tanks. An artillery hit blew off a rear portion of his vehicle dangerously close to the fuel tank; he managed to find slight cover on the ridge for the Sherman, and he and his crew continued firing, single-handedly preventing the German forces from taking their position for over an hour.

Charlie Company, across the valley, faced a fury of fire. Moses Dade led his platoon forward a short distance when his turret took a direct strike. Despite injuries from ricocheting shrapnel and extensive damage to their tank, Dade and his crew continued pushing forward. The infantry and the platoon's other tanks followed suit, struggling over snow that had drifts up to four feet deep. Frank Cochrane, leading a second platoon, took several artillery hits to his hull and turret, but like Dade he kept advancing, radioing back that his crew was "still giving 'em hell."

"Taffy"'s tank commander, Teddy Windsor, was ordered to advance on Charlie Company's outside flank. Despite the chaos they heard from hundreds of artillery shells and machine-gun nests merging into one sound across the valley, Leonard Smith and his crewmates advanced for some distance on their lone trek with no resistance. It seemed to Smith that he had once again gotten the luck of the draw.

Back at Gerimont, Preston McNeil's Dog Company received orders to halt its resupply duties. The M-5 Stuarts were to participate in a diversionary strike just outside of Gerimont to pull enemy fire off the hard-hit front. What began as a support mission quickly became an intense battle scene. The lightly armored tanks were not designed for the task, but McNeil's unit nonetheless successfully destroyed an enemy mortar team and ammunition dump.

Across the valley, Pop Gates had taken on the assignment of neutralizing a German defensive position that had devastated the 87th Infantry in the past few days. His team of ten tanks and infantry was to ascend a long, gradually rising slope defended by an organized fortification system containing dozens of machine-gun nests and self-propelled guns. Gates knew their chances of success were slim to none. But the Germans were raining fire on the American troops below. This would at least be a suicide mission—unlike the mindless orders for frontal attacks on Honskirch and Amberloup—in the service of a higher end, taking out key German artillery and antitank teams.

Gates had his tanks and infantry spread out as far as possible. He knew that their hopes of success rested on close communication, both from tank to tank and between the tankers and infantrymen, so that they could work in tandem to eliminate more entrenched defenses and then quickly spread out again to avoid becoming outflanked. The two-way headsets weren't functioning properly, so Gates chose to lead his team on foot. A barrage of fire was unleashed on them the moment they set out. But Gates ran in the midst of it, moving from tank to tank and squad to squad, calling out orders, giving hand signals, darting forward to scout enemy defenses, ducking down and firing his rifle, then dashing up again to signal routes of assault and attack plans to his men.

The German artillery took a brutal toll on the American forces; the Americans inflicted equally heavy casualties in turn. Dozens of tankers and infantrymen were gravely wounded, and many infantrymen were killed. The furious uphill battle raged for five hours. When the ridge was finally taken, only two tanks and a remnant of the infantry remained. Gates took just a moment to look down from the ridge at the battle still raging in the valley below, before going to see to the wounded.

LEONARD SMITH'S TANK CONTINUED on its solitary journey. Ten infantrymen trudged along stolidly beside and behind them. Smith could see almost nothing from his narrow loader's periscope; McBurney, through his horizontal turret sight, could see little more than slivers of white. Willie Devore was focused intently on the frozen snow immediately in front of his tracks. In their enlisted man's perpetual state of uncertainty, none of them knew exactly where they were—only that they had been told to advance in a certain direction, to neutralize any Germans encountered on the way.

Directly before them, over a slight rise, lay a wide, open field edged with woods on its far side. There seemed to be no easy way around it; approaching the field, they had a moment's choice either to advance or retreat. Smith could not see the utter exposure of the clearing, but in his headset he could hear the nervousness in the voices of crewmates Windsor and McBurney. They had no remaining illusions about the hazards of the Sherman tank, particularly when advancing with three and potentially four open flanks, beside a young, inexperienced, and frightened group of infantry. Windsor leaned out to confer with the infantry sergeant. The sergeant, too, was aware of the threat of ambush, but like Windsor he was doggedly determined to lead his troops forward as per their orders. Windsor called into his intercom mike for driver Willie Devore to proceed. Windsor, McBurney, and the accompanying infantry strained to look ahead.

Windsor radioed McBurney to zero in on the far trees; the veteran tanker had already done so. Devore took care to negotiate around the frozen bodies from previous attempts to take the field. Smith was tense, standing in position. It had been months since he'd been confined to the relative blindness of the loader's compartment. He used to complain about the narrowness of the gunner's horizontal sight-lines, but he vowed he never would again—nothing was worse than the helplessness of the loader's post, enclosed on all sides by steel walls he knew offered little more protection than air against the German antitank shells. He tried to imagine the layout of the unseen field on which everything suddenly depended, listening above the roar of the engine for the slightest hint of trouble in his headset.

What he heard in his crewmates' voices, after the first few agonized minutes, was a gathering lightness of tone that made him begin to relax.

They advanced far enough to feel certain they would make it. Far enough—exposed enough against the sea of white—that when the first 88-millimeter shell came in they knew they had no hope.

Smith yanked an AP shell off the wall and rammed it into the breech, ducked aside as the breech kicked back after firing, ramming in another and ejecting the spent cartridges in one continuous motion. McBurney fired back with both machine gun and cannon on the whitewashed German Mark IV tanks and antitank guns. They were almost indistinguishable from the snow beyond the whitecapped trees in the opposing woods. Smith was reduced to his own rote motion, the pinging of machine-gun bullets against the tank's steel sides surely devastating the infantry, stark fear in Windsor's voice calling for armor-piercing then high-explosive, calling targets to McBurney, ordering Devore to turn any way he could. Above all this was the unmistakable sound of 88s as they began crashing in, first too long and then too short, trying to bracket them with their fire, while Willie shifted gears furiously, fighting to swing them around.

Even without the chaos of motion, neither the scrambling infantry nor Willie Devore had any chance, in the unmarked snow, of spotting the buried Tellermine. The thirty-two-ton vehicle rolling across it set off a full pound of TNT—rocking the tank with such force that Smith was sure they'd taken an 88. The Sherman jerked to a halt. Windsor called for Devore to back up, but the tracks had been blown off and the wheels were spinning deeper into the snow. Stuck out in the open in this motionless flammable target, they had no time. Windsor reluctantly gave the order to evacuate.

The surviving infantry were already fleeing, alternately running and crawling, being cut down. Smith scrambled out the turret hatch with McBurney and Windsor close behind. Outside of the tank, the bullets and artillery became one deafening roar.

The snow scalded Smith's bare hands and face as he crawled under the blanket of bullets. He glanced back to make sure Willie was with him. What he saw left him horror-struck. Willie was still inside the tank, standing up in his seat with his head and torso sticking out of the driver's hatch. Smith screamed to him. The others turned to look and started screaming Willie's name as well, telling him to jump. Devore seemed frozen with fear, blind to who or where he was.

The explosion from the incoming shell was as sudden as it was devastating—Willie folded and fell. Smith lurched back toward the tank, and McBurney stopped him. From his angle of vision McBurney could see how badly Devore had been hit. The artillery strike had taken off half of Willie's head, he tried to convey to Smith over the fury of incoming fire. A second later, the tank exploded.

The bullets did not stop. McBurney pulled Smith into motion amid the tumult of falling shells. Smith followed numbly, looking only at the snow at his feet.

VISIBILITY WAS SO POOR THAT DAY that the Allied planes were able to fly only limited missions. On clear days, the German tanks had learned at great cost to keep under cover of woods; but with the fog and overcast they had no fear. One of the Panzers moved forward from the trees to fire its machine-gun and high-velocity shells on the three escaping tankers. The remaining Germans continued their barrage from the woods—infantry, a second Panzer, and two antitank guns firing 88s. They had obviously expected to face down a much larger assault force than one single Sherman. Glancing up around him, William McBurney saw no surviving American infantry.

McBurney and Teddy Windsor fired their .45-caliber submachine guns back toward the trees. Though they took out several of the white-clad infantry, it was ultimately an exercise in futility; grease guns had an accuracy of less than 50 percent at twenty-five yards, let alone over a hundred yards and moving.

Looking up for the first time, Leonard Smith was shaken by how isolated and exposed they were. It was worse than anything he'd imagined from the belly of the tank. He had no idea where Windsor was trying to lead them. He struggled, writhing across the drifts of snow.

Without warning the ground beneath him disappeared. Smith scrambled to his knees—staring directly into a pair of sky-blue eyes. It took him a moment to realize that the German soldier he faced was dead, that he'd stumbled into a shallow foxhole. He was close enough to the German to note the hollowed cheeks; the faint sandy-blond stubble on the boyish face; the eyes that were clear and not yet frozen over, indicating that the soldier must have been killed moments before. Smith considered stopping in the foxhole, but the Germans in the woods had likely spotted his position. More than that, Smith realized he didn't want to be left alone.

Windsor and McBurney had not gone far. The adrenaline rush that had accompanied their escape from the tank had passed. Initially, McBurney's every muscle had burned with an urge to action. But now he felt nothing; he seemed to be moving in place. His fingers were so numb, he couldn't find the trigger of his .45. The enemy rounds continued to fall. It occurred to McBurney with a curious detachment that these were in fact real bullets, these people he did not know were in fact trying to kill him, he was in fact here in this field, in this village and country the names of which he did not know, and there was no way out. It wasn't hopelessness that made him stop but the simple truth—it didn't matter what he did or did not do.

Leonard Smith's voice came out of nowhere. "Come on, man. Come on, man—think about the Savoy, so we can get back and do some more dancing." McBurney was stunned enough to turn. Smith paused beside him. "Let's get the hell out of here so we can get back and party."

The bullets and artillery kept falling. McBurney shook his head. "I ain't going no further. Go on."

Smith pulled at his arm. "The Savoy, man. Remember the Savoy."

"Shit, you're out of your damned mind." McBurney was ready to give up. Smith was scared, truly scared—the first time McBurney had ever seen him so. Nonetheless, with his irrepressible spirit he kept on talking about Harlem, about dancing, about the beautiful girls at the Savoy, anything to get McBurney's mind off their present situation. He refused to let McBurney lie down.

Motionless, Smith knew, they'd be zeroed in at any second. McBurney again tried to wave Smith on, but Smith stubbornly stayed with him. Summoning his last remaining reserves of energy and will, McBurney started moving again. Moments later, an incoming shell struck the spot where he'd lain.

The clearing seemed endless. The unevenness of the ground and the mist and debris sent up by the German bullets provided them with some kind of obscuring cover—but this strange combination of luck and terrain would surely run out. Smith could hear McBurney's ragged breathing beside him. The German Panzer rolling toward them showed no sign of stopping.

Over the continuing hum and pop of the bullets, neither Smith nor McBurney picked out the sound of the engine above. The first they heard of the American P-38 was the thunderous crash as it strafed the German tank, exploding the Panzer's ammunition. The plane flew on out of sight.

After a stunned moment, Windsor, McBurney, and Smith turned to look up at the blank white sky. Smith started waving; the three of them began wildly waving and cheering. The P-38 blasted past once more before disappearing—tipping its wings to acknowledge the three lone Americans far below.

BY NIGHTFALL, THE FUHRER BEGLEIT BRIGADE had started slowly falling back from Tillet: The 761st and the 87th Infantry Division had won. Amid the ravaged craters of snow and burning equipment, no precise tally of the carnage on both sides was made. The engagement had been fought ridge by ridge, each separate tank and squad of infantry waging its own individual and often seemingly futile campaign but continuing to push on. Able Company of the 761st was credited, among other successes, with knocking out an 88mm antitank gun and a self-propelled 75mm; Dog Company with killing fifty enemy soldiers and capturing ten; Charlie Company with destroying multiple self-propelled guns and machine-gun emplacements. But though the Battle of Tillet stood as a crucial victory toward the objective of the St. Hubert–Houffalize road, it had been so savage and costly a fight for the Americans that its successful conclusion did not bring any real sense of triumph.

When Leonard Smith, William McBurney, and Teddy Windsor returned to the American lines after three miles of running and crawling, they were met with faces almost as grim and utterly exhausted as their own. There was no break; surviving was the break they got. By the time Willie Devore's body was pulled from the remote forest clearing, the 761st's remaining M-4 Sherman tanks had moved on, fighting miles away.

THE COMBAT ON THE GROUND for the enlisted men continued for three more bitter weeks—but for the commanders involved, after January 9 the Battle of the Bulge was essentially over. At his Aldershorst

("Eagle's Nest") headquarters in Bavaria, Hitler tacitly acknowledged the ultimate inevitability of an Allied victory, ordering the withdrawal of the Sixth Panzer Army from the northern shoulder of the salient. The Fifth Panzer Army had already, the morning of the ninth, begun executing its own reluctantly given orders to retreat. Beaten back without securing their initial objectives, facing nightmarish supply problems, and taking casualties beside which the gruesome toll on the Americans paled, Hitler's leading generals saw the withdrawals as long overdue. General von Rundstedt and General von Manteuffel hoped, by pulling back to Germany, to preserve as many troops as possible for the decisive battle to be fought on the Russian front.

By January 9, Patton was also certain of an American victory. Looking beyond the Bulge, he told his staff to start poring over "those German maps again" for the plans for the Saar–Siegfried Line Campaign he had had so suddenly to abandon in December.

BUT FOR ALL THIS FUTURE PLANNING by the generals—and for all the crucial early command decisions like Eisenhower's immediate dispatch of the 7th and 10th Armored and Patton's lightning drive to the Ardennes to forestall disaster—the victory at the Battle of the Bulge belonged first and last to the enlisted men. American soldiers had died by the thousands holding off the initial German push in the north; thousands more had died in the furious fighting around Bastogne; and for nineteen straight days after January 9, Americans continued to take casualties in the unceasing cold.

The Germans in the north and south held to a policy of strategic withdrawal—fighting and inflicting the highest possible number of casualties as they went, placing countless roadblocks and mines in roads and fields likely to be crossed by armor, stationing heavy artillery in the high grounds to exact a punishing toll. The 761st supported the 87th Infantry Division between January 10 and 13 in heavy fighting as it advanced to seize Bonnerue, Pironpre, St. Hubert, Amberloup, and Sprimont. On January 14, the 761st was ordered to attach to the 17th Airborne Division.

Spearheading for the 17th Airborne—another young division that had suffered its own brutal baptism of fire on January 4 outside Bastogne—the 761st continued its northeastern drive toward Houffalize and St. Vith. With elements stopping only briefly for emergency maintenance, the battalion and the intrepid 17th Airborne fought from Wicourt to Vaux, Tavigny, Hautbellain (with Charlie Company there crossing briefly into Luxembourg, the fourth country in which its Shermans had seen combat), Gouvy, Thommen, and Wattermal. Leonard Smith, returning after Tillet to act as gunner with "Cool Stud"'s crew, no longer felt any sense of glory in the fight. Combat had been reduced to a set of habitual motions. Town blended into town and valley into valley; the only shift was from snow to a period of rain in which tanks and infantry alike bogged down.

The Americans were winning, but many German troops escaped east into Germany, where they would have to be faced and fought in yet another campaign. On January 26, the 761st shifted back from the 17th Airborne Division to the 87th Infantry, driving ever farther to the northeast. On January 28, the Americans regained the initial line of the German jump-off point, thus officially ending the Ardennes campaign. Sixteen thousand Americans had been killed in the Ardennes fighting, and 60,000 wounded or captured.

"THE BATTLE OF THE BULGE" WAS A TERM no American soldier would hear until long after the battle was over, a name that entered legend through Hollywood films and thousands of history books. For the enlisted men, the experience was one continuous fight that did not stop on January 28 but only pushed on farther toward Germany. After relieving elements of the 7th Armored Division at St. Vith, the 761st supported the 87th Infantry in attacking Schierbach, Huem, and Schonberg.

Every night in bivouac, Leonard Smith thought of writing a letter to Willie Devore's family in South Carolina, but he couldn't bring himself to tell Devore's mother how Willie had died. He couldn't bring himself to put to words the moment of his best friend's death alone in a frozen field 4,000 miles from home. Smith did not understand himself just what had happened. It was possible the impact of the Tellermine that had so rocked the tank had been more severe in the driver's front compartment than in the turret. Through forty straight days of combat in the Saar, through the initial week of fighting in the Ardennes, Devore had developed a reputation as one of the battalion's best drivers. Smith couldn't get his mind around the question of why Willie had seemed so confused, had hesitated and died in terror in that clearing on that bitter cold day. He would never know the answer.

9

TASK FORCE RHINE

You have fought gallantly and intelligently, and you have led all the way.

—Major General Anthony C. McAuliffe, message to the
combined attack team of the 761st Tank Battalion
and 103rd Infantry Division

In February 1945, American soldiers everywhere in Europe were faced with a peculiar situation: Though they were winning the war, the Germans did not seem to be losing. The Allies clearly had the upper hand: German armies in the west would engage in no further offensive operations after the Ardennes, and the eastern front was collapsing as well under the weight of a massive Russian attack toward Berlin that began on January 12. The Russians, having absorbed a German blitz in 1941 and taken millions of casualties in continuous combat, had since the spring of 1944 been mounting a skilled and merciless counteroffensive that brought the Red Army to the doorstep of Germany itself.

Even the most uninformed of American soldiers on the ground in western Europe had begun to realize, through their inexorable forward movement, that victory was at hand and that they were engaged in "mopping up" remaining pockets of resistance. But mopping up had perhaps never before occurred on such a grand scale, against such a determined foe, and at such a price. Hitler refused to concede defeat, ordering instead that the boundaries of the Reich be defended at all costs. The border of most importance to him was that of the Rhine.

The Rhine River runs from southeast Switzerland to the North Sea in the Netherlands, passing for most of its 820-mile length inside the German border. Given the almost total disarray of the German forces in the west in the wake of the Battle of the Bulge, Hitler's top generals argued that the best course of defense would be to withdraw the main body of their remaining troops to positions just behind the Rhine, using that natural barrier to aid in their guarding of Germany's prime industrial regions. But the Rhine had been a symbol of national identity and strength since the earliest-known German myths and legends, of a psychological importance to the German people something on the order of the Shenandoah River, Rocky Mountains, and Statue of Liberty combined—and Hitler, with his delusions of a historically determined destiny, insisted that the Rhine remain sacrosanct with his armies standing firm before it. This insistence, in turn, dictated that the "last killing ground in the west" would be that section of Germany to the west of the Rhine and east of the borders with the Netherlands, Brussels, Luxembourg, and France, a region known as the Rhineland.

The 761st would play key roles with a dizzying number of units in this final campaign, serving with four different divisions in three different U.S. armies in the fifty days between the beginning of February and the first large-scale penetrations of the Rhine—a jockeying that was not unique to the battalion but rather reflected the ever-shifting agendas of and conflicts between the leading Allied generals. In the final months of the war, as victory became ever more certain, clashes in personality and ambition within the coalition emerged with such persistence that Eisenhower likened his role to "trying to arrange the blankets smoothly over several prima donnas in the same bed." Eisenhower had chosen to pursue the "broad front" strategy he had favored ever since the breakout from Normandy, with the 21st British, 12th U.S., and 6th U.S. Army Groups attacking the Rhineland along a front measuring 450 miles; the generals involved argued bitterly against this, each one urging instead that a "single, full blooded thrust" be made in his own sector. The harshest conflict was, as usual, that between Patton (supported by Omar Bradley) and Montgomery.

According to Eisenhower's final plan for the campaign, no Allied forces would cross the Rhine until all armies had gained the river's west bank. But the priority of troops, air support, and supplies in the first phase would be given to Montgomery's 21st British Army Group (with the Ninth U.S. Army attached)—both in the interest of holding together the ever-grumbling coalition, and because Montgomery's troops held the northernmost position, closest to Germany's critical Ruhr industrial region. Patton, with his Third Army holding the middle sector of the line along the borders of Belgium and Luxembourg, raged even more fiercely than he had the previous fall at the secondary role given to U.S. troops, wondering "if ever before in the history of war, a winning general had to plead to be allowed to keep on winning." He intended to return to the "rock soup" tactics of his Lorraine campaign, moving forward whenever possible despite orders from the high command.

THE 761ST HELD ITS POSITION with the 87th Infantry near Schonberg, Belgium, less than a mile from the German border, until the morning of February 3, 1945. Its forward drive had been halted by

Eisenhower's decision to give priority to Montgomery and his 21st Army Group; on the third, the battalion received orders to turn and head northwest to Hermee, Belgium, there to attach to the 95th Infantry Division with the Ninth U.S. Army. This was the first time since their arrival in Normandy that the men would find themselves operating outside of Patton's command.

The battalion rolled 140 miles north through the battle-torn landscape along narrow roads clogged with army traffic, setting up headquarters just across the border from Hermee in the town of Jabeek, Holland, near Sittard. William McBurney, though generally cautious, was by this point tattered, gunpowder-stained, and exhausted beyond care about the potential consequences of his actions: He cursed out and threatened to beat up the battalion's diminutive supply clerk, whom he suspected of selling off unit supplies to other Allied soldiers and local civilians. He successfully managed to obtain his first change of clothing in well over a month; the new uniform felt so good to him his only regret was that he hadn't done it sooner.

Hearing McBurney describe this encounter, Leonard Smith cracked a smile for the first time in almost a month. McBurney owed his life to Smith's refusal to leave him at Tillet, and continued to try to lift his friend's spirits. Smith had always looked up to McBurney's maturity and intelligence; McBurney's ironic humor was one of the few things at this point that could alleviate his grief and sense of loss since the death of Willie Devore.

The 761st's assignment in Holland was to relieve elements of the 21st British Army Group as they prepared for the Rhineland offensive scheduled to begin on February 23. A second, concomitant assignment was to train the sizable number of replacements who were, at long last, arriving.

Replacements were a problem for both sides in the wake of the Battle of the Bulge. The Germans, with high losses in the Ardennes as well as staggering casualties against Russia, faced by far the worst manpower crisis: Entire German units were already being created of men previously disqualified from service because of stomach ulcers and hearing impairment; in January, Hitler ordered that all men up to forty-five years of age be shifted from industry into army roles. The Allies also faced dire shortages of troops, and finding replacements for specialized units like the armored forces, which normally required months of training, posed a unique problem—a problem of even greater severity for the 761st.

The Armored Force Training School had continued to train replacement tankers throughout the fighting in Europe, but none of these men were African American. The segregated Army had no choice but to put out a call among African American soldiers in service units for volunteers to fight in tanks. It was amazed at the high rate of response. Like Smith, McBurney, and McNeil when they first signed up years before, many of these volunteers were aching for the chance to fight for their country and willingly took reductions in rank to join the 761st. Christopher Navarre, who at the age of twenty-four had risen in the 590th Ambulance Company to become one of the youngest first sergeants in the Army, resigned his status to become a private in the battalion because he had found his previous work deeply troubling: On many occasions, white soldiers who were being ferried to safety by the black medics objected to being handled by African Americans. Navarre joined the 761st to fight and to avoid having to endure the insults of soldiers whose lives he was risking his own life to save.

What the fresh replacements found, when they arrived in Jabeek, was far from the gung-ho unit of old. None of the battalion's veterans had any remaining illusions about the glories of war. The 761st had only twenty operational M-4 Shermans coming out of the Bulge, and William McBurney and the others were at a low point, unable to see any end to the conflict.

Though exhausted, the men nonetheless summoned the inner strength to rise to their work, helping the overworked maintenance teams to service and repair their vehicles; training replacements in the mechanics of driving, loading, and bracketing targets; and fighting with remarkable courage when called on to support each other and the units with which they served. They were to perform with extraordinary distinction, in particular in the operation known as "Task Force Rhine."

EVEN THE MOST BATTLE-WEARY battalion members agreed that there was one bright spot in the otherwise dreary month of February—the return to the unit, on February 17, of an officer who had recently recovered from extensive injuries suffered on November 8: Lt. Col. Paul L. Bates. Bates, with his pick of assignments, had chosen to come back to the 761st. Bates's presence did not materially change conditions for the men, who had been on the line now for more than a hundred straight days; but the return of the unit commander who had shown them the highest degree of respect and honor from the time of their earliest training in the States through their first day of battle did considerably lift morale. Preston McNeil felt a spark of life return to his platoon for the grueling tasks ahead.

ON FEBRUARY 20, THE 761ST received orders to shift yet again and attach to the 79th Infantry Division, in Corps reserve with the Ninth U.S. Army. Preparations for Montgomery's "Operation Grenade" attack from Holland into the Rhineland were intensifying. On February 23, Baker Company, with the greatest number of operational vehicles, was the first unit of the 761st to move back into combat, spearheading for elements of the 79th Infantry in an attack on End, Holland. This assault was an effort to divert enemy attention from the main thrust of the Ninth Army's offensive to their south; the Shermans nonetheless encountered pockets of enemy resistance. Baker, soon to be joined by elements of Able and Dog, participated in an ongoing series of attacks to cut an enemy supply line in the vicinity of Milich, and on March 3 crossed into Germany, entering between Gangelt and Gilrath to assault the town of Schwannenberg. On March 7, the 761st minus Charlie Company worked with the 79th Reconnaissance troop to lead an attack on Kipshoven and Munchen Gladbach, twenty miles inside the Reich.

Charlie Company—generally the most battered and besieged of the 761st's units—had received a stroke of grace toward the end of February and the beginning of March, a rest of sorts: orders to move back to Mheer, Holland, to continue working with replacements as a provisional training company with its own firing and driving range. Mheer was a quiet town, and though the men worked full days, William McBurney caught his first glimpse in months of life beyond the demands of war. He began to have the feeling that there might, after all, be an end in sight. The bitter weather had finally broken and turned mild. The Dutch citizens spoke perfect English. McBurney and Leonard Smith found themselves billeted with townspeople who treated them with genuine warmth, welcoming them simply as Americans—honoring them, moreover, as liberators from the German occupation forces.

For Smith, such simple kindnesses were a welcome and pleasant surprise after the treatment he had experienced at the hands of some of the American soldiers. The men of the company joked together in the motor pool and on the firing range, and at night got together to play cards and tell stories. Smith ever so slowly began to relax and join in. Something had changed in him, he couldn't say just what. The dreams of heroic exploits that had defined his every waking thought since childhood had been stripped away with Devore's death. In Mheer, that lost hope for adventure gradually came to be replaced by the concrete present. Smith found solace in fleeting moments of shared humor around the campfire and in the presence of his friends, and otherwise resigned himself to the daily grind.

One day he looked up to see an airplane passing overhead with impossible speed. It was a jet, the first that Smith or any of the other men had seen. Fortunately, this plane was on a reconnaissance mission. Fortunately too, in a larger sense, the Germans had held back their development of the Me-262 jet aircraft until too late in the war to impact Allied air superiority.

Charlie Company's moment of recuperation at Mheer did not last long: On March 8, the entire battalion received orders to travel by train to Saverne, France, and prepare to participate in a major attack toward the German heartland by the Third and Seventh U.S. Armies on the southern flank of the Allied forces.

WHILE MONTGOMERY'S 21ST British Army Group had been driving forward across the northern portion of the Rhineland from February through early March, Bradley's 12th U.S. Army Group to the south had been furiously disobeying its orders to sit still. Bradley and Patton waged what they viewed as a guerrilla campaign to be the first to reach the Rhine, with Patton telling his staff to let the high command "learn what we're doing when they see it on their maps." The Third Army fought for a cold, bloody month to cross the rugged terrain of the Eifel region of Germany, and all the while Patton kept his battle plans and movements secret from his superiors: Told by SHAEF to bypass the key city of Trier, Patton responded simply that he had already "taken Trier with two divisions. Do you want me to give it back?" The First U.S. Army of Bradley's 12th Army Group had also been fighting steadily east, and on March 7, in one of the great feats of the war, it captured the bridge at Remagen intact and established the first Allied outpost on the eastern bank of the Rhine.

Bradley, for years the voice of caution, had become as determined as Patton that the Americans beat Montgomery's 21st Army Group into the heart of Germany. Bradley's animosity toward Montgomery had in fact become quite personal, after Montgomery, contrary to Bradley's wishes, had been given temporary control of the First U.S. Army during the Battle of the Bulge, and after a disastrous press conference in January in which Montgomery had belittled the American effort in the Ardennes (a potentially coalition-busting error corrected by Churchill's famous speech praising the courage of American soldiers before the House of Commons).

After the stunning if unauthorized successes his First and Third Armies had achieved in February and early March, Bradley argued determinedly to Eisenhower that the American forces to the south be allowed to capitalize on their gains and drive across the Saar-Palatinate region, where the German opposition was known to be weaker and thus riper for attack than that in Montgomery's zone. Montgomery's attack had indeed—despite high sacrifices by the Second British, First Canadian, and Ninth U.S. Armies—been slower than initially expected due to fierce enemy resistance and heavy flooding. Eisenhower granted Bradley permission to turn the Third Army from its previously ordered defensive stance to attack southeast in conjunction with a drive northeast by the Seventh U.S. Army of the 6th Army Group, with the goal of encircling the remaining German units defending the Siegfried Line and dashing east to the Rhine. The 761st had been ordered to Saverne, France, to spearhead one prong of this attack.

THE 761ST WAS INITIALLY TOLD to report to the Third Army; while still en route, with the men sleeping beside their tanks in freight cars heading south through the rural landscape, the battalion's orders were changed and they were instructed instead to attach to the 103rd

"Cactus" Infantry Division of the Seventh U.S. Army, commanded by Maj. Gen. Anthony McAuliffe, who had issued the famous "Nuts!" reply to the German forces surrounding Bastogne. Leonard Smith had gathered through the GI rumor mill that the train was heading back to France, but none of the men realized how close they were coming to the region that had cost them dearly in November and that they had been only too happy to leave.

Their scheduled attack would take them, in fact, on a course roughly twenty-five miles east of and parelleling their northeastern drive during the Saar Campaign. Parts of the ground gained in that campaign had since been recaptured by the Germans: The thinly spread Seventh Army, which had taken over the 761st's forward positions in December, had managed to hold the line against a second major German offensive ("Operation Nordwind") in January, but had been forced to cede small portions of terrain in Lorraine and in Alsace.

The 761st's planned drive would take it directly across this recaptured territory and straight into one of the most strongly defended sectors of the Siegfried Line. Leonard Smith and William McBurney—who had finally started to believe the end was in sight— would find themselves instead in the heat of some of the heaviest fighting the battalion had faced.

THE 761ST SET UP ITS command post eight miles northeast of Saverne, in the town of Bosselshausen, relieving the 48th Tank Battalion from the front on March 12. The 761st was to spearhead one section of a broad-front thrust by the Seventh Army scheduled to jump off on March 15, with ten full divisions attacking in concert to breach the Siegfried Line from Saarbrucken to Lauterbourg. While the men of the Seventh Army battered against German Army Group G at the Siegfried's tough defenses, to their north Patton's Third Army would catapult across the rear of the German troops to the Rhine. Patton's forces, with this rapid drive on a southeast trajectory, would "envelop their rear and pocket them so they can't get over the Rhine to fight us on the east bank."

The 761st and the 103rd Infantry Division held positions toward the southern end of the Seventh Army's zone. The battalion's initial mission for the joint campaign was to support the 103rd in penetrating the Siegfried Line in the vicinity of Bobenthal, twenty miles northeast of their line of departure.

On March 15, Charlie Company's three platoons rolled forward in the predawn darkness to the outskirts of the village of Zutzendorf to prepare for their wing of the attack. Charlie, flush with replacements and repaired equipment, was for the first time since its first day of combat operating at close to full strength. Both Smith and McBurney found themselves riding with five-man crews. The experience of waiting in the steel hulls, by now familiar to most of the men, was a new event to eager replacements like Christopher Navarre—and in this the seasoned veterans shared a measure of trepidation. While "replacements" in infantry units are traditionally regarded by the vets as expendable, the smallest mistake by any crew member of a Sherman tank would put all five men at risk.

At 6:30 A.M., the tanks were shaken with the thunder of an American preparatory artillery barrage on Zutzendorf, including a round of white phosphorus shells to cover them from surrounding enemy artillery positions. The replacements were soaked with nervous sweat, listening to terse commands in their headsets. At 6:45, the tank commanders received word from their platoon leaders to begin advancing through the smoke and haze. Their line of attack would take them along narrow roads through a series of small, fortified villages directly into the Hardt Mountains. The Germans, true to form, were to take full advantage of these natural fortifications, waging a punishing and carefully planned defense characterized by concealed mines, demolitions, roadblocks, and tank traps covered with fire.

The Shermans blasted their way through Zutzendorf but were halted just north of town by a blown bridge, which combat engineers worked to repair for several hours in the face of sporadic opposition. The tanks and infantry then continued north toward Niefern—running straight into the still more formidable obstacle of a series of mines. First Lt. Thomas Bruce, advancing with his platoon in the center, personally led his tanks across a minefield to give direct supporting fire to the attacking infantry.

To his right, the platoon commanded by 2nd Lt. Frank Cochrane had landed in the most heavily mined zone and caught by far the worst of it: Of the squad's five tanks, three were lost to Tellermines. Fortunately, no crew members were killed in the explosions. Evacuating their damaged tanks, crews took care to stay inside the marks left by their tracks to avoid antipersonnel mines. Replacement Christopher Navarre suffered injuries to his hand and leg early in the attack, but the former ambulance worker was determined to continue and refused to be evacuated.

The remaining tanks and crews kept attacking northeast—pushing forward through Mulhausen, Rothbach, Zinswiller, and Woerth in continuous fighting over the next four days. Leonard Smith, acting as gunner in "Cool Stud," fired intensely but with a sense of detachment on target after target. He peered through his periscope and horizontal sight, searching in every direction for gun posts and mortar teams. Enemy artillery was a near constant. The Germans in the battalion's zone of advance, as throughout the Rhineland, were exhausted, hungry, and much-diminished but nonetheless holding firm, building every sort of obstacle, fighting desperately, and retreating only when their posts became untenable.

First Lt. Thomas Bruce and 2nd Lt. Moses Dade both chose to lead their platoons on foot, reconnoitering enemy positions subject to small-arms and mortar fire. The tanks were pushing ever farther into the mountains, often forced to move in single file through the increasingly rugged terrain. The infantry was everywhere taking casualties. On their frequent trips back for resupplies of ammunition, Smith's tank commander, Daniel Cardell, as well as tank commander Isiah Parks and gunners William R. Burroughs and Christopher Navarre, exposed themselves beyond the line of duty to aid and evacuate wounded infantrymen in the face of heavy incoming fire.

Charlie Company successfully fought its way with the infantry across the border near Climbach, reaching the town of Bobenthal, Germany, by March 19—only to find itself given the still more difficult assignment of clearing Reisdorf, Niederschlettenbach, and Erlenbach, heavily defended towns along the Siegfried Line.

The Siegfried Line, like the Maginot, consisted of a complex series of fortifications including dragon's teeth, antitank ditches, and concrete pillboxes. In the 761st's zone, its narrow approaches were overlooked by numerous mortar, machine-gun, and artillery posts situated atop wooded hills and high cliffs.

WHILE CHARLIE COMPANY AND ELEMENTS of the 411th Regiment had continued struggling forward through the nineteenth, the main body of the 103rd's initial effort, "Task Force Cactus," had been halted to their south near Froeschwiller because of bad road conditions and difficult terrain. The 761st minus Charlie was instructed to regroup and roll forward to an assembly point near Bobenthal, and on March 21 received orders to form "Task Force Rhine"—to spearhead for a new, concentrated push with the objective of the city of Klingenmunster. Nine miles to their northeast, located just beyond the Siegfried Line and the Hardt Mountains, Klingenmunster stood as a gateway to the open plains before the Rhine River.

Task Force Rhine would include the 2nd Battalion of the 409th Infantry Regiment, a recon platoon from the 614th Tank Destroyers, the 103rd Signal Company, and a detachment of combat engineers.

The 761st's commander, Lt. Col. Paul Bates, was given the honor of leading this team. On the twenty-second, the task force rolled forward in the predawn hours to wait just south of Reisdorf.

Charlie had been engaged in a desperate battle throughout the twentieth and twenty-first to clear the approaches for this attack. Lieutenant Bruce's platoon blasted away at a series of pillboxes and camouflaged artillery posts outside of Reisdorf, while the infantry moved to locate key German positions in the steep surrounding hills. A team of American combat engineers moved forward to detonate all captured German emplacements.

Two miles to their north, Moses Dade's platoon, along with elements of the 411th Infantry, had begun attacking the town of Nieder-schlettenbach at 0700 hours on the twentieth. Like Reisdorf, Neiderschlettenbach was surrounded by enemy-held hills. Dade's tanks fought their way forward until midday, in the process assisting in destroying thirteen pillboxes and twelve machine-gun nests, and capturing intact a 75mm antitank gun. The Shermans helped clear a path for the infantry to begin entering the town but were halted in their own advance by a series of roadblocks and blown bridges.

As engineers worked to clear these obstacles, Dade's platoon—which had by now been fighting for six straight days—was relieved by 1st Lt. Harold Kingsley's platoon of Able Company. Kingsley's tanks and their accompanying infantry pressed on, only to be stopped after a short distance by a concentrated barrage of antitank, mortar, and sniper fire. Kingsley dismounted and personally scouted the thickly wooded hills for possible approaches to the German positions. Discovering a well-entrenched and hidden series of pillboxes and anti-tank posts, Kingsley remained in his precarious forward position. He called in target coordinates and directed fire from his Shermans to knock out ten pillboxes, helping clear the way for the infantry. Then he directed elements of his platoon to an exposed position, which caused the remaining Germans to redirect their fire. While they were so distracted, American forces were able to attack and completely destroy the German emplacement.

The Germans were heavily entrenched throughout the town: Able Company's S. Sgt. Johnnie Stevens noted countless Mark IVs and antitank guns. First Lt. Maxwell Huffman, who had taken over the company from David Williams, entered the town against Staff Sergeant Stevens's advice to help direct his tanks. Huffman, a white replacement from Newell, South Dakota, who had joined the unit early in December, had in Captain Williams's opinion initially been too gung ho for his own good; however, he had proven a quick study, and by the time he assumed command at the Battle of the Bulge, he had earned the respect of Williams and the enlisted men. On March 20, advancing through the town of Niederschlettenbach with his tank's top hatch open, Huffman was struck by sniper fire. He died of his wounds five days later.

MOSES DADE'S PLATOON REJOINED the fight at Niederschlettenbach on the twenty-first; the unit, having lost several of its tanks to mines and enemy fire, was rounded out later in the day by the remaining tanks and men of Cochrane's battered platoon, and continued attacking. Both Leonard Smith and William McBurney rode in this combined platoon, as did Christopher Navarre and "Iron Man" Warren Crecy. Navarre had heard the stories of Crecy's courage under fire from the other battalion members but was stunned to witness it himself. When Crecy's gunner, William Burroughs, knocked out a pillbox on a hill, Crecy immediately manned the .50-caliber machine gun to take out the enemy soldiers exiting the bunker—ducking down and shutting his hatch just as return 88mm artillery exploded yards away.

Cochrane's platoon fought its way to Niederschlettenbach using fire and movement tactics, with two tanks rushing forward while another two stood back to provide covering fire, followed by another pair of tanks. Engineers of the 411th Regiment bridged the Lauter River under heavy fire, and Cochrane's tanks continued fighting their way forward on the road between Niederschlettenbach and Erlenbach—a narrow corridor overlooked by cliffs containing numerous pillboxes connected by communications tunnels.

William McBurney's Sherman, commanded by Teddy Windsor, rolled directly into a concealed tank trap, becoming completely immobilized in the enemy ditch. Windsor, as he had at Tillet, reacted quickly—calling for covering fire from Leonard Smith's nearby tank and the tanks commanded by Isiah Parks and Warren Crecy. Crouched inside the turret, McBurney steeled himself to dismount on Windsor's signal. It was only a matter of time before the nearby artillery zeroed in, and they had no choice but to try to break out. Through his gunner's sight, McBurney had seen enough to know there wasn't much chance all five crewmen would make it.

Leonard Smith's tank was moving forward to give covering fire. Smith, too, could tell the situation for his friend's crew was dire. The enemy positions in the surrounding hills were well-hidden and widely dispersed. As the artillery barrage began—with his own tank now fully exposed—Smith furiously fired his 76mm cannon and .30-caliber machine gun on the enemy posts. He refused to let McBurney down. Crecy and Parks rolled forward to create a cross fire.

McBurney, Windsor, and crewmates John Safford, Mozee Thompson, and Robert Thrasher dismounted. Looking only at the ground immediately around them, they could hear the sickening familiar rush of incoming artillery and the deafening reply from their own tanks. They crawled on their bellies along the road, McBurney now the most determined among them. He had been through too much, he reasoned—too damned much—to go out this way.

Encouraging each other, the five men had crawled for over a quarter of a mile back the way they'd come. Up ahead, McBurney caught sight of a pillbox they had previously cleared. They were, he thought, home free—until with a sudden earsplitting *whrack* the pill-box exploded into smoke. Stunned, it took him a moment to realize that the post had been detonated by a team of American combat engineers. They'd made it.

Windsor immediately took over another tank and got back in the action. McBurney, left for the moment without a Sherman, was glad for the brief respite after this second dismounting of a tank of Windsor's under fire. In the battalion's remaining actions, McBurney was to be given command of his own tank.

Cochrane's platoon fought on in a fury of fire throughout the night, clearing the Niederschlettenbach–Erlenbach road—destroying seven pillboxes and ten machine-gun nests—and reducing the town of Erlenbach itself. They were briefly relieved the following day by a platoon of Able; when this platoon's advance was halted by a blown bridge near Gundershoffen, all M-4 Shermans were ordered to join the main body of Task Force Rhine.

TASK FORCE RHINE, ASSEMBLED and waiting near Reisdorf, received its orders to jump off at 4 P.M. on the twenty-second. The column traveled single file along the narrow road, led by Baker Company, followed by elements of Able. Members of Lieutenant Bruce's platoon of Charlie Company, who had engaged in bitter fighting to reduce the town's approaches, waved encouragement and pulled to the side as their fellow Shermans passed. Lieutenant Colonel Bates chose to remain with the task force's lead platoon throughout the coming attack.

The combined team spread out to take up firing positions on the southern perimeter. The tanks battered at the town continuously for more than an hour, while foot soldiers of the 409th Infantry Regiment fought their way through the high grounds on either side. Reisdorf fell to this joint assault; the team next assaulted and successfully destroyed a series of enemy pillboxes northeast of town.

Charlie's actions along the Niederschlettenbach–Erlenbach road had forestalled any possibility of relief for the now-embattled Germans. Continuing on past Reisdorf, the task force split into two columns—one headed along the narrow unpaved road toward Birkenhardt, the other along a well-paved road toward Bollenborn. The 409th's foot soldiers riding astride the tanks looked watchfully in every direction around them. The tankers and infantry had been instructed to fire at any- and everything that moved along the way: They were advancing in conjunction with a push to their left (west) by the 42nd Infantry Division and to their right (east) by the 36th, and a halt by any of these units would greatly endanger the others.

The column advancing on Birkenhardt was stopped at the northeast edge of town by a heavy barrage of antitank fire. Lt. Colonel Bates pulled them back from this potentially suicidal charge and called for preparatory artillery. When communications with the American forward artillery observer were disrupted, the 761st's Russell C. Geist moved up in a light tank, directly exposing himself to incoming enemy artillery to adjust and call back coordinates for the American guns. The Shermans then rolled through, firing at all possible machine-gun and antitank positions—but the artillery had done its work well, leaving the town little more than scattered piles of rubble. The infantry fanned out through the smoke-filled streets to solidify their hold.

The column moving along the better-paved road to Bollenborn had met with obstacle after obstacle. The Germans, anticipating a major armored push along this route, had positioned a series of dragon's teeth and an extended roadblock, which combat engineers moved forward to clear. A concealed 75mm gun on the outskirts of Bollenborn opened fire as the team was preparing to resume its forward thrust—destroying two of the 761st's Shermans (though both crews managed to evacuate safely). The remainder of the Bollenborn team withdrew to join the already progressing Birkendhardt column. The combined team's immediate objective was the town of Silz, located in the middle of some of the toughest Siegfried defenses in their sector.

Night was falling as the task force rolled on. Bates had been told that his team would meet up at Silz with elements of the 10th Armored Division, a stalwart of Patton's Third Army, advancing from the opposite side of town. But Bates's forward scouts were unable to catch any sign of the division's tanks. The 10th Armored had in fact—owing to a communications error not uncommon in wartime—never been given any such orders.

All Lieutenant Colonel Bates knew was that his team had unexpectedly found itself without support in the center of the Siegfried Line. He conferred with Baker Company's 1st Lt. Harold Gary and Sgt. Ervin Latimore, both of whom wanted to go forward. In the situation as they understood it, it was imperative for the success of all units on the line that they continue their advance.

Night fighting in Sherman tanks was an intense, surreal experience. Sherman battalions generally used night for maintenance work and sleep. Approaching Silz, the 761st's drivers bulled their way forward through the darkness without benefit of headlights, which would only have made them targets, desperately scanning the ground for potentially ruinous mines and bomb craters. The tank commander, gunner, and bow gunner anxiously searched for their next targets, helped only by stray flares and the ghastly uncertain illumination of incoming artillery or whatever it was they themselves had last struck and set on fire. As they rolled forward into Silz, Lieutenant Gary and Sergeant Latimore dealt with the situation by unleashing ammunition in every direction at once and so changing night to day.

The tanks and infantry sped forward in the eerie, surging light of countless fires, with the foot soldiers joining in, shooting steadily into the ditches and hills beside the road. The tankers for the most part could hear only the rattle of their engines, the boom of incoming shells, the crash of their own cannon fire, and the endlessly barked coordinates on their headsets, but the unceasing cascade of noise gave them a sense of the violence occurring outside the tanks.

Just beyond Silz, tank fire set off an enemy ammunition dump; shells continued exploding in the inferno for hours after they had passed. The task force continued its race east toward the town of Munchweiler. Leading the attack, Sergeant Latimore encountered a vast retreating column of enemy trucks, towed guns, and horse-drawn artillery. Latimore and his lead tanks had taken this column by surprise: Determined to eliminate the enemy guns before they could engage the American column in a firefight, Latimore's Sherman tanks charged forward. What followed was a virtual slaughter, with the Germans managing to get off only scattered return fire.

The 761st's tanks pushed directly into the German troops, reducing the column to a series of burning metal hulks. Terrified German soldiers ran toward the Americans, pleading to surrender. Sergeant Latimore was wounded in the fray, but refused to be evacuated.

Farther on, the tanks were met with a heavy barrage of antitank fire. Latimore located the German emplacements by their gun flashes against the darkness, directing his team to overrun the positions. The tanks sprayed the posts with machine-gun fire; the enemy crews fled.

Lieutenant Colonel Bates had been knocked off his feet earlier in the attack by the jolt from an 88mm artillery shell. Warren Crecy dismounted his tank amid a continuous rain of incoming fire and ran forward to carry Bates to safety.

THE TASK FORCE CONTINUED EAST from Munchweiler, reaching the outskirts of its final objective of Klingenmunster shortly before 2 A.M. The tanks and infantry were pushed back by intense fire from permanent German artillery and machine-gun installations around the city. The American team had outrun its artillery support, but the men had no intention of stopping and chose to make do. The 761st's tanks and

assault guns regrouped and took up positions in the countryside surrounding Klingenmunster. They unleashed a punishing barrage until
fires raged throughout the city.

The tanks and infantry then moved forward again, meeting this
time with only sporadic mortar and sniper fire. The burning city had
been reduced to an empty, almost apocalyptic landscape. As they
advanced, the German defenders broke ranks and ran, retreating into
the night; those few resisters were killed in brief, bloody engagements.
Klingenmunster was fully cleared by 4:35 A.M. The 761st and the 103rd
Division had successfully completed their assignment: They had blasted
a path in their sector leading through some of the most entrenched
defenses of the Siegfried Line to the open Rhine plains beyond.

THE 761ST MOVED EAST as far as Insheim, taking numerous German
POWs—finding that many of the German soldiers, aware that the
vaunted Siegfried had been breached, were now quite willing prisoners. Back on the road between Silz and Munchweiler, American units
advancing along the battalion's path were shocked at the level of violence in its wake: So dense was the wreckage that before the rear elements of the task force column could pass, a tank 'dozer had to be
brought forward to push the still-smoking vehicles and countless bodies of horses and German soldiers off the sides of the road. In the final
tally, between March 20 and 23, the 761st was credited with clearing
seven towns; destroying more than 400 vehicles, 80 heavy weapons,
and thousands of machine guns, mortars, and rifles; as well as inflicting over 4,000 casualties against soldiers of fourteen different German divisions.

The punishment taken by American units and the ground gained
as they fought all along the Seventh Army's front succeeded in form-
ing one edge of a pincer around German Army Group G. Closing the
pincer from the north, in the space of just ten days, Patton's Third

Army claimed an estimated 37,000 enemy soldiers killed or wounded, captured 81,692 prisoners of war, and was firmly established along the banks of the Rhine. In the 103rd Infantry Division's zone, elements of the Seventh Army's 14th Armored Division pushed forward through the break Task Force Rhine had created (advancing as well through a parallel break in the 36th Division's zone) and prepared to cross over.

10

THE RIVER

You will wait there for the Russians.

—FINAL ORDERS, 761ST TANK BATTALION
MAY 5, 1945

Leonard Smith caught his first glimpse of the Rhine River on March 30, 1945, near the battle-scarred city of Oppenheim, Germany, looking out the top hatch of his M-4 Sherman tank. It was, as perhaps it was bound to be, an anticlimactic moment. To reach this mythic gateway into the heart of Hitler's Third Reich, Smith had logged well over a thousand combat miles, had watched several of the best men he would ever meet lose their lives, and had killed so many German soldiers that he'd lost track. The Rhine, by this point, had cost so much in spirit and blood that for the twenty-year-old it had no meaning or value; it was just another river. Smith was simply trying to survive.

The territory the battalion's tanks traversed along the west bank of the Rhine in their road march from Insheim had been captured by American troops one week before. The unit's veterans nevertheless looked out their hatches with the cautious stance they termed "half-in, half out, mostly in": They had learned that anything, from snipers to mines to stray mortar and artillery teams, was possible at any time.

The battalion had unexpectedly received its orders two days before to attach to yet another division for another campaign, its seventh division for its fourth campaign in five months. This was surely to be the last; but then, the men had thought so on almost every prior occasion. Their instructions were to travel north on the thirtieth to Oppenheim, there to cross the Rhine and roll on to Langenselbold, where they would attach to the 71st Infantry Division. The 71st Infantry, which had fought two divisions west of the 103rd in the Seventh Army's recent assault on the Siegfried Line, was itself on the move that day to Langenselbold, with orders to transfer from the Seventh to the Third U.S. Army. The 761st was thus to complete the war with a reunion of sorts, a return to Patton's command, fighting in the general direction that had in one way or another defined their every waking hour since the first artillery blasts in the predawn darkness of November 8 in France: east.

The battalion's new orders had again cut short its maintenance period; maintenance crews, working around the clock with inadequate supplies, finagled elaborate deals for replacement parts. The tanks were a patchwork of spare machinery that somehow, someway, most of the time, kept moving. Most of the men were still wearing their uniforms of months before, and could not remember the last time they'd had a chance to bathe. Based on their prior experiences of unit transfer, they could expect on their arrival to be viewed by the majority of this latest infantry division with suspicion and unease.

Though they knew to prepare themselves, knew to expect this initial attitude toward the fact that they were African American, it had never entirely lost its power to surprise and sting.

But in all of this, the men had come to feel a peculiar, contrary sort of pride, an even stronger sense of identity the more ragged, rejected, and uprooted they became: They were, as they often wryly repeated among themselves, indeed a "bastard battalion."

THE UNIT'S MASSIVE ARMORED VEHICLES crossed the wide span of the Rhine on a heavy pontoon bridge previously erected by Third Army engineers. This crossing had been secured in secrecy on the night of March 22 by the 5th Infantry Division—an action that was, as Patton and Bradley both later gleefully announced, the first assault crossing of the Rhine in modern times. The Third Army had beaten Montgomery's troops across the river by the space of a single day. Patton himself first traversed the river on March 24, commemorating the occasion with his usual flair by stopping in the middle of the bridge at Nierstein to "take a piss in the Rhine. I have been looking forward to this for a long time."

Had there been any slight doubt remaining as to the inevitable outcome of the war in Europe, it should at this late date have disappeared. By the time the 761st reached its banks a week later, the supposedly impenetrable Rhine had been bridged along over two hundred miles of its length by numerous divisions of six Allied armies, and American armored spearheads had smashed their way to positions as far east as Fulda and Kassel, two hundred miles from Berlin. To the east, elements of the Russian army had liberated Poland and were building up arms and men for their direct assault on Germany's capital city. But Hitler, increasingly removed from reality in his Berlin bunker, kept waiting for a miracle.

With the Führer's fixed refusal to surrender, the final contours of battle were set: The war would continue until American and British forces moving east met up with Russian troops moving west some-where in Germany. Eisenhower's plan of action called for Mont-gomery's First Canadian and Second British Armies to push toward Bremen and Hamburg; the Ninth and First U.S. Armies to fight in concert to encircle the Ruhr industrial region and then drive east; and the First French and elements of the Seventh U.S. Armies to push east toward Nuremberg and south to meet up with Allied forces battling through northern Italy. Patton's Third U.S. Army was to push as far east as possible across Germany toward Austria and Czechoslovakia.

THE 761st TANK BATTALION reached the 71st Infantry Division's headquarters at Langenselbold, outside of Frankfurt, on April 1. Its road march of 134 miles from Insheim had for the most part been uneventful, though Able Company's Floyd Dade encountered a small patch of resistance he found comical, if only in retrospect, when his tank became mired in the mud. Dade, looking out to see a fence fifty yards away, decided to venture forth to see if he could gather some of its posts to brace his spinning tracks; his crewmates refused to go with him. Muttering to himself, the ever-industrious Dade placed one post under the right-side tracks and went back for another. On this second trip, a concealed German 88mm antitank gun announced its pres-ence—one shot rocketed directly over his head, a second falling short. Remembering that the Germans bracketed targets like clockwork, he dove away just as a third shell crashed where he'd been standing. The tank itself, fortunately, was beyond range; Dade crawled back and waited with his crew until an ordnance unit came to retrieve them.

On their arrival at Langenselbold, the battalion's letter compa-nies were split up, with Able, Baker, and Charlie assigned, respec-tively, to the 71st Division's 5th, 14th, and 66th Infantry Regiments, and Dog assigned to the 71st Reconnaissance troop. Their initial orders were to eliminate a stubborn pocket of resistance in the woods near Leisenwald, Waldenburg, and Budingen, composed of elements of the crack 6th SS Mountain Division Nord.

Almost utterly surrounded by American forces, the SS troops still refused to surrender. On April 1 and 2, the 761st's tanks and accompanying infantry spread out over a wide area to complete the unit's encirclement. They faced a furious series of attempts to break out all along the pocket's perimeter. Able moved through the woods to circle Waldenburg, and spearheaded for the infantry in taking the towns of Buches and Budingen; Dog Company aided the 71st Reconnaissance Troop several miles away in capturing two armored supply dumps near Lake Rotenbach; the 761st's Assault Gun Platoon supported elements of the 66th Regiment at Speilberg, Streitburg, and Leisenwald. Outside of Leisenwald, several of the battalion's assault gun tanks were saved by the actions of a private in the 71st—who spotted four German soldiers with Panzerfausts and ran across an open field under enemy fire to warn the tanks of their location.

Baker Company supported the 14th Infantry Regiment in advancing north across a ravine in the face of small-arms fire. Infantry Pfc. Irving Boone was amazed to see one of Baker's officers dismount to guide the unit's tanks with hand signals in the midst of heavy firing. Farther on, in a desperate firefight to stop an SS convoy on the Nieder Mockstadt–Ober Mockstadt road, two of Baker's spearhead tanks were hit by artillery fire crossing an open field. Both crews abandoned their Shermans. Later, the driver of the second tank reentered his smoking vehicle to back it out of the line of fire so that it could be repaired for future use.

Charlie Company took up strategic positions along the southern and eastern edges of the pocket to forestall the escape of SS troops. Charlie's tanks waited patiently just beyond a thick woods. A group of German soldiers attempting to break out had been cut off from behind by elements of the 71st Infantry: Sighting the imposing line of Sherman tanks, they realized that they'd be slaughtered if they tried to advance. The Germans were stuck just inside the forest, but they gave no sign of willingness to surrender. Pop Gates ordered his tanks to fire into the woods; still the Germans refused to come out. Then Gates had an idea to end the standoff: His tanks had been firing low, but he told Leonard Smith and his other gunners to raise their fire to explode the treetops, unleashing a fury of shrapnel and falling branches. After only a few minutes of this treatment the Germans finally emerged, waving white cloths and calling out, *"Kamaraden."*

What followed as the Germans walked toward the tanks spoke to one of the 761st's more curious experiences on the battlefields of Europe. Some of the troops they'd faced had seemed utterly terrified of black soldiers (a fear that was due, they had learned from civilians, to the savage reputation of French Senegalese soldiers fighting in World War I; a common question asked by German soldiers relieving fellow soldiers in the trenches was "Are there any Africans opposite?"). Gates had ordered his tank crews to stay buttoned up inside their vehicles until the SS troops reached them, then to direct them back to surrender to the 71st Division's white infantrymen.

One of Charlie's tankers mistakenly opened his hatch when the troops were still a short distance away. The Germans saw him and called out, *"Schwarze Soldaten!"* running and stumbling back toward the woods. After a warning volley, the Germans realized they had no choice. One of the captured officers, whose men had encountered the 761st's widely dispersed tanks in every direction for miles around, asked a bemused Pop Gates, "How many Negro Panzer divisions *are* there?"

BY APRIL 4, AFTER THREE DAYS of intense fighting, the pocket of holdouts from the 6th SS Mountain Division had almost all been killed or captured. The battalion and the 71st Infantry received orders to head toward Fulda and Meiningen, mopping up any forces encountered on the way.

For Leonard Smith, looking cautiously out the top hatch of "Cool Stud," the landscape all around contained a paradox. The battalion had entered combat during the bleakest of Novembers and fought its way through brutal winter months into a dreary March. But here, just when they were entering into the ultimate heart and source of every anguish they'd endured, there flourished a sheer beauty and variousness of nature the likes of which Smith had never seen. The sky each day was tinctured a different blue, and valleys drenched with emerald green turned to fields of countless frail flowers and burgeoning woods threaded by cool streams. This, somehow, was "enemy" country. Even the generally taciturn William McBurney was moved by the breathtaking sights.

The direction in which they were moving was, as ever, east; by April 7, they had already crossed the north-south centerline through Germany. In these final weeks of war, the battalion's tanks were more dispersed than they had been in any prior campaign: Their initial mission with the 71st Infantry Division was to secure the wide swath of territory left behind the advancing 11th Armored Division (which had matured from its baptism of fire near Bastogne into an accomplished unit). Patton, believing that the swiftest advance would bring the swiftest end to the war, had ordered his armored divisions simply to smash forward as far and fast as possible without concern for securing territory or flanks. In their wake, the armored spearheads left a kind of no-man's-land where the unexpected was to be expected even more than usual. This was the terrain the tanks of the 761st, often moving by ones and twos along with groups of infantry, were fanning out to clear. Everywhere, quiet mild towns alternated unpredictably with scattered snipers and larger pockets of determined holdouts. On the road near Meiningen, the 761st's Sgt. Jonathan Hall faced the disturbing spectacle of a wounded SS officer slashing his own throat with a razor, gasping and choking to death yards from Hall's tank, rather than endure surrender.

For the gentle-hearted Preston McNeil, the mystery and strangeness of war was evident even more in Germany's civilian population than in the landscape. The battalion's tanks, following their daily assigned trajectories, moved through countless small towns never knowing their precise locations and only rarely learning their names; tank crews often caught only the slightest glimpse because of their ongoing wariness of snipers. These were "cow towns," small collections of neat, squat stone houses with firewood stacked along their outer walls. In one of the first such towns his tank helped to clear, Preston McNeil stopped in the middle of the market square for a break. The streets seemed utterly deserted. The infantry had already been house to house; McNeil enjoyed the chance to stretch, and he leaned comfortably against the side of his tank as he ate his rations.

When he finished, he threw his food scraps into what seemed to be a garbage pile. He turned back when a quick movement caught his eye—a frightened, hollow-cheeked child was pulling out the food that he'd just tossed aside. It disturbed McNeil to see a child going through garbage while he himself had food. He called to the boy to come over; the boy started backing away until McNeil held out more food. The boy took it and ran off. Gradually, a small group emerged from the seemingly deserted houses and shops. They'd been scared into hiding, it seemed, as much by the rumor of savage *"Schwarze Soldaten"* as by the recent fighting; most of them had never before seen anybody with dark skin.

In town after town, McNeil found the same pattern, an initial fear and suspicion replaced by a startling and genuine warmth, glimpses of a vast, struggling humanity where he had expected to find only enemies. It made the reasons behind the carnage he had seen, and the horrors he would soon witness, an even greater and more troubling mystery.

THE MEMBERS OF THE 761ST had begun to sense that the end could not be too long in coming. With the exception of the few days of vio-

lence surrounding Task Force Rhine, it had been some time since the
unit had encountered anything like the fire of its initiation to combat
in France or the well-armored opposition in the Ardennes. The farther
the men pushed into Germany, the more rapid seemed their advance,
the farther apart the ongoing pockets of resistance, and the greater
the number of willing prisoners they took. The soldiers they captured
were nothing like those they had earlier faced, but rather a testament
to just how far the Reich had fallen. Leonard Smith was amazed to
see increasingly haphazard units of old men and boys so young that
many of them didn't shave yet.

On April 11, the battalion's separate units and the 71st Infantry
began closing in on the medieval town of Coburg, a scant fifty miles
from the eastern border with Czechoslovakia. On Coburg's outskirts,
they encountered the stiffest resistance they had faced in days from
scattered machine-gun nests, Panzerfausts, mortar fire, and a period
of harrassment by Luftwaffe planes. The 11th Armored Division had
moved east of the town the day before; the 71st Infantry, 761st, and
Combat Command B of the 11th Armored fought their way to a complete encirclement of Coburg, and the mayor finally surrendered. Dog
Company's light tanks and a group of infantry were ordered forward
the following day to clear Coburg of snipers, shooting out a number of
upper-level windows.

That afternoon, the 761st enjoyed a rare break in the now-
secure town—in a comfort aided by their commandeering of all the
fresh chicken and eggs they could find, several feather beds, and a
vast quantity of cognac. Preston McNeil admonished his men to save
some of the cognac for later, then sought out Charlie Company and
spent time catching up with his friends Smith and McBurney, whom
he hadn't seen for almost two weeks. But like most of their rests, this
one proved shorter than hoped or expected: The men were soon
ordered to advance to the southeast.

On April 14, they attacked the town of Kulmbach, fifteen miles north of the city of Bayreuth. Working closely together, the Shermans fired on targets signaled by the infantry as the 71st Infantry spread out within the town—fortunately discovering no hidden snipers.

Just outside of Kulmbach, Cpl. Fred Brown's tank of Baker Company stopped for a moment. As Brown was climbing up to reenter the turret, a sudden burst from a concealed enemy 88mm exploded directly overhead. Brown, a Bronx native who had been with the battalion since its earliest days, later died of his injuries.

The 66th Infantry Regiment, supported by Charlie Company, was moving to attack an airfield and aeronautical school in a wooded area north of Bayreuth. Charlie's tanks fired on a series of machine-gun nests positioned across a field while the infantry, with extraordinary courage, crossed the open ground by alternately running and diving to their stomachs amid a hail of German bullets.

In the thick of the firing, Charlie Company's 1st Sgt. William Burroughs dismounted his tank to locate a hidden machine-gun position that was devastating the infantry. Burroughs, a replacement who had given up rank to join the unit and who had earned special mention in Task Force Rhine, was shot above his left eye. Evacuated to an army hospital, Burroughs survived but lost his eye.

The 761st and the 71st Infantry advanced to the outskirts of Bayreuth, where fanatical holdouts had previously refused to consider a surrender ultimatum. Together with elements of the 71st and 65th Infantry Divisions and 11th Armored Division, the 761st shelled the city continuously for two days. The shattered city's defenders finally surrendered on April 16.

NEWS TRAVELS STRANGELY through a battalion—often with amazing rapidity, but occasionally, in a group as dispersed as the 761st was at this time, by fits and starts. For much of the battalion, the news of President Franklin Roosevelt's death on April 12 was delayed. Able

Company's Walter Lewis was rolling along a road in the second half of April, past a large group of German POWs being shepherded by American infantrymen. A few of the GIs spotted Lewis's fifty-gallon canister of raw cognac from Coburg, which he'd strapped to the rear of his Sherman. They asked Lewis for a taste, and he told them to jump on and help themselves. One of the GIs said, "Too bad about Roosevelt, isn't it?" This was the first Lewis had heard of the President's fatal cerebral hemorrhage.

Quite by accident, one of the first Americans in Europe to learn of Roosevelt's death had been the Third Army's commander: In bed at his headquarters, Patton had just tuned his radio to the BBC to set his watch when the news broke. Patton immediately woke Bradley and Eisenhower, who happened to be staying with him; the three had "quite a discussion as to what might happen," but agreed that the tragedy was unlikely to have any marked effect on Allied battle plans.

Hitler, hearing the news that night inside his Berlin bunker, reached a different conclusion. This was the miracle he had long been expecting: This great event would somehow compel the Americans to withdraw from the war, the British would follow, and the Third Reich would be saved. Hitler ordered renewed resistance, delusional in his overestimation of the number of German troops remaining.

There was no possibility that any of the Allied armies would withdraw. The Red Army had entered Germany and by April 11 was approximately thirty miles from Berlin. Montgomery's forces were simultaneously clearing northern Holland and heading east toward Bremen. Elements of the First and Ninth U.S. Armies had sealed off the Ruhr pocket and were successfully subduing the 325,000 German troops contained within; other elements were pushing east, with the 2nd Armored Division reaching the Elbe River at a point fifty-five miles from Berlin. By April 12, the Third Army's advance teams had traversed most of Germany's width, with the 4th Armored driving past Jena and the 6th Armored capturing a bridge over the Weisse-Elster River.

For some time, the real question had been not *what* would happen in Europe but rather *how* it would happen—more specifically, how far the American and British forces would push in their advance toward the Russians. At February's Yalta conference, Churchill, Roosevelt, and Joseph Stalin had agreed on rough spheres of influence, with the city of Berlin being granted to Stalin. But by early April, the Red Army's advance had been slower than expected due to ongoing resistance, while the Americans and British were gaining ground faster than they'd planned. Churchill urged Eisenhower to continue east as far as possible and attempt to beat the Russians to Berlin. In light of the Cold War, the justification behind and ramifications of Eisenhower's ultimate decision will forever be debated by historians.

Eisenhower based his decision in part on a belief that the Russians had already paid for the city in lives: Eight out of every ten German soldiers killed in the war had been killed by members of the Red Army in the brutal battles of the eastern front, and the Russians had taken more casualties than all other Allied countries combined. Further, Omar Bradley had cautioned Eisenhower that subduing the entrenched defenders of the city could cost as many as 100,000 American casualties (it did, in fact, eventually cost 300,000 Russians killed or wounded); and there was no guarantee that the United States would not afterward be forced to give it back. Eisenhower was also concerned about the possible existence of a "National Redoubt," a secret cache of arms somewhere in southern Germany and northern Austria where intelligence reports indicated that fanatical holdouts might wage an ongoing guerrilla war.

The Supreme Allied Commander ordered a stop line for the Allied forces roughly following the contours of the Elbe and Mulde Rivers. The Third Army was instructed to halt its eastward advance toward Czechoslovakia and turn south to take out the rumored National Redoubt.

THE SHIFT SEVERAL DEGREES FARTHER to the south of their axis of advance did not have an immediate, appreciable impact on the enlisted men's day-to-day existence. The 761st continued rolling rapidly forward day after day, firing in support of the 71st Infantry wherever resistance was encountered. Smith's tank was most often assigned to ride beside McBurney's; the two friends became ever closer, looking forward to bivouacking at night, when they could kick back, rib each other, and talk about what they were going to do when the war was over. They weren't planning future careers. After five months on the front, their goals were simpler and more concrete: specific lists of hot foods that didn't come from C-ration cans, hot showers whenever they wanted them, and the freedom simply to sit still without worrying about snipers and artillery fire.

On April 17, as the Third Army began its reorientation to the south, the 71st Infantry Division and 761st were shifted from command of the army's XII Corps to XX Corps and ordered to push south-southeast from Bayreuth toward the city of Regensburg. The 11th Armored's spearheads had remained with XII Corps; in their southward attack, the 761st and infantry were now both claiming and mopping up new territory as they went. They advanced rapidly down the autobahn toward Amberg.

The badly damaged Luftwaffe had been using the pavement along the highway's centerline as a landing and takeoff strip: The battalion's Shermans shot down a number of planes and destroyed landing lights as they went, while firing on enemy soldiers in the adjacent woods. Fanning out to claim a number of small towns, they were soon spread over such a wide area and moving so quickly that supplies became a problem. The men were forced even more than usual to supplement their meager rations by living off the land. They discovered, as did many hungry GIs throughout Germany, that a grenade strategically dropped in a lake or stream would serve up large quantities of fish. By this point, anything beat their C- and K-rations staple.

On April 18, near the town of Neuhaus, the Able Company tank commanded by S. Sgt. Johnnie Stevens was called to support a group of infantrymen pinned down by a machine-gun emplacement on a hill. Stevens left his Sherman and crawled fifty yards forward to scout out the enemy position. He looked up to see that the machine-gun nest was much closer than he'd realized, in fact just yards away. There was no way he'd make it back to the tank unseen. He took a deep breath, jumped up, and charged directly at the emplacement, throwing his grenades. A nearby infantry lieutenant, who had watched Stevens's solitary advance in disbelief, immediately leapt up and ordered his men to charge along with him. Stevens's actions, as well as the covering fire provided by his crew and the support of the infantry lieutenant, allowed the Americans to take the position without another American casualty; nine Germans were killed and thirty-six captured.

Charlie Company worked closely with the 66th Infantry Regiment in assaulting Neuhaus and clearing portions of the surrounding Veldensteiner Forest. Hitler's propaganda minister, Hermann Goering, had a castle on a high bluff just beyond Neuhaus. Several of Charlie's crew members, including Christopher Navarre, headed back after piecemeal fighting in the surrounding woods to tour the castle. The Germans had already removed most of Goering's treasures, but Navarre looked in wonderment at a series of secret passageways, an elevator leading to the dining room, and the marbled walls of the huge master bath.

The Allied tanks and infantry continued their forward push—claiming, against scattered resistance, the towns of Auerbach, Schwandorf, Burglengenfeld, Regenstauf, Kurn, Pirkensee, and Zeitlern. Moving through the astonishing beauty of the Sulzbach Valley, they were fast approaching their objective of Regensburg, at the meeting point of the Regen and Danube Rivers. The Germans had heavily fortified the city and refused a demand that they surrender it. The 65th Infantry Division advanced to take up positions beside the 71st

Infantry and the 761st. The battalion's light and medium tanks, 81mm mortars, and 105mm assault guns worked alongside division artillery to rain fire on the city's inhabitants. With no secure crossing into the city, their role was confined to a peripheral, supporting one. Infantrymen crossed the river on assault boats and spread throughout the streets in fierce house-to-house combat. Regensburg finally surrendered on April 26.

THE BATTALION'S TANKS CROSSED THE BRIDGE at Regensburg over the opaque brown waters of the Danube and rapidly advanced, their operations now almost entirely confined to mopping up. Early on the morning of May 2, Able Company tanks were the first to reach the Inn River—the boundary line, in their sector, between Germany and Austria. Able fired across at enemy positions on the opposite side, destroying two machine-gun nests and clearing the way for the infantry to advance over the bridge. The bridge, however, was too weak to hold the weight of the M-4 Shermans. Able's members waited impatiently in the town of Ering for two days before receiving permission to move upriver to the dam at Egelfing. The battalion's other companies were already there, anxiously waiting for the go-ahead to proceed across. If the forced move east had been the sole defining mission of their lives through some of the war's most brutal moments, then here, when they could all feel that the end was close, the men were not about to put up with being stopped: They thoroughly intended to go east as far as they possibly could. At 7:30 A.M. on May 4, Charlie Company's Shermans became the first of the 761st to start across the Inn River.

Egelfing was not the safest of bridges. The span of the tanks' tracks was wider than the road across the dam and there were no guardrails; it was a considerable drop to the river's icy waters below. Pop Gates instructed tank commanders and drivers to stay inside their vehicles and the rest to walk behind—but if Leonard Smith had come this far in a Sherman, he was determined to go all the way. Gates could only smile and shake his head, glad that Smith, though more somber and guarded than before, still had some of that willfulness and high-spiritedness Gates had always admired even when it drove him to distraction.

THE TANKS ALMOST IMMEDIATELY encountered scattered fire as they fanned out and pushed forward to support the advancing infantry. In a small woods that was most likely situated in the vicinity of Lambach and Wels, Leonard Smith's "Cool Stud" tank and William McBurney's tank accompanied a squad of infantry. The foot soldiers encountered intense fire from an enemy machine-gun position in a clearing up ahead. The infantry commander called back for the two Shermans to eliminate it. Advancing into the field, McBurney saw a long fence with an enemy team firing from a machine-gun nest beside a high gate. He called coordinates to his gunner, who took out the emplacement with a high-explosive blast.

McBurney then ordered his driver to roll forward. Knocking over the heavy gate, they entered into what seemed a kind of compound, a collection of barracks. McBurney had seen a POW camp before and assumed this must be another. No German soldiers were anywhere to be seen.

Everywhere, slowly at first and then in increasing numbers, figures emerged from the buildings. Leonard Smith's crew cautiously watched from their turret, their hatches half-closed. They didn't know what they were seeing; it took a moment to realize that these impossibly frail figures were men.

The compound they had entered was a branch of a Nazi concentration camp. The enlisted men, like most Americans at the time, had never heard the term "concentration camp." When the Red Army had liberated the vast complex at Auschwitz in its push across Poland, most Westerners had dismissed its descriptions of the camp as Russian propaganda. This error was soon corrected when the Third U.S. Army discovered its first camp at Ohrdruf, Germany—a branch camp of Buchenwald—early in April. Eisenhower toured the camp, then ordered all commanders and all noncombat units in the area, as well as all German citizens of the surrounding towns, to do the same. Eisenhower also summoned all available members of the Allied press corps to document the atrocities committed at Buchenwald, so that what could not previously have been imagined could never afterward be denied.

Hitler's campaign to eradicate the Jewish people had begun shortly after he seized full control of the German government in 1933. The first concentration camp, Dachau, had been opened that year; others soon followed. German Jews were gradually stripped of all political rights and freedoms and shipped in increasing numbers to these camps. Jewish men, women, and children, as well as political prisoners and other "undesirables," were literally worked to death. Forced to live on daily rations of watery soup and scraps of bread, they died by the thousands from malnutrition, exposure, exhaustion, and widespread disease. Random executions by SS guards were commonplace. Nazi doctors performed barbaric medical experiments on live prisoners, including children. One type of camp was reserved almost exclusively for Jews: Death camps, like those at Auschwitz and Treblinka, were not work camps but rather holding pens for mass executions. As the borders of the Reich expanded beginning in 1938 into Austria, Czechoslovakia, Poland, Hungary, France, and Russia, Jews in each new territory were either shot to death by special SS squads or shipped to the growing number of camps. Unsatisfied with the pace of the annihilation, Hitler in 1942 ordered the "Final Solution," the construction of gas chambers at the death camps that were capable of killing up to 4,000 people at once. By war's end, the Nazis had murdered six million Jews.

The camps that members of the 761st witnessed in Austria (some of the tankers and infantry had earlier freed a camp outside of Straubing, Germany) fell under the general jurisdiction of Mauthausen. The largest of the camps in the 71st Division's sector, Gunskirchen Lager, housed 15,000 inmates, mostly Hungarian Jews. The scattered camps the tankers and infantry, by twos and threes, discovered in the region were branch and work camps, not the vast concentration and extermination complexes. Although only a portion of that great evil, what the men witnessed was brutality enough to remember forever.

Smith and McBurney did not know what to do as the crowd of skeletal figures around them grew. They began to hand down their rations, unaware that this could be dangerous for people in a near-starving condition; they and the stunned foot soldiers behind them were soon admonished by officers to cease performing what had seemed acts of mercy. Several of the infantrymen were vomiting. The filth of the compound and the sheer human suffering contained within its walls—as well as the knowledge that this suffering had been deliberately, consciously, inflicted—were horrors beyond words.

Smith and McBurney had been inside the camp for only ten minutes when the two Shermans received orders from the infantry to pull out. The surrounding territory had not yet been fully secured, and the infantry captain asked McBurney's team to advance against a possible counterattack. With such compounds being discovered throughout the region and continuing pockets of resistance being encountered, the commanders didn't know what was going on and wanted the support of all available American tanks.

ON MAY 4, SHERMANS OF THE BATTALION engaged German troops in a brief firefight at Wels and supported the infantry in capturing a civilian airstrip on the eastern edge of town that had been taken over for military use. Those who had seen the camps fought with increased purpose, destroying a number of hangars and riddling several planes attempting to take off with .50-caliber machine-gun fire. After downing a Junkers transport plane, they took grim satisfaction in surveying the still-burning wreckage containing the bodies of dozens of German soldiers who'd attempted to escape.

Able Company tanks, continuing to press forward on the highway outside of Lambach, were halted by intense fire from a large enemy force in the surrounding woods. Hoping to block the American armored advance, the Germans were well-entrenched with numerous machine-gun emplacements and antitank guns. The Shermans left the highway and fanned out into the woods, unleashing a furious rain of fire on all sides.

The German troops were so overwhelmed by the rampaging tanks that survivors of the initial barrage quickly held up their hands in surrender. In the brief but heavy combat action, Able claimed two Mark IV Panzers, two machine-gun nests, four Panzerfausts, and a large number of enemy dead. Three hundred German soldiers surrendered; a thousand more had previously surrendered at Lambach. There was no hope for the Reich and no reason for any of these troops to resist any longer, though scattered groups continued until the bitter end.

THE BATTLE OF BERLIN, WHICH BEGAN with a massive Russian assault on April 16, had waged for two weeks, a house-to-house, hand-to-hand fight costing tens of thousands of lives and hundreds of thousands of casualties, including countless civilian losses. (In a futile attempt to symbolize a united people, the Nazis had not allowed the civilian population to evacuate.) On April 30, the Soviets flew the Russian flag over the German parliament at the center of the city. Hitler, in his underground bunker, dictated one last vicious statement against "international Jewry and its helpers" before marrying his mistress and, together with her, committing suicide by poison.

The last fanatical holdouts in Berlin surrendered to the Red Army on May 2. Members of the First and Ninth U.S. Armies in the northern half of Germany had encountered Russians at the Elbe River as early as April 25. Patton's Third Army had pushed across a broad front into Austria and Czechoslovakia, and Omar Bradley, concerned that Patton would ignore his designated stop-line, telephoned to repeat, "You hear me, George, goddamnit, *halt!*" Only the formalities of the German surrender remained.

On May 5, the men of the 761st received what proved to be their final order of the war: "You will advance to the Enns River and you will wait there for the Russians." They began rolling east toward the town of Steyr. The same day, Hitler's successor, Admiral Karl Doenitz, was already attempting to negotiate the terms of the German surrender. Eisenhower responded that there were to be no "terms": Nothing less than unconditional surrender would be accepted.

LATE ON THE AFTERNOON OF THE FIFTH, the Able Company platoon commanded by Teddy Weston was the first of the 761st to approach the bridge on the western bank of the Enns River at Steyr. Weston saw no one across the river in the territory assigned to the Soviets. Intrigued, he walked across the bridge, still seeing no sign of any troops. He walked back to his tank and waited. The battalion's other units slowly began pulling into Steyr.

Leonard Smith saw a curious sight when he arrived: a gradually increasing stream of German soldiers and civilians crossing the bridge toward the American lines. They were terrified, it seemed, of the advancing Russian troops. In their advance across Russia in 1941, the Germans had engaged in a brutal, organized campaign of rape, torture, and murder; many of the Russian troops, in crossing German territory, responded in kind. The 761st, positioned overlooking the river, were told to direct the frightened German soldiers back to surrender to the 71st Division. At a number of crossing points in this area alone, the 71st was to claim no fewer than 80,000 prisoners.

Looking out across the river, Smith and the others began to doubt that the Russians would ever reach them. Then, after several days in Steyr spent marshaling POWs and cleaning their equipment, they finally heard the rumble of advancing armor. A number of Russian tanks rolled to a stop on the other side of the river. Crews emerged from the tanks and started walking over the bridge toward them. Standing warily beside the American tanks, Smith had no idea what to expect, no idea how the Russians would react to this face-off with U.S. tanks and in particular with black soldiers. He became conscious of a woman's voice shouting, "America! America! America!" A heavyset Russian female tanker ran up and scooped Smith into a hug so tight that he was afraid she was going to damage his rib cage. After two thousand combat miles and 183 straight days on the front lines of France, Belgium, Luxembourg, Holland, Germany, and Austria, through almost impassable weather and terrain and the deaths of valiant close friends and comrades, the 761st Tank Battalion's war had come to an end.

11

HOME

We love, we marry, we create families

and we hope for the best.

—MARGARET CRECY, WIFE OF MAJOR WARREN CRECY

After a period of several months spent performing occupation duties near Teisendorf, Germany, the men of the 761st began making their separate journeys back to the United States. According to the Army's "points" system, their designated dates of departure varied based on how long they had served, and each soldier was to be sent back to the city from which he had enlisted years before. Preston McNeil and Leonard Smith, two of the battalion's earliest members, were among the first to leave, traveling together to arrive at Camp Kilmer, New Jersey, in time to surprise their families and friends three days before Christmas on December 22, 1945. William McBurney should have been with them but instead spent his Christmas at an Army hospital in Europe, suffering from an upset stomach brought on by his indulgence, after the deprivations of wartime, in donut after donut just out of the hot grease of a Salvation Army mess truck.

Floyd Dade, like more than a hundred other members of the battalion, chose to reenlist in Europe. Many more battalion members contemplated reenlistment, but after being advised that there was no guarantee the old unit would remain together they demurred; some were also troubled by what they perceived as arrogance and disdain toward them by new and untested white officers just rotated in from the United States. As they made their separate journeys home over the next few months and years to cities and small towns scattered throughout the country, the 761st's veterans, along with a group of over 1.2 million African American veterans of World War II, were to find themselves in many ways more at the beginning of a struggle than at the end.

ON FEBRUARY 13, 1946, a decorated young sergeant who had served for fifteen months in the Pacific Theater boarded a bus following his honorable discharge at Fort Gordon, Georgia, to travel to his North Carolina home. The bus made a rest stop in Batesburg, South Carolina. Sgt. Isaac Woodward Jr., still wearing his uniform, went in to use the "colored" rest room; when he returned, the bus driver cursed at him for taking too much time. Woodward took exception to the verbal abuse and an argument broke out, whereupon the driver called for police. On their arrival, the driver demanded that the local sheriff place Sergeant Woodward, who did not drink, under arrest for public drunkenness. Woodward denied the accusation; Sheriff Linwood L. Shull then beat Woodward with a blackjack and, at the end of the vicious attack, thrust the end of a nightstick into his eyes. The severely injured Woodward was denied medical treatment and locked in a jail cell overnight; the next day, after a sham hearing, he was found guilty of the charge of drunkenness and fined fifty dollars. He finally made his way to the Army hospital in Spartanburg, South Carolina, for treatment. Sergeant Woodward's corneas had been so badly damaged in the attack that he was left permanently blind.

Linwood Shull was later tried and acquitted by an all-white jury of federal charges of assault; as his verdict was read, the all-white South Carolina courtroom erupted in cheers. The prosecuting U.S. attorney had failed to present any witnesses other than the bus driver, and the defense attorney regularly referred to Woodward using racial epithets, though cautioned against doing so by Federal District Judge J. Waties Waring. Judge Waring was so outraged by the callous treatment of Sergeant Woodward that he would later recall the case as being crucial in the legal reasoning that led him to strike down, in 1950, school segregation in South Carolina, a case that was ultimately decided as part of the epochal *Brown v. Board of Education.*

The Isaac Woodward incident was a particularly brutal and emblematic example of the larger experience of repatriated African American soldiers: Having served the nation with distinction during the largest and most violent conflagration in human history, they returned to second-class status and with expectations that were in direct conflict with those of many of their white compatriots, who expected life in the United States—with its racial castes and customs—to go on as if the war had never happened, and who reinforced the unwillingness to change with lynchings and beatings of African American veterans throughout the South. The NAACP would use the sense of moral outrage and revulsion sparked by Woodward's case and others to enlist national politicians, including President Harry Truman, in the cause of racial justice.

THE 761ST TANK BATTALION'S VETERANS returned home without ticker-tape parades or fanfare to resume their daily lives in a country in which, in most southern and border states, they could not vote, use public facilities, sit beside whites in buses or at lunch counters, provide their children with an equal education, or find work at anything but the most menial of jobs. In the metropolitan areas of the North, their lives were circumscribed in more subtle but nonetheless enduring ways: The VHA loans, for instance, which fueled so much of the postwar economic expansion and prosperity, did nothing to help them attain homes and financial security for their families in the thousands of all-white Levittowns and other booming suburbs, as they were redlined into existing ghettos; they experienced, as well, various sorts of oblique and unstated employment discrimination. They returned to discover that what Ruben Rivers, Samuel Turley, Willie Devore, and dozens of others had given and what they themselves had endured for their country was not acknowledged or even believed. In the segregated postwar America of the 1940s and '50s, the battalion's service might as well not have happened; it meant almost nothing.

The battalion's beloved commander, Lt. Col. Paul Bates, returned to America to find himself in a period of deep confusion, haunted not only because of what he had seen in combat but even more so because "I couldn't put behind me all the contradictions I'd encountered, and how badly my men had been treated." He was also stunned to witness and learn more over time about the true dimensions of the racial divide back home. He began a long campaign to help bring his men their due.

But if their native country and countrymen had not changed and were not immediately ready to receive them, something was different: the men themselves. They knew what they had accomplished in the war as a unit and as individuals. They had worked in combat on equal footing with white troops, some of whom had come to acknowledge them, and they had performed beyond all expectations. They had succeeded in the worst of terrain and weather conditions against far superior German equipment, in vehicles that were essentially mobile death traps. They had stood up for one another in the face of extraordinary losses, and had kept going back and continuing to stand up for 183 straight days. In England, France, Holland, Austria, and Germany, they had experienced at first hand—and, for most of them, for the first time—a larger, unsegregated world, a world in which they were viewed by civilians directly and simply as human beings, not categorized by the color of their skin.

They came back to the United States with a different sense of life's possibilities, and they expected more from their countrymen and from themselves. In cities and small towns throughout the country, others of the 1.2 million African American veterans of World War II expected the same—and over the next ten years, veterans like Medgar Evers, sacrificing their jobs, their lives, putting their families at risk, would demand a share of the American Dream for themselves and their children. Their war experiences and heightened expectations were in many ways the spark that ignited a revolution in the way Americans lived and understood their society: Their questioning of whether the first fully democratic nation on paper would fulfill its promise, their questioning of the real meaning of the Declaration of Independence and the United States Constitution, developed into the American civil rights movement.

Though there were no well-known civil rights leaders among the veterans of the 761st, their numerous accomplishments had been important in paving the way for the integration of the military—a landmark step toward true equality that was firmly established as policy (though it would take several years to implement fully) by Executive Order 9981, signed on July 26, 1948, by President Truman, which stated, "It is hereby declared to be the policy of the President that there shall be equality of treatment and opportunity for all persons in the armed forces without regard to race, color, religion, or national origin." And as the 761st's veterans returned to their home cities and towns and gradually began to put their lives together, to start careers, to marry, to raise children, they were to lead in countless other quiet but nonetheless significant ways.

Capt. Charles "Pop" Gates thought he had seen enough of the military—more specifically, of the racial prejudice he and his men had encountered in the service both at home and overseas—and fully intended to leave it. He began studying veterinary medicine at the Tuskegee Institute in Alabama, but chose to return to his native Kansas City, Missouri, before completing his degree in order to care for his ailing mother. He took a job at the local post office. In 1949, he received a call asking whether he would be willing to run the 242nd Engineer Battalion, a newly created African American Missouri National Guard unit. Gates was about to refuse the offer when he heard a Missouri congressman comment that blacks were incapable of running a military outfit. To prove the congressman wrong, he accepted the post, intending to serve for just one year. He eventually rose to the rank of lieutenant colonel, leading hundreds of black troops in what became one of the most distinguished units in the Fifth Army area until his retirement in 1964. At Camp Clark, Missouri, three streets were named after outstanding National Guardsmen: one after President (and former Missouri Senator) Harry Truman, one after a general from Cape Girardeau, and one after Charles Gates.

Floyd Dade, in charge of battalion equipment in Europe after the war ended, supervised as the battle-scarred M-4 General Sherman tanks were driven up on flatcars and taken to the equipment depot to be cut up for scrap: The battalion, filling up with replacements, trained now on the better-armed and better-armored M-26 Pershing tanks. Upon his return to the States and honorable discharge from the military in 1947, Dade completed his education at City College of San Francisco and Elkhart University, working for ten years as a dental technician and then becoming supervisor of school custodians in the San Francisco Unified School District until his retirement in 1986. Twice married—to his second wife for more than thirty-five years—Dade raised three daughters and three sons, and he has been an extremely active presence in community, church, and veterans' affairs.

Christopher Navarre, the Army ambulance worker who gave up his rank to join the 761st, was branded as a troublemaker by whites in his Louisiana hometown when he attempted to register to vote and encouraged others to do the same; the decorated veteran subsequently decided to return to the military, serving with distinction in Korea, rising to the rank of sergeant major, and later serving as a warrant officer.

Able Company's S. Sgt. Johnnie Stevens left the military to return to his native Georgia, working as a cook at the only job he could find there before deciding to migrate north to New Jersey. He began working for the New Jersey Transit Authority as a long-distance bus driver in 1947, one of the first African Americans to hold such a position, and became actively involved in mentoring local youth.

Capt. David J. Williams returned to the States to complete the education he had deferred in order to enter the military, earning his degree from Yale in 1947. He married and raised three sons, working as a stockbroker with E. F. Hutton & Co. His true work and passion, however, was writing about his experiences with the 761st so that the sacrifices of the men would not be forgotten. His tireless campaigning to this end would be instrumental in the battalion's fight for recognition.

Lt. Col. Paul L. Bates remained in the military after the war, working among other assignments at the Pentagon and at an officers' college at Fort Leavenworth. Bates was helped in his readjustment to life back in the States following World War II by his longtime girlfriend, the "Taffy" after whom his storied tank had been named. He married Taffy and raised two sons. He remained beloved by and in constant touch with the veterans of the 761st until his death in 1995 at the age of eighty-six. Bates and his family established a scholarship at Bates's alma mater, Western Maryland College, for descendants of members of the 761st.

WARREN CRECY, UNIVERSALLY REVERED by the battalion as the most courageous of its soldiers, their "Iron Man," received a battlefield commission from sergeant to the rank of 2nd lieutenant in May 1945. Crecy volunteered to remain in Europe and did so for five years, serving at one point as a prison officer during the Nuremberg trials. In 1950, he returned to the States to serve in the slowly desegregating army as the commander of an all-white unit at Fort Benning, Georgia. When the Korean War began, he received orders to once again serve in combat duty.

In October 1952, Crecy was injured by a mortar blast as he was dismounting his tank under fire to aid a disabled tank in his unit. The mortar shattered his eardrums and severed his lower jaw. His internal injuries were so extensive that he was not expected to live. On regaining consciousness, however, Crecy's first concern was the status of his men: He had to be physically restrained from crawling through hostile fire to find them.

Crecy was transferred to a military hospital in San Francisco. He had a permanent tracheotomy, and a plastic block was surgically inserted to replace his jaw. In his long, difficult recovery, Crecy exhibited a valor beside which even his battlefield actions paled, visiting other patients left with permanent disabilities and disfigurement to encourage them in their struggles. He became the officer in charge of the hospital's supply store, receiving a commendation for hiring and striving to help other recovering patients. He returned briefly to limited active duty at the Presidio. His injuries caused him severe pain for the remainder of his life. He hoped more than anything to recover fully enough to be able to return to a tank battalion, and was heartbroken in 1965 when, as a major, he was ordered to retire with full disability.

Crecy did not attend the yearly reunions of the 761st Tank Battalion because, he said, he didn't want his fellow tankers to feel pity for him. But in the years following his return from Korea, he would sit for hours reading the battalion's unofficial history, *Come Out Fighting*, reminiscing about his fallen comrades and the accomplishments of the unit in Europe. Crecy's son, Warren G. H. Crecy Jr., graduated from West Point in 1976, and later that year Crecy finally attended his first reunion of the 761st. On October 26, 1976, he died of the ongoing complications from his war wounds. Crecy was buried with full military honors in Arlington National Cemetery.

WHEN HE RETURNED TO NEW YORK CITY in the winter of 1945, Leonard Smith was twenty-one years old. He was at a loss as to what to do with the rest of his life. He had no skills other than those he had learned in the military, and "tank gunner" was not a profession immediately translatable to the civilian world. But he had learned one invaluable skill in the service, largely through his relationship with Pop Gates—that of listening to his elders—and when an old man from his neighborhood suggested he go into the civil service, Smith took his advice, beginning by cleaning up subway cars, then working for the sanitation department, then driving a city bus. Figuring he had nothing to lose, he eventually took the exam to join the police force and was accepted by the New York City transit police, a position he would hold until his retirement.

Preston McNeil worked for a number of years at a company in the city that made wrought-iron furniture, before trying, like his friend Smith, to join the police force. He passed his test, but the distinguished veteran was disqualified, in a quirk of history, because the labor union for the furniture company where he was employed had been designated in those Cold War years as a "communist" organization. He appealed and was eventually cleared of these charges, but still he was not put on the list for a job; the New York City police force of that time, the 1940s and 1950s, was an almost exclusively white organization and Smith's hiring by the transit police had been the exception rather than the rule. McNeil began working instead at the post office.

William McBurney went to mechanical drafting school and was awarded his degree—but found that despite his qualifications, among them a Bronze Star for valor, no one would hire him. Like McNeil, he took the test to join the police force but was not put on the list. He had married and started a family; there was nothing to do but look for another job. He took an entry-level job at a plastics factory in the Bronx.

AS THEY RETURNED TO BEGIN their lives as civilians, Smith, McBurney, McNeil, and most of the battalion's other members talked less and less to people outside the unit about what they had seen and done during the war. Smith found that even people he'd considered close friends often didn't believe him. The men were confronted with the commonly held notion that not one black had fought—let alone fought in the famed Sherman tanks—during World War II.

The service roles that the majority of African American soldiers performed in the war were crucial to the Allied victory—including maintenance, engineer, and ambulance duties, as well as the construction of the Alaska Highway through Canada and the Lido Road in Burma. But tens of thousands of African Americans did, in fact, see combat. Twenty-two African American units fought in the European Theater of Operations, including nine field artillery battalions, an antiaircraft battalion, eight combat engineer battalions, and the 761st and 784th Tank Battalions (the 784th entered battle near Eshweiler, Germany, in January 1945). African American combat units in Italy included the 92nd Infantry Division and the 758th Light Tank Battalion; in the Pacific, they included elements of the 93rd Infantry Division, two coast artillery battalions, and an antiaircraft barrage balloon battalion. When the replacement situation in Europe grew dire in 1945, thousands of African Americans—many more than the 2,500 requested—volunteered to take up rifles beside white infantrymen.

Part of the reason the men of the 761st remained invisible to history concerned the type of unit to which they belonged: The separate tank battalions, phased out after the war in favor of the combined-arms infantry division of the present day, were officially considered a part of whatever division they were attached to at the time and were not mentioned by name in most history books. Whether black or white, none of the separate battalions has truly been given the recognition it deserves for its efforts.

The 761st suffered additionally from being an African American unit. Capt. David Williams, Capt. Charles Gates, Capt. John Long, Capt. Ivan Harrison, and Lt. Col. Paul Bates all believed that race was at times a factor in the underreporting of the accomplishments of their battalion. The Army of that time, and particularly the officer corps, was heavily populated with white Southerners, and there is reason to believe that many lost records, valor citations, and petitions for commendations were deliberately misplaced or destroyed. Like the Ancient Mariner of Coleridge's poem, the battalion's members found themselves with an anguished tale they urgently wanted to tell but with no one to listen to or believe them.

THE 761ST BEGAN WHAT WOULD become an arduous fight for official recognition in June 1945, when Capt. Ivan Harrison submitted a request that the unit be considered for a Presidential Unit Citation, also known as the Distinguished Unit Citation. The paperwork for this request included a four-page narration of the unit's combat actions from October 31, 1944, to May 6, 1945; a damage report listing, among other statistics, its documented 331 enemy MG nests, 58 pillboxes, and

461 wheeled vehicles destroyed or captured, 6,246 enemy killed, and 15,818 captured (with a note explaining that these totals were low, as they did not fully reflect those achieved in combined operations with infantry); the 71 battalion tanks destroyed by the enemy; the 3 officers and 31 enlisted men killed in action; and the 296 Purple Hearts awarded to its members (8 with clusters), 8 battlefield commissions, 8 Silver Stars, and 62 Bronze Stars (three with clusters). These latter totals would later be revised to 11 Silver Stars and 70 Bronze Stars.

Also included with Harrison's submission were letters of commendation for outstanding achievement from XII Corps commander Maj. Gen. Manton S. Eddy; 26th Infantry Division commander Maj. Gen. Willard S. Paul; 103rd Infantry Division commander Maj. Gen. Anthony C. McAuliffe; and 71st Infantry Division commander Maj. Gen. Willard G. Wyman; as well as mention of the high verbal praise received from the 17th Airborne's Maj. Gen. William Miley.

The 761st Tank Battalion's request was denied on August 18, 1945, by Third Army Headquarters, with a statement reading, in part: "1. Not favorably considered. 2. After a careful study of the 761st Tank Battalion described in basic communication, it is considered that the action, while commendable, was not sufficiently outstanding to meet the requirements for a unit citation. . . ." General Eisenhower's office, following the Third Army's evaluation, formally denied the request on February 12, 1946.

THE THIRD ARMY COMMANDER HIMSELF had been quoted in *Stars and Stripes* as saying that "the Negro tank battalion attached to my command fought bravely in the critical Battle of Bastogne" and that its soldiers were "damn good soldiers"—but there were nowhere to be found any other indications that George Patton had changed his opinions about the capabilites of African Americans in battle. Patton, who died from injuries sustained in an automobile accident in Germany in

December 1945, remains a complex, enigmatic figure with as many if not more tragic flaws than strengths. But though the members of the 761st scanned his biographies in the years that followed, finding only negative, if any, references to African Americans, most were aware that it was on Patton's request that they had first been given the opportunity they had hoped and trained for—the opportunity to fight: Their story remains a part of his, and his of theirs. Patton was, along with Douglas MacArthur, the only Allied general whom the Germans truly feared, and most members of the battalion remain proud to have served in his army.

FOLLOWING THE REJECTION of their submission for a Presidential Unit Citation, veterans of the battalion submitted repeated requests over the years for this decision to be reviewed, arguing that the case had not been given just and fair consideration. All such requests were denied. Congressman Frank Annunzio from Illinois had become a champion of the battalion's cause when the matter was brought to his attention by a member of his district. In 1977, Annunzio discussed the battalion with Congressman John Conyers of Michigan, and Conyers sent a letter detailing the 761st's ongoing fight to the Secretary of the Army, Clifford Alexander. Alexander decided to reopen the case. Army researchers assigned to review the case noted that "there are clear indications that racial discrimination and inadvertent neglect on the part of those in authority, at the time the recommendations were originally considered, may have been a factor in the disapprovals" and "that the climate created by the Army commanders could only have made it difficult to provide proper recognition for a 'Negro' unit during the period 1944–1947. . . ."

The initial evidence was reexamined, along with substantial information gathered during seven months of intensive research through the National Archives, the Army Library, the Library of Congress, the Office of the Chief of Military History, and the Eisenhower

Library. On January 24, 1978, thirty-three years after the conclusion of the war in Europe, President Jimmy Carter signed the orders and awarded the 761st Tank Battalion the Presidential Unit Citation for Extraordinary Heroism.

THE END OF THIS STRUGGLE for recognition marked the beginning of another fight, led primarily by Able Company's Capt. David Williams. On November 23, 1944, four days after the fierce battle for Guebling and Bourgaltroff, France, Williams had handed paperwork to the battalion's acting commander, Lt. Col. Hollis Hunt, recommending S. Sgt. Ruben Rivers for a posthumous Medal of Honor. Hunt seemed indifferent, at best, to his request. Able Company's clerk later swore, in an affidavit supporting Williams's assertion, that he had indeed processed this recommendation. The paperwork, however, was either lost or destroyed at some point after this—no record of it exists in Army archives.

In 1978, Captain Williams, who was greatly encouraged by the awarding of the Presidential Unit Citation, began in earnest another fight—tirelessly lobbying congressmen and the Army for Rivers to be considered for the Medal of Honor. Four hundred and thirty-three Medals of Honor had been awarded to soldiers in World War II, but none of the 1.2 million African Americans who served had yet received the honor.

In 1993, the Pentagon established a committee of military historians, based at Shaw University, to comb military records and determine whether recommendations for African American soldiers in World War II to receive the Medal of Honor had been justly and properly considered. Members of the 761st submitted the names of Ruben Rivers, Samuel Turley, and Warren Crecy to this committee and testified to their heroism.

In 1996, the Shaw University team forwarded the names of nine

African American soldiers to Congress and the President to be considered for the Medal of Honor despite the Army's 1952 cutoff date for World War II honors; seven were eventually accepted. Rivers's name, owing largely to the efforts of Williams and author Joe W. Wilson Jr. to make his story known, was included in that list. Rivers's "lost" paperwork was not uncommon; of those seven, four had had paperwork, like Rivers's, submitted that also disappeared. Though no direct proof of overt racism could be discovered in any of these cases, there was, as the report indicated, a climate that encouraged such omissions.

On January 13, 1997, at a White House ceremony, seven African American soldiers were awarded the Congressional Medal of Honor by President Bill Clinton. Two of these men, 1st Lt. John R. Fox and 1st Lt. Vernon J. Baker (the only soldier still alive and able to receive his medal in person), had served with the 92nd Infantry Division in Italy. The 92nd Infantry was poorly trained and poorly led by white southerners, most of whom were openly contemptuous of their men; the black troops received a grossly unjust yet enduring reputation for cowardice under fire. Throughout its tenure in combat, beginning in the summer of 1944, the 92nd was assigned to cover areas far beyond the frontage ordinarily given an infantry division.

On Christmas Day 1944, 1st Lt. John R. Fox, with Cannon Company of the 366th Infantry Regiment, volunteered to act as a forward artillery observer in the town of Sommocolonia, located in Italy's Serchio Valley. Fox's unit was stretched impossibly thin, with a 1,000-man battalion assigned to a thirty-mile front. The Germans and Italian partisans were easily able to infiltrate the line. At 4 A.M. on December 26, a heavy German artillery barrage announced the beginning of a German assault. The greatly outnumbered infantry were forced to withdraw from Sommocolonia, but Fox and several others volunteered to remain behind in the house where they had set up their observation post. By 8 A.M., German soldiers were visible throughout the streets. Fox called on his radio for the 598th Field

Artillery Battalion to fire on the German positions. At 11 A.M., Fox placed a second call—received by a friend of his, the 598th Artillery's Lt. Otis Zachary. Fox's post was about to be overrun completely. Fox called for the artillery's 105mm howitzers to fire directly on his own coordinates. Zachary refused to give this order, turning to the battalion's commanding colonel. The colonel radioed Fox for details; Fox responded, "There are hundreds of them coming. Put everything you've got on my OP!" The shaken colonel called to division headquarters for approval and received it. Zachary had no choice but to give the order for four of the artillery battalion's heavy guns to "converge, sheath"—walking their fire steadily forward until all came together simultaneously on Fox's position. When a counterattack later reclaimed Sommocolonia, Fox's shattered body was discovered surrounded by the bodies of a hundred German soldiers. Lieutenant John R. Fox was recommended at the time for a Distinguished Service Cross, but the paperwork was lost for almost forty years.

Early in 1945, the men of the beleaguered 92nd Division received what were essentially suicide orders to attack German positions frontally along a mountainous region made still more difficult by the man-made fortifications of Gen. Albert Kesselring's "Gothic Line." Some units (as had assorted white troops in Europe) broke up under the intense fire; many more fought on. First Lt. Vernon Baker commanded a platoon of Company C with the 370th Infantry Regiment. On April 5, 1945, Baker, who had recently recovered from a previous combat wound, was ordered to lead his twenty-five-man team in an assault on Castle Aghinolfi, a mountain stronghold located near the town of Viareggio. Baker led his platoon forward through concentrated fire from several machine-gun emplacements. Spotting the slit of a German bunker in the hillside, Baker crawled ahead to empty his rifle into the hole; then he took out a nearby machine gun nest; then he blasted open another dugout with a grenade, running inside and killing the stunned German occupants with a submachine gun he had pulled off a dead soldier. Baker's commander, a white captain, had apparently seen enough action and told Baker he was heading back to the rear to gather "reinforcements. " Baker and his platoon fought on, waiting in vain for these nonexistent reinforcements. Of Baker's original platoon of twenty-five men, all but six were killed.

The third of the African American soldiers to be awarded the Medal of Honor by President Clinton, Pvt. George Watson, served in the Navy with the 29th Quartermaster Regiment. On March 8, 1943, near Porloch Harbor, New Guinea, Watson's ship was heavily damaged by Japanese bombers. In the confusion of the mass evacuation, life rafts quickly became separated from the ship. Watson chose to remain in the water, pulling other soldiers who could not swim to the rafts. Watson continued these lifesaving efforts for an extended period of time, eventually becoming so exhausted that he could not himself reach the boats. He was dragged down by the undercurrent created by the sinking ship. His body was never recovered.

The fourth African American to receive the Medal of Honor for his service in World War II, Pfc. Willy F. James Jr., fought with the 413th Regiment of the 104th Infantry Division. The 104th was originally created as an all-white unit; in December of 1944, however, the shortage of replacements in the American Army was so acute that a call was put out to black service units for volunteers, and Willy James was among those who signed on. On April 7, 1945, as part of the First U.S. Army's efforts to clear Germany's Ruhr Pocket, James's unit was ordered to secure a vital crossing over the Weser River. James acted as lead scout for his platoon, moving forward to draw enemy fire near the town of Lippoldsberg. James was pinned down by the intense barrage for more than an hour; he then returned to his platoon through the ongoing fire to report extensively on the entrenched German positions. In the platoon's following assault, James volunteered to walk point. When his platoon leader was mortally wounded, James ran to his aid and was himself struck and killed by enemy fire.

S. Sgt. Edward A. Carter Jr. was also a replacement; Carter had originally been assigned to a supply unit in Europe, but voluntarily gave up his rank to serve as a private with an infantry unit attached to the 12th Armored Division. On March 23, 1945, near Speyer, Germany, Carter was riding on a tank along with several other infantry-men. The tank came under heavy bazooka and small-arms fire from a nearby warehouse. Carter volunteered to lead a team on foot across an open field to eliminate the German positions. Two members of Carter's four-man team were killed in this assault, and one was wounded. Carter himself was hit five times and forced to take cover. Eight enemy riflemen advanced on Carter's position, hoping either to capture him or to ascertain that he was dead. Carter killed six of the Germans and captured the other two. Then he crossed the exposed field back to the American line, using the two prisoners as a human shield; these prisoners were interrogated, yielding vital information on enemy positions.

The sixth Medal of Honor recipient, 1st Lt. Charles L. Thomas, served with the 614th Tank Destroyer Battalion, an African American battalion, like the 761st, that trained at Fort Hood and was first com-mitted to combat in France in November 1944. On December 14, 1944, Thomas volunteered to lead a tank destroyer platoon in an assault on the town of Climbach, five miles from the German border. Thomas's 250-man company would act as a decoy, making a frontal assault up a hill, drawing the brunt of the German fire while American infantry sneaked through the woods and entered the town. Thomas's armored scout car, riding point, was almost immediately hit by tank and artillery fire; the window shattered, spraying Thomas with glass and metal shards and rupturing the vehicle's tires. Thomas nonetheless jumped on top of the disabled vehicle and manned the .50-caliber machine gun. Hit numerous times in his chest, legs, and left arm, Thomas was eventually forced to take cover beneath his vehicle—but continued to direct the team, refusing to be evacuated until he was sure his men were well-placed. Thomas's unit, which suffered 50 percent casualties in the assault, succeeded in making possible the capture of Climbach.

The final recipient of the Medal of Honor was the 761st Tank Battalion's S. Sgt. Ruben Rivers. Rivers's medal citation, granted fifty-two years after the date of his death, read: "For extraordinary heroism in action during 15–19 November 1944, toward Guebling, France. Though severely wounded in the leg, Sergeant Rivers refused medical treatment and evacuation, took command of another tank, and advanced with his company in Guebling the next day. Repeatedly refusing evacuation, Sergeant Rivers continued to direct his tank's fire at enemy positions through the morning of 19 November 1944. At dawn, Company A's tanks began to advance towards Bougaktroff [*sic*], but were stopped by enemy fire. Sergeant Rivers, joined by another tank, opened fire on the enemy tanks, covering Company A as they withdrew. While doing so, Sergeant Rivers' tank was hit, killing him and wounding the crew. Staff Sergeant Rivers' fighting spirit and daring leadership were an inspiration to his unit and exemplify the highest traditions of military service."

Rivers's nephew, George Livingston, and Rivers' sisters, Grace Rivers Woodfork and Anese Rivers Woodfork—the last of his siblings to wave good-bye as his train left the Holtulka, Oklahoma, station—were present at the White House ceremony.

SOME OF THE MOST PERSONALLY painful memories of wartime for members of the 761st had occurred before they ever left the States—in their training at Camp Claiborne, Louisiana, and Camp Hood (now Fort Hood), Texas, in the deep hostility they faced from the civilian population and other soldiers there. Leonard Smith, along with many others of the battalion, had vowed that he would never return to either location. But in 1993, fifty years after the unit's departure from

Camp Hood, a local woman named Beverly Taylor who had learned of the unit's struggles there and in Europe began lobbying the post commander for a monument to the 761st. She had searched Fort Hood's military museums, finding no mention of the battalion.

In 1993, a temporary monument was dedicated on the site near the main gate, where, in 1996, ground was broken for a permanent monument to the unit. On October 16, 1994, Fort Hood's Headquarters Avenue was redesignated 761st Tank Battalion Avenue. On June 30, 1995, the main processing center at the post was named in honor of Ruben Rivers.

The mayor of Killeen, Texas, retired colonel Raul Villaranga, had learned of the 761st's history and invited the unit back for a reunion. The general membership of the battalion voted to accept this invitation for a reunion in August 1996. Many of the battalion's members, who were understandably still anguished over their eleven months of gross mistreatment there when they wore the uniform of their country, did not attend. Those who did, Leonard Smith among them, were moved by the great efforts on the part of the mayor and civilians of the city to acknowledge what they had endured. One of the city's main streets was renamed "761st Tank Battalion Boulevard," and they were given the key to the city. Smith had chosen to go back with no small measure of trepidation. But local residents whom Smith had never met came up to him as he walked down the street, introducing themselves and telling him that their grandparents or parents had lived in all-white Killeen at the time, and that they were sorry for what he'd faced.

SMITH AND MANY OTHERS in the battalion had for years carried memories of what they witnessed at the concentration camps in Germany and Austria in the final days of the war. Battalion members have visited Jewish organizations and school groups throughout the country to share these memories and to testify to the horrors they saw. Smith and other liberators were honored at the Simon Weisenthal Foundation in California, and Smith participated in the Holocaust Documentation and Education Center's oral history project; a copy of his interview is currently housed at the United States Holocaust Memorial Museum in Washington, D.C. Smith still counts the small role his unit was able to play in the liberation of the camps as among the proudest of its actions.

FOLLOWING THE END OF WORLD WAR II, the 761st Tank Battalion continued its occupation and training duties until it was deactivated in Germany in 1947. The battalion was reactivated at Fort Knox, Kentucky, as a training unit, and was permanently deactivated on March 15, 1955. As many of its members have passed away, part of the great wave of approximately 1,000 World War II veterans who die each day, their reunions grow ever smaller. At its peak in the 1960s, more than four hundred veterans of the battalion attended the yearly gatherings; in the last few years, the number has dwindled to around thirty.

THROUGH THE LONG YEARS of the absence of any public or official recognition for their battalion, one source of acknowledgment deeply meaningful to many veterans of the 761st has been their recognition by veterans of some of the units with which they served. Battalion members continue to receive the division newsletters of the 26th Infantry and 17th Airborne Divisions, among others. They felt a particularly close bond to the 26th, the first unit beside which they fought. More than fifty years after the war, when Floyd Dade visited France with his wife, this close bond was evidenced by an extraordinary, uncanny encounter with Oscar Jensen, a member of the 26th Division's 101st Infantry Regiment.

Jensen described this meeting: "In August 1995, I had the pleasure of making a trip to the ETO with my son and son-in-law. . . . Our tour began by first visiting the Normandy Beaches and then traveling east along the path of the YD [26th Yankee Division]. . . . While viewing the church at Ste. Mere Eglise where the paratrooper mannequin still hangs from the spire, we met an African American gentleman and his wife. After a brief conversation we found that we had both landed nearby . . . and then discovered we had both joined the battle in the Lorraine area. He had been a tanker with the 761st Tank Battalion. I expressed my surprise, as they had supported the YD in that region. I mentioned that I had brought a photo from the November 27, 1944 'Stars and Stripes' taken during the battle for Guebling."

This photograph was of "two tanks, one knocked out and being used by the other as a shield." The picture had been taken on the eastern side of Guebling on November 18. The knocked-out tank belonged to the 4th Armored Division; the second vehicle, which was positioned to guard the crossroads at the edge of town overlooking Bourgaltroff, belonged to the 761st. It was in fact Floyd Dade's tank. Jensen continues, "I had ducked under that tank's gun to enter the adjacent barn. This man of our chanced meeting was the fellow with his head sticking out of the hatch of that tank! He also had that photo with him and also planned to visit that same spot! We were both dumfounded! This after 51 years!!!!"

WILLIAM MCBURNEY REMAINED in plastics for thirty-five years, becoming a foreman and eventually rising to the position of plant manager of a factory in New Jersey. Preston McNeil continued working at the post office until his retirement. McNeil and his wife of many years raised a family of their own and then, though they had little money to spare, the deeply religious couple adopted five children, all siblings, so that they could remain together.

Leonard Smith worked for more than twenty-five years for the

New York City transit police before retiring. He was married several times. Over the years, he found that he thought more and not less about his time with the 761st. He thought often about his best friend, Willie Devore. He had called Willie's family shortly after the war ended—but found that it would have been too painful for them to hear the details of their son's death. Devore is still buried overseas, and Smith has made a number of trips to Europe to visit his grave in the American military cemetery in Luxembourg.

During a visit nearly fifty years later to the memory-filled region around Tillet, Belgium, Smith came across a surprising and startling memorial. In the middle of a town square in Bastogne, a lone Sherman tank with a hole in its side from an antitank gun stands as a monument to the sacrifices of American soldiers in the fierce combat that took place there during the Battle of the Bulge. Smith has described the inital sighting of the tank as one of the most significant moments of his life.

He has remained one of the battalion association's most active members. The foster child from Queens who first volunteered for the military because he was looking for high adventure, and learned through the grim realities of combat the emptiness of such hopes, had found something else instead. It would take him years to realize what had happened to him, what he had been too young in 1945 to voice or even begin to understand: In the heat of Louisiana and Texas and in the endless dark fields and snow-covered woods of bitter-cold France, Belgium, and Germany, beside a ragged, often bewildered, and yet determined group of young men who somehow managed to wake every morning under the worst of circumstances and keep pushing forward no matter what they experienced from the enemy or what was said about them by their allies, and who never let each other down, he had found his home.

Endnotes

Chapter One: Volunteers

20 "The colored man only waits . . ." William S. McFeely, *Frederick Douglass*, W. W. Norton, New York, 1991, p. 218.

25 "You got to have a mean coon . . ." David J. Williams, *Hit Hard*, Bantam Books, New York, 1983, p. 18.

27 "Bullying, abuse and physical violence . . ." Judge Hastie, as quoted in Lou Potter with William Miles and Nina Rosenblum, *Liberators: Fighting on Two Fronts in World War II*, Harcourt Brace Jovanovich, New York, 1992, pp. 71–73.

Chapter Two: Soldiers

35 "Wars may be fought . . ." George S. Patton, quoted in Carlo D'Este, *Patton: A Genius for War*, HarperCollins, New York, 1995, p. 607.

37 "The tank is a special, technical . . ." Patton, "Comments on Cavalry Tanks," *Cavalry Journal,* Vol. 30, July 1921, quoted in *Patton,* D'Este, p. 299.

37 "exactly right . . ." Stephen Ambrose, *Eisenhower,* Vol. 1, pp. 71–72, quoted in *Patton,* D'Este, p. 299.

47 "You know what . . ." Paul L. Bates, speech given at the Fort Hood 761st Tank Battalion Monument Banquet, February 11, 1994, quoted in Joe W. Wilson Jr., *The 761st "Black Panther" Tank Battalion in World War II,* McFarland & Company, Jefferson, NC, 1999, p. 33.

47 "I'm going to come out fighting!" Ivan H. Harrison, interview with Joe W. Wilson Jr., conducted August 23, 1996, quoted in *The 761st "Black Panther" Tank Battalion,* Wilson, p. 38.

51 "Robinson, I want to commend you . . ." Jackie Robinson, "Jackie Tells Own Story," *Washington Post,* August 23, 1949, quoted in *The 761st "Black Panther" Tank Battalion,* Wilson, p. 39.

51 "Robinson, I don't care how . . ." Ibid.

52 "one of the most serious problems . . ." Gibson, quoted in *Liberators,* Potter, pp. 119–20.

52 "All the reports coming up to Washington . . ." Trezzvant W. Anderson, *Come Out Fighting: The Epic Tale of the 761st Tank Battalion 1942–45,* The Advocate Press, New Haven, CT, 1979, p. 15.

54 "arthritis, chronic, nonsuppurative . . ." Arnold Rampersad, *Jackie Robinson: A Biography,* Alfred A. Knopf, New York, 1997, p. 98.

54 "physically disqualified for general military . . ." Ibid.

55 "go on and drive the bus . . ." Virginia Jones, Deposition, July 19, 1944, quoted in *The Liberators,* Potter, p. 126.

55 "Will you move to the back?" Ibid.

56 "There's the nigger that's been . . ." Jackie Robinson as told to Alfred Duckett, *I Never Had It Made,* G. P. Putnam's Sons, New York, 1972, p. 31.

56 "Quit fucking with me." Robinson, as quoted in Jules Tygiel, "The Court-Martial of Jackie Robinson," *American Heritage,* August/September 1984, pp. 34–39. Reprinted in *The 761st Tank Battalion & Allied Veterans Association of World War II, Celebrating their 37th Annual Reunion,* August 28–September 1, 1985.

56 "They were enlisted men . . ." *I Never Had It Made,* Robinson, p. 31.

56 "nigger lieutenant" Tygiel, "The Court-Martial of Jackie Robinson."

56 "did not seem to recognize me . . ." *Jackie Robinson,* Rampersad, p. 103.

56 "in an effort to try to be . . ." Ibid.

56 "disrespectful and impertinent . . ." Ibid.

57 "Don't you know you've got no right . . ." *I Never Had It Made*, Robinson, 31.

57 "uppity nigger" Ibid., p. 32.

57 "arrest in quarters" *Jackie Robinson*, Rampersad, p. 104.

57 "that he had been alerted . . ." *I Never Had It Made,* Robinson, p. 32.

59 "at ease" *Jackie Robinson,* Rampersad, p. 107.

59 "if he had ever called Jackie Robinson . . ." Paul Bates, speech at Fort Hood Monument Banquet, quoted in *The 761st "Black Panther" Tank Battalion*, Wilson, p. 43.

60 "Whosoever shall relieve . . ." Articles of War, United States Statutes at Large 2 (1789–1848) pp. 359–372, Ninth Congress, first session, Chapter 20, quoted at freepages.military.rootsweb.com.

Chapter Three: ETO

67 Infantrymen who were pulled off . . . Belton Y. Cooper, 3rd Armored Division, interviewed in Rob Lihani, *Suicide Missions: Tank Crews,* A&E Television Networks: The History Channel, 2000.

69 "the German Army was no longer a factor . . ." Quoted from Liddell Hart, "Notes for History: Talk with Jim Rose," October 28, 1944, quoted in Stanley P. Hirshson, *General Patton: A Soldier's Life,* HarperCollins, New York, 2002, p. 513.

70 "how little the enemy can do . . . " George S. Patton Jr., to Beatrice Ayer Patton, APO 403 New York, August 8, 1944, Patton Papers, quoted in *General Patton*, Hirshson, p. 512.

70 "we can be in Germany . . ." Patton Diary, August 21, 1944; Patton to Beatrice Ayer Patton, APO 403 New York, Aug. 21, 1944, quoted in *General Patton*, Hirshson, p. 525.

70 "a great general" Colonel Robert S. Allen, *Lucky Forward: The History of Patton's Third U.S. Army,* The Vanguard Press, New York, 1947, p. 24.

71 "As far as I can remember . . ." Patton Diary, January 26, 1944, quoted in *Patton*, D'Este, p. 568.

71 "But it only goes as far east . . ." Oscar Koch, *G2: Intelligence for Patton*, Army Times/Whitmore, Philadelphia, 1971, p. 61, quoted in *Patton*, D'Este, p. 577.

72 "What in the world . . ." *Hit Hard*, Williams, p. 125.

73 "This is a rather hard thing for me . . ." Quoted in *Liberators*, Potter, p. 148.

75 "Each, in his appropriate sphere . . ." Quoted in *The 761st "Black Panther" Tank Battalion*, Wilson, p. 49.

75 "a living nightmare of bloody hell" *Come Out Fighting*, Anderson, p. 29.

76 "just like a barroom fight . . ." Transcript of George S. Patton Jr., Press Conference, Sept. 7, 1944, Patton Papers, Library of Congress, quoted in *Patton,* Hirshson, p. 531.

Chapter Four: Blood Brothers

79 "Men are true comrades . . ." J. Glenn Gray, *The Warriors: Reflections on Men in Battle*, Harper & Row, New York, 1959, p. 46, quoted in Stephen E. Ambrose, *Band of Brothers,* Simon & Schuster, New York, 1992, p. 22.

80 The majority of those . . . Belton Y. Cooper, *Death Traps: The Survival of an American Armored Division in World War II,* Presidio Press, Novato, CA, 1998, p. 8.

85 "make real history" *Lucky Forward*, Allen, p. 163.

87 "Men, you are the first Negro tankers . . ." Mary Penick Motley, ed., *The Invisible Soldier: The Experience of the Black Soldier, World War II,* Wayne State University Press, Detroit, 1987, p. 152.

87 "gave a very good first impression . . ." Martin Blumenson, *The Patton Papers, Volume II,* U.S. Army Military History Institute, Carlisle Barracks, PA., 1945, p. 567, quoted in *The 761st "Black Panther" Tank Battalion,* Wilson, p. 53.

93 "it took some doing . . ." Patton to Beatrice Ayer Patton, APO 403 New York, Nov. 8, 1944, Patton Papers, quoted in *General Patton*, Hirshson, p. 554.

93 "I think this has been the longest day . . ." *Patton,* D'Este, p. 668.

93 "Don't take council . . ." Patton Diary, Nov. 8, 1944, quoted in *General Patton*, Hirshson, p. 554.

93 "like the constant slamming of heavy doors" Ibid., p. 555.

102 Lewis never forgot it. Walter Lewis, *Diary of a Gunner*, quoted in *Liberators,* Potter, p. 172.

107 "I'm going to get 'em" Harry K. Tyree, interview with Joe Wilson, June 1994, quoted in *The 761st "Black Panther" Tank Battalion,* Wilson, p. 66.

Chapter Five: Field of Fire

114 "as it was my birthday . . ." Ladislas Farago, *Patton: Ordeal and Triumph,* Ivan Oblensky, New York, p. 666.

115 "They've got us surrounded again . . ." This quote has been variously attributed; however, *Time* magazine, October 13, 1961, cites Lt. Col.

Creighton Abrams, who in World War II commanded the 37th Tank Battalion of the 4th Armored Division, as does historian Christopher Gabel. Abrams later served as the commander of U.S. forces during the Vietnam War.

115 Three regiments of infantrymen . . . *General Patton,* Hirshson, pp. 555–56.

116 When a German shell penetrated . . . *Death Traps,* Cooper, p. 67. Cooper served as an ordnance officer with the spearhead 3rd Armored Division.

116 "I'm hit hard as hell" Johnnie Stevens interview with Joe W. Wilson Jr., July 4, 1994, quoted in *The 761st "Black Panther" Tank Battalion,* Wilson, p. 79.

120 "I'm already through . . ." *Come Out Fighting,* Anderson, p. 36.

121 They were the ones who had to clean . . . *Death Traps,* Cooper, p. 20.

122 "What the fuck can you do to me? . . ." *Hit Hard,* Williams, p. 196.

122 by a certain class . . . Ibid., pp. 216–17.

127 "This is one order . . ." David J. Williams, speech given at the MOH Conference, February 27, 1994, quoted in *The 761st "Black Panther" Tank Battalion,* Wilson, p. 91.

129 "Simply with driving steadily . . ." Hugh M. Cole, *United States Army in World War II: The European Theater of Operations: The Lorraine Campaign,* Historical Division, Department of the Army, Washington, D.C., 1950, p. 520.

129 The ground-bearing pressure . . . *Death Traps,* Cooper, p. 24.

130 "Commander to driver . . ." Steven J. Zaloga, *Sherman Medium Tank 1942–45,* Osprey Publishing, Oxford, 1978, p. 13.

131 "never seen a better demonstration . . ." *Come Out Fighting,* Anderson, p. 39.

133 "How in the hell can I go back . . ." *Hit Hard,* Williams, p. 209.

133 "Division should pinch out this sector . . ." Ibid., p. 210.

134 "I see them. . . ." David J. Williams, speech given at MOH Conference, February 27, 1994, quoted in *The 761st "Black Panther" Tank Battalion,* Wilson, p. 95.

135 "who drew large arrows . . ." Christopher R. Gabel, *The Lorraine Campaign: An Overview, Sept.–Dec. 1944,* Combat Studies Institute, Ft. Leavenworth, Kansas, 1985, quoted at www.cgsc.army.mil.

136 "I've never seen a tank company . . ." *Hit Hard,* Williams, p. 217.

136 "There were no sounds . . ." Ibid., p. 218.

Chapter Six: The Saar

139 "the traditional invasion route . . ." *The Lorraine Campaign*, Gabel.

150 "The fight we are now having . . ." Patton to Gilbert R. Cook Papers, APO 403, New York, Dec. 10, 1944, Gilbert R. Cook papers, Eisenhower Library, Abilene, Kansas, quoted in *General Patton*, Hirshson, p. 564.

150 "more important for young officers . . ." Alden Hatch, *George Patton, General in Spurs,* Julian Messner, New York, 1950, p. 147, quoted in *Patton*, D'Este, p. 665.

151 "We are not going to be stopped . . ." *Lucky Forward,* Allen, pp. 190–91.

156 "keep their heads down" *Hit Hard,* Williams, p. 237.

158 "Lt. General George S. Patton's . . ." Quoted in *The 761st "Black Panther" Tank Battalion*, Wilson, p. 118.

158 "It is with extreme gratification . . ." *Come Out Fighting*, Anderson, p. 44.

158 "I consider the . . ." Ibid.

159 By contrast, to capture . . . *The Lorraine Campaign,* Gabel.

159 "The German defenders were critical of, but grateful . . ." Ibid.

160 "The corps commanders . . ." Ibid.

160 "he preferred to forget it" *General Patton*, Hirshson, p. 544.

160 "Every defensive position . . ." *Lucky Forward,* Allen, p. 195.

161 "It is my belief . . ." Gay Diary, Dec. 10, 1944, and Dec. 13, 1944, quoted in *General Patton*, Hirshson, p. 566.

161 "I don't know what it means . . ." *Patton,* Farago, p. 697, quoted in *General Patton*, Hirshson, p. 570.

Chapter Seven: The Bloody Forest

163 "It just looked almost endless . . ." Private Bart Hagerman of the 17th Airborne Division, transcription from *American Experience: Battle of the Bulge: The Deadliest Battle of World War II,* WGBH Educational Foundation, Boston, 1994, 2002.

164 "electric" John S. D. Eisenhower, *The Bitter Woods: The Battle of the Bulge,* G. P. Putnam's Sons, New York, 1969, reprint, with an introduction by Stephen E. Ambrose, Da Capo Press, New York, 1995, p. 257.

166 nothing so much as upstate Vermont Danny S. Parker, *Battle of the Bulge: Hitler's Ardennes Offensive, 1944–1945,* Combined Publishing, PA, 1991, reprint, Da Capo Press, New York, 2001, p. 50.

167 "drive like hell!" Patton Diary, Dec. 20, 1944, quoted in *Patton,* D'Este, p. 682.

168 "you could spit across it" *Battle of the Bulge*, Parker, p. 200.

168 Historian John S. D. Eisenhower . . . *The Bitter Woods*, Eisenhower, p. 409.

170 "lance this boil" *Battle of the Bulge*, Parker, p. 209.

170 "Some call it luck, some genius . . ." Patton Diary, quoted in Mitchell Kaidy, "Who Really Liberated Bastogne," 87th Infantry Division website, www.87thinfantrydivision.com.

172 the dense woods and rugged terrain . . . *Battle of the Bulge*, Parker, p. 49.

173 "on a likely target as a New Year's . . ." George Forty, *Patton's Third Army at War*, Scribner's, New York, 1978, p. 140, quoted in *Patton*, D'Este, p. 694.

174 In his December 22 surrender . . . *Battle of the Bulge*, Parker, p. 175.

175 "hornet's nest" Hugh M. Cole, *United States Army in World War II: The European Theater of Operations: The Ardennes: Battle of the Bulge,* 1965, reprint, Washington, D.C.: Center of Military History, United States Army, 1994, p. 643.

176 "three of the tanks were burning . . ." 87th Infantry Division Association, *Stalwart and Strong: The Story of the 87th Infantry Division*, Flourtown, PA, 1993, quoted in *The 761st "Black Panther" Tank Battalion*, Wilson, p. 125.

177 "dangerous gap" *The Ardennes: Battle of the Bulge,* Cole, p. 644.

178 "could win this war now" Patton Diary, Dec. 27, 1944, quoted in *General Patton*, Hirshson, p. 586.

178 "tired little fart" Ibid.

179 "had to try to push . . ." Peter Elstob, *Hitler's Last Offensive*, London, 1971, pp. 381–82, quoted in *Patton,* D'Este, p. 699.

179 "a complete misunderstanding of the problem . . ." Gay Diary, Dec. 30, 1944, quoted in *General Patton*, Hirshson, p. 588.

179 "badly disorganized" *Battle of the Bulge,* Parker, p. 241.

179 "we can still lose this war" Ibid., p. 247.

180 "I'm going to speak for my whole company . . ." *Hit Hard*, Williams, pp. 267–68.

182 "go very damn slow . . ." Ibid., p. 275.

182 "There's no one to take my place . . ." Ibid., p. 276.

183 "chilled thoroughly . . ." Ibid., p. 277.

Chapter Eight: Tillet

187 "To introduce into a philosophy of war . . ." Quoted in *Battle of the Bulge*, Parker, p. 307.

188 "fanatical" *Battle of the Bulge,* Parker, p. 218. Danny Parker calls the unit "fanatically dedicated."

189 "difficult to follow because so much . . ." *The Bitter Woods*, Eisenhower, p. 23.

190 "Each Battalion will be prepared . . ." *The Ardennes: Battle of the Bulge*, Cole, p. 641.

190 when pilots did fly . . . *General Patton*, Hirshson, p. 581. Brig. Gen. Otto Weyland, commander of the XIX Tactical Air Force, is quoted as saying, "It was white when you looked down, white when you looked up, white when you looked out that way."

190 "How men live, much less fight . . ." Quoted in *Patton*, D'Este, p. 699.

191 Staff Sergeant Curtis Shoup . . . Medal of Honor citation, www.homeofheroes.com.

192 "the most moving experience" Patton Diary, January 8, 1945, quoted in *Patton*, D'Este, p. 695.

194 "still giving 'em hell" *Come Out Fighting*, Anderson, p. 50.

202 "those German maps again" *Lucky Forward*, Allen, p. 271.

Chapter Nine: Task Force Rhine

205 "You have fought gallantly and intelligently . . ." *Come Out Fighting*, Anderson, p. 76.

206 "last killing ground . . ." Ken Ford, *The Rhineland 1945: The Last Killing Ground in the West,* Osprey Publishing, Oxford, 2000, title page.

207 "trying to arrange the blankets smoothly . . ." Eisenhower quoted in Franklin M. Davis Jr., *Across the Rhine*, Time-Life Books, Alexandria, VA, 1980, p. 22, quoted in *Patton*, D'Este, p. 703.

207 "single, full blooded thrust" *Patton*, D'Este, p. 704.

207 "if ever before in the history of war . . ." Patton, quoted in Ibid., p. 705.

207 "rock soup" Ibid., p. 704.

212 "learn what we're doing when they see it . . ." Patton Diary, Feb. 26, 1945, quoted in *Patton,* D'Este, p. 706.

212 "taken Trier with two divisions . . ." quoted in Harry Semmes, *Portrait*

of *Patton*, Paperback Library, New York, 1970, p. 240, quoted in *Patton*, D'Este, p. 708.

215 "envelop their rear and pocket them . . ." *Lucky Forward*, Allen, p. 326.

Chapter Ten: The River
227 "You will wait there . . ." *Come Out Fighting*, Anderson, p. 89.

229 "take a piss in the Rhine . . ." Patton Diary, March 24, 1945, quoted in *Patton*, D'Este, p. 712.

229 The war would continue until American and British forces . . . *Patton*, D'Este, p. 702.

231 Infantry Pfc. Irving Boone was amazed . . . Gerald McMahon, *The Siegfried and Beyond*, The 71st Infantry Division Association, Cleveland, 1993, quoted in *The 761st "Black Panther" Tank Battalion*, Wilson, p. 167.

232 "Are there any Africans opposite?" Leonard G. Shurtleff, "France at War: Tirailleurs Senegalais," The Great War Society, www.worldwar1.com.

232 "How many Negro Panzer divisions . . ." *The 761st "Black Panther" Tank Battalion*, Wilson, p. 168.

234 "cow towns" Ibid., p. 169.

237 "Too bad about Roosevelt . . ." Walter Lewis, *Diary of a Gunner*, quoted in *Liberators*, Potter, p. 229.

237 "quite a discussion . . ." Gay Diary, April 12, 1945, and Patton Diary, April 12, 1945, quoted in *General Patton*, Hirshson, p. 628.

246 "You hear me, George . . ." *Patton*, D'Este, p. 728.

Chapter Eleven: Home
249 "We love, we marry . . ." Margaret M. Crecy, speech given at the MOH Conference, February 27, 1994, quoted in *The 761st "Black Panther" Tank Battalion*, Wilson, p. 238.

252 "I couldn't put behind me . . ." Bob Armbruster, *Alumni Profile of Paul Bates (31)*, Western Maryland College, 1994, quoted in *The 761st "Black Panther" Tank Battalion*, Wilson, p. 229.

253 "It is hereby declared to be the policy . . ." Quoted in Robert B. Edgerton, *Hidden Heroism: Black Soldiers in America's Wars*, Westview Press, Boulder, CO, 2001, p. 164.

260 "Not favorably considered . . ." White House Central File, Jimmy

Carter Presidential Library, quoted in *The 761st "Black Panther" Tank Battalion*, Wilson, pp. 239–40.

260 "the Negro Tank Battalion . . ." *Stars and Stripes*, photostat copy in *The 761st "Black Panther" Tank Battalion*, Wilson, p. 267.

261 "there are clear indications . . ." White House Central File, Jimmy Carter Presidential Library, quoted in *The 761st "Black Panther" Tank Battalion*, Wilson, p. 241.

262 Hunt seemed indifferent . . . *Hit Hard*, Williams, pp. 217–18.

263 On Christmas Day 1944 . . . The source material for the combat actions of the Medal of Honor recipients described in the following passages are Medal of Honor citations as published in www.homeofheroes.com; Joseph L. Galloway, "Debt of Honor," *U.S. News & World Report*, May 6, 1996; and Edgerton, *Hidden Heroism*.

267 "For extraordinary heroism in action during 15–19 November . . ." Rivers Medal of Honor Citation, published at www.homeofheroes.com.

269 "In August . . . This after 51 Years!!!" Oscar Jensen, 26th Infantry Division Newsletter, *Yankee Doings*, December 1999, Vol. LXXX, No. 4, p. 22.

Select Bibliography

Books

Allen, Colonel Robert S. *Lucky Forward: The History of Patton's Third U.S. Army.* New York: The Vanguard Press, 1947.

Ambrose, Stephen E. *Band of Brothers: E Company, 506th Regiment, 101st Airborne From Normandy to Hitler's Eagle's Nest.* New York: Simon & Schuster, 1992.

Anderson, Trezzvant W. *Come Out Fighting: The Epic Tale of the 761st Tank Battalion 1942–45.* 1945. Reprint. New Haven, CT: The Advocate Press, 1979.

Cole, Hugh M. *United States Army in World War II: The European Theater of Operations: The Lorraine Campaign.* Washington, D.C.: Historical Division, Department of the Army, 1950.

————. *United States Army in World War II: The European Theater of Operations: The Ardennes: Battle of the Bulge.* 1965. Reprint, Washington, D.C.: Center of Military History, United States Army, 1994.

Cooper, Belton Y. *Death Traps: The Survival of an American Armored Division in World War II.* Novato, CA: Presidio Press, 1998.

Courtney, Pfc. Richard D. *Normandy to the Bulge: An American Infantry GI in Europe During World War II.* Carbondale & Edwardsville: Southern Illinois University Press, 1997.

D'Este, Carlo. *Patton: A Genius for War.* New York: HarperCollins, 1995.

Edgerton, Robert B. *Hidden Heroism: Black Soldiers in America's Wars.* Boulder, CO: Westview Press, 2001.

Eisenhower, John S. D. *The Bitter Woods: The Battle of the Bulge.* New York: G. P. Putnam's Sons, 1969. Reprint, with an introduction by Stephen E. Ambrose, New York: Da Capo Press, 1995.

Farago, Ladislas. *Patton: Ordeal and Triumph.* New York: Ivan Oblensky, 1964.

Folkestad, William B. *The View from the Turret: The 743rd Tank Battalion During World War II.* Shippensburg, PA: Burd Street Press, 2000.

Ford, Ken. *The Rhineland 1945: The Last Killing Ground in the West.* Oxford: Osprey Publishing, 2000.

Franklin, John Hope. *From Slavery to Freedom: A History of Negro Americans,* 3rd. ed. New York: Alfred A. Knopf, 1967. Reprint, New York: Vintage Books, 1969.

Gabel, Christopher R. *The Lorraine Campaign: An Overview, September–December 1944.* Fort Leavenworth, Kansas: Combat Studies Institute, 1985.

Hirshson, Stanley P. *General Patton: A Soldier's Life.* New York: HarperCollins, 2002.

McFeely, William S. *Frederick Douglass.* New York: W. W. Norton, 1991.

Miller, David. *The Illustrated Directory of Tanks of the World: From World War I to the Present Day.* Osceola, WI: MBI Publishing, 2000.

Motley, Mary Penick, ed. *The Invisible Soldier: The Experience of the Black Soldier, World War II.* Detroit: Wayne State University Press, 1987.

Parker, Danny S. *Battle of the Bulge: Hitler's Ardennes Offensive, 1944–1945.* Pennsylvania: Combined Publishing, 1991. Reprint, New York: Da Capo Press, 2001.

Potter, Lou, with William Miles and Nina Rosenblum. *Liberators: Fighting on Two Fronts in World War II.* New York: Harcourt Brace Jovanovich, 1992.

Province, Charles M. *Patton's Third Army: A Daily Combat Diary.* New York: Hippocrene Books, 1992.

Quarrie, Bruce. *The Ardennes Offensive: US VII & VIII Corps and British XXX Corps: Central Sector.* Oxford: Osprey Publishing, 2000.

Rampersad, Arnold. *Jackie Robinson: A Biography.* New York: Alfred A. Knopf, 1997.

Ritgen, Helmut. *The Western Front 1944: Memoirs of a Panzer Lehr Officer,* translated by Joseph Welsh. Winnipeg, Manitoba: J. J. Fedorowicz Publishing, 1995.

Robinson, Jackie, as told to Alfred Duckett. *I Never Had It Made.* New York: G. P. Putnam's Sons, 1972.

Russell, Frank M. *The Saar: Battleground and Pawn.* Stanford: Stanford University Press, 1951.

Terkel, Studs. *The Good War: An Oral History of World War II.* New York: Pantheon, 1984.

Townshend, Charles, ed. *The Oxford Illustrated History of Modern War.* New York: Oxford University Press, 1997.

Weinberg, Gerhard L. *A World at Arms: A Global History of World War II.* Cambridge: Cambridge University Press, 1994.

Williams, David J. *Hit Hard.* New York: Bantam Books, 1983.

Wilson, Joe W., Jr. *The 761st "Black Panther" Tank Battalion in World War II.* Jefferson, NC: McFarland & Company, 1999.

Zaloga, Steven J. *M3 & M5 Stuart Light Tank 1940–45.* Oxford: Osprey Publishing, 1999.

Zaloga, Steven J. *Sherman Medium Tank 1942–45.* Oxford: Osprey Publishing, 1978.

Military Maps

U.S. Army in World War II Atlas: The European Theater. Minnetonka, MN: The National Historical Society, 1996.

Periodicals

Associated Press. "Overdue But Not Forgotten." *Dallas Morning News,* April 28, 1996.

Galloway, Joseph L. "Debt of Honor." *U.S. News & World Report,* May 6, 1996, pp. 28–41.

Holmes, Steven A. "Some Notable Old Soldiers Fight to Avoid Fading Away." *The New York Times,* September 2, 2002.

Jensen, Oscar. "A Memorable Visit to the ETO." *Yankee Doings: 26th Division Newsletter,* Vol. LXXX, No. 4, December 1999.

Sikes, David. "WWII Battalion Honored." *Killeen Daily Herald,* August 23, 1996.

Tygiel, Jules. "The Court-Martial of Jackie Robinson." *American Heritage,* August/September 1984, pp. 34–39. Reprinted in *The 761st Tank Battalion & Allied Veterans Association of World War II, Celebrating their 37th Annual Reunion,* August 28–September 1, 1985.

Van Gelder, Lawrence. Paul Bates Obituary. *The New York Times,* February 25, 1995.

Wilson, Dale E. "A Time to Live; A Time to Die: The Sad Saga of Staff Sergeant Ruben Rivers." *Negro History Bulletin: African Americans and World War II, 50th Anniversary of World War II Commemorative Issue,* December 1993, pp. 51–55.

Videos

Lennon, Thomas, and Mark Zwonitzer. *American Experience: Battle of the Bulge: The Deadliest Battle of World War II.* Narrated by David McCullough. A Lennon Documentary Group Film, produced for American Experience. Boston: WGBH Educational Foundation, 1994, 2002.

Lihani, Rob. *Suicide Missions: Tank Crews.* Produced by Rob Lihani. A&E Television Networks: The History Channel, 2000.

Stahl, Norman. *America's Black Warriors: Two Wars to Win.* Produced by Mort Zimmerman. With closing comments by General Colin Powell, U.S. Army (Ret.). A&E Television Networks: The History Channel, 1998.

Internet Sites of Interest

"26th Infantry Division 'Yankee Division.'" www.grunts.net; www.globalsecurity. org; www.military.com.

"71st Infantry Division Official Web Page." www.geocities.com

"The Seventy-First Came to Gunskirchen Lager." Produced by the 71st U.S. Infantry Division in May 1945, after their liberation of the Gunskirchen concentration camp in Austria. With foreword by Major General Willard G. Wyman. Reprinted at www.remember.org.

"87th Infantry Division Association." Contains numerous articles and wartime recollections written by members of the 87th "Golden Acorn" Division.

www.87thinfantrydivision.com.

"History of the 103rd Infantry Division." www.grunts.net

"TheTroubleshooters.com." Website of the 702nd Tank Battalion of Patton's Third U.S. Army. Contains articles on tank equipment and performance, and recollections of unit veterans. www.thetroubleshooters.com.

www.homeofheroes.com. Website featuring Congressional Medal of Honor citations.

Acknowledgments

The authors would like to thank the following friends and colleagues for their contributions to the realization of the book:

Michael Hurd, Hanna Broda, Sloan Harris, Alan and Harriet Dresher, Matthew Greenfield, Craig McEwen, Roger Scholl, and Sarah Rainone.

We would like to give special acknowledgment and thanks to Deborah Murphy.

Index

Adams, Clifford, 97
Adamson, Capt. Garland "Doc,"
    49–50, 94, 118–19, 190
African American soldiers in Ameri-
    can military, history, 17–20, 30
    "Buffalo soldiers," 18, 19
Allied leaders, meeting in Tehran,
    44–45
Anderson, Alexander, 112
Anderson, Trezzvant, 86–87
Annunzio, Frank, 261
Ardennes. See Battle of the Bulge
Armstrong, Emile, 112

Ashly, Thomas, 49
Austria, 241, 246
    761st Able Company, 246
    Steyr, 246–47

Baker, 1st Lt. Vernon, 264–65
Ballard, Sgt. Moses, 147
Barbour, 1st Lt. Samuel (or Charles),
    90, 115–16, 122
Bates, Lt. Col. Paul L., 29, 32, 46–47,
    51, 57, 58, 68, 72, 81–82, 86,
    123
    postwar, 252, 255–56, 259

reads Articles of War to 761st,
  60–61
return to 761st, 210
Saar Campaign and wounding, Nov.
  8, 89, 92, 93–94, 100, 121
tank, "Taffy," 43, 255
Task Force Rhine, 217–23
Battle of the Bulge, 2, 163–85
  air support, 198, 200–201
  Bastogne, 165, 166–68, 169–70,
    178, 214
  casualties, 180, 183, 184, 185, 191,
    198, 202, 203
  civilian casualties, 181
  end of, 203
  First Army in, 163, 164
  German forces, 164, 167–68,
    170–71, 175, 176, 178, 179,
    187–88, 189, 194, 195, 201
  German surrender demand and
    Gen. McAuliffe's famous reply,
    167, 174
  January 3, Allied counterattack,
    178–85
  St. Hubert Hwy, 174–76, 188, 201
  761st Able Company, 180–85,
    188–89, 190, 192–201
  761st Baker Company, 173–76, 189
  761st Charlie Company, 170–77,
    180, 181, 188–89, 190, 192–201
  761st Dog Company, 180, 190–91,
    201
  761st Gates command, 177–78,
    190, 192–93
  Seventh Army, 164
  Third Army sent to, 164, 167, 174
  Tillet, 177–78, 179, 180, 181–85,
    187, 190–204, 270
  weather, 171, 173, 174, 175, 177,
    180, 190, 192–93
Battle of Hurtgen Forest, 129, 151
Bear, Capt. Gerald M., 56, 58–59
Belgium, battles and battle sites
  Amberloup, 177

Bastogne, 165, 166–68, 169–70
Bonnerue, 175, 176. 187–88
Gerimont, 177, 178, 180, 181, 182,
  183, 184, 188, 195
Haies de Tillet Forest, 174, 176,
  177, 180
Hermee, 208
"High Ardennes," 171
Houffalize, 178, 179, 203
Jenneville, 175–76
Moircy, 175
Nimbermont, 171
Offagne, 169, 173, 180
Pironpre, 175, 176, 187–88
Remagne, 171–72, 175, 176
Rondu, 171
St. Vith, 203, 203
Schonberg, 164, 204, 207–8
Tillet, 177–78, 179, 180, 181–85,
  190–204, 270
Bond, Jessie, 185
Boone, Pfc. Irving, 231
Bradley, Gen. Omar, 68, 69, 135, 164,
  207–8, 212–13, 229, 237, 246
Bragg, Pvt. Thomas, 182, 184
Branch, Cpl. Buddie, 147
Brisbane, Thomas, 14
Briscoe, Robert, 112
Brooks, Charles, 184
Brown, Cpl. Fred, 236
Bruce, Lt. Thomas, 216, 218, 221
Bryant, Mose, 136
Burroughs, William R., 217, 219, 237
Byrd, L. C., 101

Campbell, Walter, 116
Camp Breckinridge, Texas, 59
Camp Claiborne, Louisiana, 5–6, 21,
  28–32
Camp Clark, Missouri, 254
Camp Hood (Fort Hood), Texas, 33,
  36, 39, 43–44, 46–51
  German prisoners at, freedom
    greater than black servicemen, 52

monument and other memorials to 761st, 267–68
reunion at, 268
travel off base, racial problems and, 42–43, 51–52, 55–59
Camp Kilmer, New Jersey, 58, 249
Camp Shanks, Orangeburg, New York, 64–65
Camp Siebert, Alabama, 55
Camp Upton, New York, 12
Camp Wheeler, Georgia, 59
Cardell, Daniel, 100, 101, 146, 152, 217
Carter, S. Sgt. Edward A., 266
Carter, Jimmy, 262
Chapman, Carlton, 101
Chatmon, Earnest, 110
Christy, Walter, 37
Churchill, Winston, 45, 213, 238
Clark, Hollis, 41, 140, 141, 173
Cochrane, S. Sgt. Frank, 110, 146, 147, 148, 193, 216, 219, 220, 221
Codman, Lt. Col. Charles R., 93
Coleman, 1st Lt. Kenneth, 108–9, 112
Collier, George, 110
Come Out Fighting, 257
Congressional Medal of Honor, 100
   African American recipients, 263–67
   fight for award to Ruben Rivers, 262–63, 267
Conway, S. Sgt. Henry, 126, 136, 193, 194
Conyers, John, 261
Cooper, Theodore, 112
Crecy, Warren "Iron Man," 21
   Battle of the Bulge, 172
   death of Horatio Scott and, 112, 114
   in England, 72
   in France, 84
   postwar, 256–57
   Saar Campaign, 107, 112, 117–18, 141–42
   in 761st Charlie Company, 114

in 761st Dog Company, 42, 46, 112, 114
in 761st Service Company, 24
as tank commander, 23
Task Force Rhine, 219, 220, 224
valor of, 107, 112, 117–18, 172, 219, 262
wife, Margaret, 48, 249
Culin, Sgt. Curtis G., 69
Culin, Maj. Gen. Frank, 169

Dade, Floyd, 47–48
   France, yearly visits to, 269–70
   in Germany, 230–31
   postwar, 254–55
   reenlistment, 250
   Saar Campaign, 91, 97–98, 102, 125, 132, 134, 135, 156, 158
Dade, 2nd Lt. Moses, 193, 194, 216, 218, 219
Dawley, Brig. Gen. Ernest A., 52
Devers, Lt. Gen. Jacob, 164
Devore, Willie, 48, 142
   Battle of the Bulge, 168–69, 173, 175, 181, 192, 196–98
   at Camp Hood, 39
   death of, 198, 201, 204
   deployment for ETO, 65–72
   as driver, 24, 39, 120, 175
   in France, 84
   in New York City, 65
   Saar Campaign, 103, 120, 144
   in 761st Headquarters Company, 24
Douglass, Frederick, 18, 20
Dunn, Lane, 146, 148

Eddy, Maj. Gen. Manton S., 92–93, 158–59, 260
Edwards, Corp. James, 100
85th Infantry Division, 32
Eisenhower, Gen. Dwight D., 37, 69, 70, 84, 135, 164, 166, 178, 179, 207–8, 213, 229–30, 237, 238, 243, 246, 260

England
  African-Americans, 68, 71, 72–74
  21st British Army Group, drive into
    Germany and, 207–8, 212
  Wimborne, 73, 74, 77
English, Capt. Richard, 114, 152
European Theater of Operations
    (ETO), 45
  African American units in, 258–49
  Allied commanders, clashes
    between, 207–8, 212–13
  Allied commanders at Verdun,
    164–65
  Battle of the Bulge, 2, 163–85
  casualties, 151
  dangerous optimism of Allies, 69–70
  liberation of Paris, 69
  logistical problems, 75–76
  Germany, subduing of, plan for,
    229–30
  Normandy invasion (Operation
    Overlord), 1–2, 45, 53, 80–81
  October, 1944, various operations,
    84
  Omaha Beach, 80–81
  Operation Cobra, 68–69
  Operation Grenade, 210–11
  push for Germany, Montgomery
    and, 206–7, 229
  "Red Ball Express," African Ameri-
    can quartermaster regiment, 76
  Saar Campaign, 2, 59, 71, 75, 84,
    93–161
  Sherman tanks, casualties and
    problems with, 53, 66–67, 76,
    80, 82
  Task Force Rhine, 217–25
  troopships for, 67–68
  Yalta Conference, 238
Ewing, Roderick, 135

Fletcher, Autrey, 110
Fort Knox, Kentucky, 14–17, 20–21
  black officer training, 28

disparity in training for African
    Americans, 16–17
  segregation at, 17
Fort Riley, Kansas, 30
442nd Regimental Combat Team,
    100th Battalion ("Nisei" Japanese
    Americans), 32
Fox, Lt. John R., 263–64
France, battles and battle sites, 85–86
  Albestroff, 149
  Benestroff, 128, 129, 137–38
  Bezange-la-Petite, 99, 101
  Bidestroff, 149
  Bosselhausen, 214
  Bourgaltroff, 119, 123–28, 129,
    133–35
  Château-Salins, 104–5
  Dieuze, 128, 129, 131, 137, 139,
    159
  Guebestroff, 131
  Guebling, 119, 123–28, 129,
    132–33, 136, 139, 149, 159
  Hill 253, 92, 100, 101
  Honskirch, 129, 142, 145
  Les Pieux, American camp at, 81, 82
  Maginot Line, 154–56
  Marimont, 136, 149
  Metz, 115, 128, 156, 158, 160
  Morville-les-Vic, 104, 105–6,
    108–12, 113, 114, 138, 145,
    148, 159
  Munster, 142–45
  Oermingen, 154, 155
  Rodalbe, 119, 127, 129
  Saare-Union, 129
  St. Nicholas-de-Port, bivouac at,
    83–84, 86, 89, 90
  Sarreguemines, 129, 150, 157
  Sarre-Union, 152–54, 158, 160
  Saverne, 212, 213
  Torcheville, 138, 142
  Val-de-Bride, 131
  Vic-sur-Seille, 96–99, 101–2
  Vittersbourg, 145

Woefling-les-Sarreguemines, 156,
157–58
Wuisse, 113, 115–16, 119–20, 124,
165–66

Gary, 1st Lt. Harold, 223
Gates, Lt. Charles A. "Pop," 30–31,
72, 83, 103, 142
African American Missouri
National Guard Unit and, 254
Assault Gun Platoon, 131, 138, 143
Battle of the Bulge, 168, 169,
177–78, 181, 190, 195–96
dinner in Bidestroff, 149–50
German invasion and, 232, 241–42
Headquarters Company com-
mander, 46, 107–8, 123
Patton and, 149
postwar, 254, 259
Saar Campaign, 107–8, 156
Saar Campaign, Nov. 22, attack on
Honskirch, 145–49.
Gay, Maj. Hobart R., 161, 179
Geist, Russell C., 49, 123, 147–48,
222
Germany, battles and battle sites
Allied invasion, 229–47
Battle of Hurtgen Forest, 129, 151
Bayreuth, 236
Berlin, 238, 246
Birkenhardt, 222
Bobenthal, 215, 217
Bollenborn, 222
civilians and American troops,
233–34
Coburg, 235
concentration camps and Holo-
caust, 242–44
Erlenbach, 220, 221
Inn River, Austrian border, 241–42
Insheim, 225, 228
Lambach, 245
Langenselbold, 230
Kipshoven, 211

Klingenmunster, 217, 224–25
Kulmbach, 235–36
Nazi resistance to invading Allies,
231
Neuhaus, 240
Niederschlettenbach, 218, 219,
220, 221
Regensburg, 240–41
Reisdorf, 218, 221, 222
Remagen, 212
Rhine River, 206–7, 227–28
Rhine River crossed by Patton, 229
Saarbrucken, 129, 150, 214
Schwannenberg, 211
761st Able Company in, 230, 231,
237–38, 240, 241, 245
761st Baker Company in, 230, 231
761st Charlie Company in, 230,
231–32, 236, 239, 240, 241–44
761st Dog Company in, 230, 231
Siegfried Line, 71, 75, 84, 85, 114,
128, 129, 135, 150, 155,
160–61, 214, 217, 225
Silz, 222–24, 225
surrender, 246
Tiesendorf, 249
Third Army and 761st crosses into,
158
Trier, 212
Wels, 244
Zutzendorf, 215–16
Goering, Hermann, 240
Goines, George, 147
Graham, Ardis, 148
Gray, J. Glenn, 79
Greenwood, Frank, 146–47, 148
Grow, Maj. Gen. Robert, 92–93

Hagerman, Pvt. Bart, 163
Hall, Elwood, 148
Hall, Felix, 26
Hall, Sgt. Jonathan, 233
Hammond, 1st Lt. Robert, 96, 98, 99,
120, 123–28, 134–36

Harrison, Capt. Ivan H., 30, 47, 48, 259
  Saar Campaign, Nov. 8–9, 100, 109
Hastie, William, 27
Hill, Corp. Raleigh, 110
Hilliard, Ivory, 136
Hitler, Adolf, 69
  Battle of the Bulge and, 169–70, 174, 178, 187, 201–2
  refusal to surrender, 229–30, 237
  Rhine, defense of, 206–7, 209
  suicide, 245
HMS *Esperance Bay*, 67–68
Holland
  End, 210
  Jebeek, 209
  Mheer, 211
  Montgomery in, 237
  761st in, 208
  761st Able Company, 211
  761st Baker Company, 210–11
  761st Charlie Company, 211, 212
  761st Dog Company, 211
Huffman, 1st Lt. Maxwell, 219
Hunt, Lt. Col. Hollis, 121–22, 123, 136, 262

Italy
  Allied advance in, 45, 52–53
  92nd Infantry Division, 263–65

Jackson, Austin, 118
James, Pfc. Willy F. Jr., 265
James, Sgt. Walter, 133, 182
Jennison, Sgt. John, 118
Jenson, Oscar, 269–70
Johnson, Lt. Jay E., 99
Johnson, Sgt. Robert, 147–48, 169
Jones, James, 151
Jordan, James, 184

Kahoe, 1st Lt. Joseph, 96, 97, 99, 101, 119–20, 123–28
Kilburn, Maj. Gen. Charles, 169

King, Sgt. Roy, 106
Kingsley, 1st Lt. Harold, 218
Kitt, Sgt. William, 193
Koch, Oscar, 161

Latimer, Philip, 152
Latimore, Sgt. Ervin, 223–24
Lear, Lt. Gen. Benjamin, 32–33, 52
Lewis, Gunner Walter, 101–2, 126, 183–84, 238
Lofton, Willie, 112
Long, Capt. John, 259
Louis, Joe, 47, 55
Luxembourg, 761st in, 203
Lyons, Lt. Col., 124, 125, 127, 133, 135

MacArthur, Gen. Douglas, 60
Mann, Claude, 101
Marshall, Gen. George, 70
McAuliffe, Gen.Anthony, 167, 174, 214, 260
McBurney, William, 1, 2–3, 5, 9–12, 19, 44, 63, 116
  Battle of the Bulge, 166, 168–69, 172, 173, 177, 192–201
  at Camp Claiborne, 22–23
  at Camp Hood, 39
  at Camp Upton, 14
  Channel crossing, 79
  concentration camp entered, 242–44
  deployment for ETO, 58, 63–72
  in England, 72
  at Fort Knox, 14, 20–21
  in France, preparing for battle, 87–88
  German invasion and, 233, 239, 242
  as gunner, 23, 40, 117, 131
  in Holland, 208, 209, 211
  postwar, 258, 270
  racial incident, Alexandria and, 31–32
  return to U.S., 250

Saar Campaign, 95, 103, 112, 117, 130, 131, 137–38, 140, 143–44, 145, 157
  in 761st Headquarters Company, 24
  tank, "Taffy," 43, 143, 192, 194
  Task Force Rhine, 214, 219, 220–21
  trench foot, 150–51
McHenry, Capt. Irvin, 104, 131
McIntyre, Harold, 126
McNair, Lt. Gen. Leslie, 33, 38–39
McNeil, John, 106
McNeil, Preston, 12–13, 19, 44, 118
  Battle of the Bulge, 165, 166, 180, 191, 195
  at Camp Claiborne, 22–23
  at Camp Hood, 42–43, 48
  at Camp Upton, 14
  Channel crossing, 79
  deployment for ETO, 64–72
  in England, 72, 74
  at Fort Knox, 14–15, 20–21
  in France, 84, 87
  German invasion and, 233–34, 235
  in Holland, 210
  postwar, 257–58, 270
  racial discrimination, Texas, 42–43
  racial incident, Alexandria and, 31–32
  return to U.S., 249–50
  Saar Campaign, 91, 95, 112, 118, 123, 157
  in 761st Dog Company, 42, 95
  in 761st Service Company, 24
  as tank commander, 23, 42
Miley, Maj. Gen. William, 260
"Million-dollar wound," 54
Montgomery, Field Marshal Bernard, 75, 84, 178, 207–8, 210, 230, 237
Mucklerath, Pvt. Ben, 56
Murphy, Sgt., 185

Navarre, Sgt. Christopher, 209, 216, 217, 219, 240, 255
Nelson, S. Sgt. James, 183
Nimitz, Adm. Chester, 60
969th Field Artillery, African American battalion, 167

Osby, Dennis, 110

Pacific Theater of Operations (PTO), 45, 53, 60
  African American units in, 258–49
Parks, Isaiah, 217, 220
Patton, Gen. George S., 35, 69–71
  addresses 761st, 86–87
  artillery preparation to "soften" enemy lines, 124–25
  assault on Honskirch and, 149
  Battle of the Bulge, 164–65, 167, 169–70, 173, 178–79, 190, 191–92, 202
  casualties of ETO campaigns, 76
  clashes over drive into Germany, dislike of Montgomery and, 178, 207–8, 212–13, 229
  drive toward Germany, 70, 75–77, 212–13
  German invasion, 233, 246
  injunction to lieutenants, 74–75
  integration of rifle units by, 77
  Operation Cobra, 68–69
  racist stereotyping by, 77, 87, 260
  "reconnaissance by fire," 117
  Rhine crossed by, 229
  Roosevelt's death, 237
  Saar Campaign, 2, 59, 71, 75, 84–86, 92–93, 102–3, 114–15, 128, 129, 139, 150, 159–60
  761st assigned to, 74
  761st, opinion of, 260–61
  Siegfried Line and, 71, 75, 77, 128, 129, 135, 150, 160–61
  tank warfare and, 37
  Task Force Rhine, 214–15

Third Army of, 2, 69, 70, 71, 74, 76, 85, 214–15, 230
Verdun, France, allies meet at, 164–65
wife, Beatrice, 70
Paul, Maj. Gen. Willard, 131, 158, 260
Pershing, Gen. "Black Jack," 18, 19
Porter, Herbert, 106

Racism and segregation
American North, 9
American South, Jim Crow and, 13, 18–19, 22, 25–28, 31–32, 42–43, 51–52, 54–59
in Army Air Corps, 9, 11–12, 18
black soldiers in race riots, 18–19
Camp Hood, Texas, travel off base, racial problems and, 42–43, 51–52, 54–59
England and, American servicemen in, 71, 72–74
fact-finding mission, Justice Department, 27
field showers and, 154
Jackie Robinson, court-martial of, 54–59
Lee Street Riot, Alexandria, Louisiana, 27
military training, disparity in, for African Americans, 16–17
murders of black servicemen, 26–28, 31
postwar, with African American war veterans, Isaac Woodward incident, 250–51
slurs and name-calling, 157
segregation of troopships, 68
in U.S. Army, 9, 20, 50
war veterans and fight for equality, 253–54
"Red Ball Express," African American quartermaster regiment, 76
Rivers, S. Sgt. Ruben

Congressional Medal of Honor, 262–63, 267
death of, 135–36
Fort Hood building named for, 268
Saar Campaign, 98–99, 120, 124–28, 132–36
Roberson, Ray, 126
Robinson, Everett, 132
Robinson, 2nd Lt. John Roosevelt "Jackie," 50–51, 53–60
Robinson, Sugar Ray, 55
Rollins, James, 118
Roosevelt, Eleanor, 20, 44, 73
Roosevelt, Franklin Delano, 20, 45, 238
death of, 237–38
Ross, Nathaniel, 106
Russia, 45, 53, 206, 237, 238, 242–43, 245, 246–47

Saar Campaign, 2, 59, 71, 75, 114–15, 160–61
air support (XIX Air Tactical Command), 103, 105, 124, 128, 130, 155
battles, November 8–9, 93–112
battles, November 11–21, 136, 137–42
battles, November 22–December 14, 142–59
casualties and costliness of, 119, 129, 135, 149, 159, 161 (see also 761st)
commencement of, 84–85
ending, 158–60
entry into Saarland, 139–40
German divisions in, 99, 127, 133, 152
German tactic against tanks, 108
key objectives achieved, 150
living conditions, 761st, 140–42, 150–51, 154
noncombat casualties, flu and trench foot, 150–51

obstacles facing, 85

761st, Able Company, 96–99, 101–2, 104–5, 113, 115–16, 119–20, 121–22, 123–28, 132–36, 149

761st, Baker Company, 93, 94–95, 101, 105–6, 128, 129, 138–39, 145, 147, 153, 156

761st, Charlie Company, 93, 94–95, 99–102, 104, 105, 107, 108–12, 113, 114, 121, 128, 129, 138–39, 142–49, 153, 156

761st crosses in Germany, 158

761st, Dog Company, 93, 95, 100, 104, 106–7, 112, 118, 128, 129, 137–38, 145, 151, 156

761st, Headquarters Company, 93, 95, 100, 104, 107–8, 112, 128

troops and tank battalions in, 88

weather problems, 85–86, 92, 103, 120–21, 140

See also France, battles and battle sites

Safford, John, 220

Saunders, S. Sgt. Samuel F., 100

Savoy Ballroom, Harlem, New York, 65, 144, 200

Scott, Horatio, 21, 48, 72

death of, 111–12

Sears, Col., 160

741st Tank Battalion, 80

743rd Tank Battalion, 80

758th Tank Battalion, 19, 57, 59

761st Tank Battalion

Able Company, 24, 41, 47, 49, 72, 89–90, 91 (*see also* Battle of the Bulge; Germany; Saar Campaign; Task Force Rhine)

African American officers, 29–31

armored patch worn, 24

attached to 87th Division, 156–57, 160, 165, 203, 207

attached to 103rd "Cactus" Division (7th Army), 213–14, 215

attached to 95th Division (9th Army), 208

attached to 17th Airborne Division, 203

attached to 71st Infantry Division, 228–47

attached to the 79th Infantry Division (9th Army), 210

attached to 26th "Yankee" Division, 74–75, 81, 82, 89, 91, 129, 269–70

Baker Company, 24, 41, 90, 91 (*see also* Battle of the Bulge; Germany; Saar Campaign; Task Force Rhine)

as "bastard battalion," 81–82, 89

billeted in Wimborne, England, 73, 77

black officers, 29–30, 49–51, 71

casualties, 2, 97, 100, 101, 106, 108–12, 116, 135–36, 149, 153, 180, 183, 184, 185, 215, 219, 236

Channel crossing, 78, 79–80

Charlie Company, 2, 24, 41, 49, 90, 91 (*see also* Battle of the Bulge; Germany; Saar Campaign; Task Force Rhine)

Charlie Company mascot, rooster, 128, 139, 152

combat record, summary of, 6

commendation from XII Corps, 158–59

courage under fire and medals awarded, 122, 136, 260

creation of, 6, 19–20

delay in being deployed, 44, 52–53

demobilization, 249–58

deployment for ETO, 58, 63–72

desegregation of American military and, 17

Dog Company (in M-5s), 41–42, 49, 90, 91 (*see also* Battle of the

Bulge; Germany; Saar Campaign; Task Force Rhine)
"grease gun," weapon issued to tankers, 91
Headquarters Company, 24, 30, 41, 49, 90, 91 (*see also* Battle of the Bulge; Saar Campaign)
history making, as first African American armored unit deployed in battle, 77
Jackie Robinson in, 50–51, 53–60
lack of recognition postwar, and fight for justice, 251, 255, 258. 259–62
maneuvers in the Kisatchie National Forest, 32–33
motto, 47
nickname, "black panthers," 47
ordnance units, 121
outstanding performance in training and maneuvers, 52–53
Patton's address to, 86–87
Presidential Unit Citation request, 259–60, 261–62
pride and battle-hardened spirit, 229
recruits join, 47–48
replacements, ETO, 209, 215
Rhine crossed by, 229
R&R lost, 156–57
Saar Campaign (*see* France, battles and battle sites; Saar Campaign)
Service Company, 24, 41
Sherman tank chosen for, 33
Simon Weisenthal Foundation, honors from, 269
size of battalion, 47
tanks delivered to, for ETO, 77–78
tank names, 1, 2, 43
training, Camp Claiborne, 6, 21, 22–24, 28–32
training, Camp Hood, 33, 36, 39–42, 43–44, 46–51
training, Fort Knox, 14–17, 20–21, 28

vehicle maintenance, 23, 121, 149, 158
veterans, 250, 269–70 (*see also individuals*)
white officers, 28–29, 49, 71
784th Tank Battalion, 19–20, 49
Sherman, William Tecumseh, 18. *See also* Tanks, U.S. armored force
Shivers, Sgt. George, 116
Shoup, S. Sgt. Curtis, 191
Simmons, Coleman, 148
Simmons, Nathaniel, 101
Simpson, Corp. Dwight, 111–12
Smith, Leonard, 1, 2–3, 5–9, 19, 41, 44, 48, 81, 113–14, 117, 138, 142, 154, 166, 203, 211–12
as assistant gunner, 23
Austrian invasion, Steyr, 246–47
Battle of the Bulge, 165, 166, 168, 169, 172, 173, 176, 177, 181, 188–89, 191, 192–204
at Camp Claiborne, 14, 15, 21, 22, 30–31
at Camp Hood, 36
Camp Hood reunion, 268
Channel crossing, 79
concentration camp entered, 242–44, 269
death of Willie Devore and, 198, 204, 208, 211
deployment for ETO, 64–72, 78
"Doc" Adamson and, 50
in England, 72
in France, 83, 84, 87
German invasion and, 227–29, 232, 233, 235, 239, 242
in Holland, 208, 211–12
as loader, 40
"Pop" Gates and, 30–31, 46, 48, 72, 83, 131, 138, 142, 168, 242
postwar, 257, 270–71
racial discrimination, off-base travel, Texas, 42–43

racial incidents, Alexandria,
  Louisiana, 25–26, 31
return to U.S., 249–50
Saar Campaign, 93, 95–96,
  100–101, 102, 103–4, 112, 117,
  123, 130, 140, 143–45, 152,
  153, 157
segregation and, on base movies, 49
in 761st Headquarters Company, 24
tank ("Cool Stud"), 1, 2, 43, 78, 95,
  102, 104, 139, 152, 203, 216
Task Force Rhine, 214, 216, 219,
  220–21
Stalin, Joseph, 45, 238
Stevens, S. Sgt. Johnnie, 116, 193,
  194, 219, 240, 255
Stewart, Sgt. James, 147, 153
Stimson, Henry, 20

Tanks, German armored force, 37–38
  artillery used on, 67
  Mark IV Panzer (Panther) tanks, 1,
    38, 39, 47, 67, 76, 133
  Panzerfaust (bazooka), 66, 106
  technology developed for, 38
  Tiger Tank, 38, 67, 76, 133
Tanks, U.S. armored force, 37
  armored divisions vs. "bastard bat-
    talions," 82
  Armored Force Replacement Train-
    ing Center, Fort Knox, 14,
    20–21, 209
  artillery carried on Sherman, 78,
    117–18
  casualties and problems with Sher-
    man Tank, Normandy invasion,
    53, 66–67, 69, 76, 80, 82,
    100–101
  code of rescue, 136
  cold and, 140
  crew and positions in tank, 16, 23,
    39–41, 76, 97
  "Duckbills" added for mud, 86, 97
  guidelines, 89

"Hell on Wheels" 2nd Armored
  Division, 70
intercom communication, 143
M2 Medium, 38
M4 firing sequence, 130
M4A3E8 "Easy Eight" Sherman,
  78
M4 Medium Sherman, 1, 2, 15,
  35–36, 38–39, 76, 82, 86
M5 Stuart Light, 15–16, 22–23,
  35, 37, 195
M26 Pershing, 38, 39
name and history of, 36–37
nicknames for, 130
100-hour maintenance checks, 121
"rhinoceros" prongs for, 69
"tank traps," 46, 109–10
training periods for, 44
Task Force Rhine, 217–25
  accomplishments, 225–26
  casualties, 215, 219
  Patton's Third Army, plan for,
    214–15
  761st, extraordinary distinction in,
    210, 225
  761st Able Company, 218–21
  761st Baker Company, 221,
    223–24
  761st Charlie Company, 212, 214,
    215–17, 218–25
  troops in, 217–18
Tates, Joseph, 153
Taylor, Beverly, 268
Taylor, Herman, 184
Tedder, British Air Marshal Arthur,
  164
Thomas, 1st Lt. Charles L., 266–67
Thompson, Mozee, 220
Thrasher, Robert, 220
Truman, Harry, 20, 251
Turley, Sgt. Sam, 105, 110, 112, 262
Tuskegee Airmen (99th Fighter Pur-
  suit Squadron), 20
Tyree, Harry, 107

U.S. Army
  Armored Force created, 1940, 70
  "bastard battalions," 81–82
  battalions, rifle and tank, 89
  black engineering battalions, 24, 26
  black MPs, 25–26
  black servicemen and racial incidents in the South, 26–28, 42–43, 51–52, 54–59
  companies, 89
  divisions, 81
  opposition to black tank battalion, 63–64, 72
  Patton and integration of, 77
  platoons, 89
  racial discrimination within, 44
  regiments, 89
  segregation on base, 49
  segregation of troopships, 68
  Tank Destroyer Center, 52
U.S. Third Army, 2, 69, 70, 71, 74, 76, 81, 153
  4th and 6th Armored Divisions, 83, 88, 92, 92–93, 114, 119, 128, 131, 160
  80th Division, 164, 167
  87th "Golden Acorn" Infantry Division, 156–57, 160, 165, 169–76, 179, 188, 191, 195, 202–3, 207
  Germany, invasion and, 230
  90th Infantry Division, 191–92
  101st Infantry Regiment, 89, 90, 93, 104, 114, 115, 123–28, 132–36, 152
  104th Infantry Regiment, 89, 90, 91, 96, 97, 98, 120, 149, 152, 156
  replacements, 151
  Saar Campaign, movement and placement of troops, 88, 128–27
  71st Infantry Division transferred to, and German invasion, 228–47
  761st assigned to, 74–75, 81, 82, 89

691st Tank Destroyer Battalion, 90
328th Infantry Regiment, 89, 90, 93, 99, 114, 131, 143, 144–45
345th Infantry Regiment, 170–73
347th Infantry Regiment, 173, 174–76
XII Corps, 81, 82, 88, 92–93, 102, 105, 115, 128
XX Corps, 81, 88, 115, 128
26th "Yankee" Infantry Division 82, 88, 89, 91, 99, 101, 104, 105, 114, 116, 121, 128, 129, 153, 164, 167, 174, 189–90, 269–70
  See also Battle of the Bulge; Saar Campaign

Waring, Judge J. Waties, 251
Watson, Corp. Alfred L., 99–100
Watson, Pvt. George, 265
Welborn, James, 146, 147, 148
Weston, S. Sgt. Teddy, 124, 134, 182, 246
Whitby, James, 106
Williams, Lt. David J., 29, 49, 72, 219
  Battle of the Bulge, 169, 180–85, 188, 190
  postwar, 255, 259
  Saar Campaign, 88–90, 91, 96, 97, 98, 104–5, 121–22, 123–28, 132–36, 156
Wilson, Joe W., Jr., 263
Windsor, Sgt. Teddy, 1, 2–3, 192, 193, 196–201, 220–21
Wingo, Maj. Charles, 49, 58, 60, 72, 94, 100, 122
Woodard, S. Sgt. Harvey, 100, 101
Woodson, Sgt., 183, 184
Woodward, Isaac, 250–51
Wyman, Maj. Gen. Willard G., 260